Risk Management in
the Outdoors

A whole-of-organisation approach for education, sport and recreation

Risk Management in the Outdoors is essential reading for students and practitioners involved in outdoor education, sport, recreation and tourism. Written by an expert author team, it explores the value of the outdoors in a society that is increasingly risk-averse, but at the same time pushes the commodification of high risk and extreme activities.

Drawing upon the risk management process from the International Standard on Risk Management, ISO 31000, this text adopts a whole-of-organisation approach to risk management. It covers:

- organisational sustainability
- legal issues
- program design
- activities
- severe weather scenarios
- incident analysis.

Risk Management in the Outdoors provides direction on how best to manage the 'downside' of risk taking while maximising the potential benefits. Each chapter contains focus questions, case studies, action points for practitioners, plus further questions and activities.

Tracey J. Dickson is Associate Professor of Tourism Management in the Faculty of Business and Government, University of Canberra.

Tonia L. Gray is Associate Professor in the Faculty of Education, University of Wollongong.

Risk Management in
the Outdoors

A whole-of-organisation approach for education, sport and recreation

Edited by Tracey J. Dickson and
Tonia L. Gray

CAMBRIDGE
UNIVERSITY PRESS

CAMBRIDGE UNIVERSITY PRESS
Cambridge, New York, Melbourne, Madrid, Cape Town,
Singapore, São Paulo, Delhi, Tokyo, Mexico City

Cambridge University Press
477 Williamstown Road, Port Melbourne, VIC 3207, Australia

Published in the United States of America by Cambridge University Press, New York

www.cambridge.org
Information on this title: www.cambridge.org/9780521152310

First published 2012

Cover design by Eggplant Communications
Typeset by Aptara
Printed in China by Printplus Co. Ltd.

A catalogue record for this publication is available from the British Library

National Library of Australia Cataloguing in Publication data
   Dickson, Tracey J.
   Risk management in the outdoors : a whole of organisation approach
   for education, sport and recreation / Tracey J Dickson, Tonia Gray.
   9780521152310 (pbk.)
   Risk management – Australia.
   Outdoor recreation – Law and legislation – Australia.
   Recreation – Law and legislation – Australia.
   Gray, Tonia L.
  346.94032

ISBN 978-0-521-15231-0 Paperback

Never forget that life can only be nobly inspired and rightly lived if you take it bravely and gallantly, as a splendid adventure in which you are setting out into an unknown country, to face many a danger, to meet many a joy, to find many a comrade, to win and lose many a battle.

Annie Besant, 1847–1933

To all those who inspire adventure, joy and friendship through activities in the outdoors.

Contents

List of tables   *page* xi
List of figures   xiii
List of contributors   xiv
Preface   xvii

1 An introduction to risk, adventure and risk management   1
Tracey J. Dickson
Focus questions   1
Introduction   2
Risk, adventure and the outdoors   3
Why adventure and the outdoors?   4
A whole-of-organisation approach to risk management   7
Philosophy   9
People, equipment and environment   9
Social and political context   9
Child protection and the nanny state   10
The risk management process   13
Expanding the steps in the risk management process   17
Communicate and consult and monitor and review   21
Conclusion   21
References   21

2 Organisational sustainability and risk management   25
Brian Weir & Tracey J. Dickson
Focus questions   25
Introduction: what is sustainability?   25
Organisational sustainability and risk management   28
What is sustainability in an organisational sense?   29
How will we know our organisation is sustainable?   34
Some strategies to assist   36
Points for action for practitioners   39
References and further resources   40

3 The legal context for outdoor activities and programs 43

Lyn Ainsworth & Jon Heshka

Focus questions   43
Introduction   44
The concept of 'reasonableness'   45
Risk management standard AS/NZS/ISO 31000: 2009   46
Work health and safety: statutory liability   47
Key operational areas of responsibility   49
Special characteristics of participants   50
Obligations   51
Reasonably practicable   54
Penalties   55
Relationship with civil liability   55
Law of negligence: breach of duty of care   55
Some other legal issues to consider   58
Using the law to mitigate risk: civil liabilities legislation   59
Recreational activities and dangerous recreational activities   60
Risk management when something goes wrong   62
Recent cases   62
Points for action for practitioners   65
References and further resources   66

4 The organisational context of risk management   69

Tracey J. Dickson & Anne Terwiel

Focus questions   69
Introduction   70
Strategic management: an overview   72
Accreditations and reviews   76
Knowledge management and knowledge transfer   78
Moving beyond strategic management   78
Leadership and power   82
Training, development and education   86
Conclusion   87
Points for action for practitioners   88
References and further resources   89

5 The real physical risks: putting it into perspective   91

Tracey J. Dickson

Focus questions   91
Introduction   92
Research on incidents in outdoor, adventure and sporting activities   95
Overview of the available research   109
Conclusion   111
Points for action for practitioners   111
References and further resources   112

6 Program design and activity selection   116

Eric Brymer & Tonia L. Gray

Focus questions   116
Introduction   117

Contextualising risk   118
Holistic program design   122
Programs and activity design   123
Activity standards and industry norms   124
Staff skills and qualifications   126
Conclusion   127
Points for action for practitioners   128
References and further resources   129

7 Program evaluation   132
Tonia L. Gray & James T. Neill

Focus questions   132
Introduction   133
Historical dimensions of program evaluation   135
Aspects of evaluation   135
What are the main approaches to program evaluation?   137
What steps are involved in program evaluation?   141
Common practices in program evaluation   145
Conclusion   145
Points for action for practitioners   146
References and further resources   146

8 Risk communication   150
Clare Dallat

Focus questions   150
Introduction   151
Research insights   157
Practical applications for risk communicators   158
Conclusion   161
Points for action for practitioners   161
References and further resources   162

9 Technology, risk and outdoor programming   164
James T. Neill & Tonia L. Gray

Focus questions   164
Introduction   168
What is technology?   169
Reasons for using technology in the outdoors   171
Types of technology in outdoor programming   173
Level of technology in outdoor programming   173
Technology, risk and safety   174
Technology becoming passé   177
Audio and video availability on mobile devices   178
Location tracking   178
Conclusion   179
References and further resources   179

10 Severe weather   183
Paul Colagiuri

Focus questions   183
Introduction   184

Severe weather events and the outdoor industry   186
Managing risks associated with severe weather   187
Severe weather events   191
Points for action for practitioners   200
References and further resources   202

11 Learning from injury surveillance and incident analysis   204
Tracey J. Dickson

Focus questions   204
Introduction   205
Are we safe?   206
Why investigate injuries and incidents?   207
Different paradigms   207
Injury surveillance   210
Accident and incident prevention   213
Gathering data   216
Environmental extremes   217
Incident and injury investigation and analysis   220
Organisational learning, learning organisations and knowledge
management   223
Conclusion   224
Points for action for practitioners   224
Glossary of terms   225
References and further resources   226

Appendix: Examples of risk analyses   231
Index   238

Tables

1.1 Generational characteristics *page* 11
1.2 Steps in the risk management process 14
1.3 Risk analysis matrix 19
1.4 Risk analysis matrix: examples of acceptable and unacceptable
levels of risk 20
2.1 Examples of economic, social and environmental sustainability
indicators 35
3.1 Occupational Health and Safety (OHS) and safety legislation 67
4.1 Examples of different leadership scenarios 84
4.2 Potential responses of 'followers' to types of leadership power 85
5.1 Exercise and recreation participation data for people aged
15 years and over in select activities (organised and
non-organised) 2009 94
5.2 Summary measures for sports- and recreation-related injury
hospitalisations 97
5.3 Injury rates (hospitalised) per 100 000 participants across
selected activities, 2002–03 98
5.4 Key indicators for sports-related hospitalisations 2004–05 99
5.5 Frequency of injuries across selected sport and recreational
activities 2004–05 100
5.6 Top 24 leisure/sporting activities at time of death of young
people < 25 years of age: 1 July 2000 – 31 December 2008 103
5.7 Serious harm accidents in NZ education settings 1 July 2004 –
30 June 2009 106
5.8 Rate of NZ adventure and outdoor injuries resulting in serious
harm and fatalities by activity 2004–09 106
5.9 Challenge ropes course incidents (1981, 1986, 1991) 108
7.1 Characteristics of qualitative and quantitative research designs
in educational research 137

7.2 Types of measurement instruments that may be used for
     outdoor and experiential education research and evaluation   138
7.3 The eight LEQ-H factors and descriptions   139
7.4 Why use mixed research methods?   141
8.1 The nature of risks   154
9.1 Reasons for using technology in the outdoors   171
9.2 Technologies used in planning and conducting
     outdoor programs   174
9.3 Examples of low, moderate and high outdoor activities   175
9.4 Positive and negative effects of technology on positive and
     negative risk in outdoor programs   176
9.5 Possible approaches to one technology: podcasting in
     outdoor education   179
10.1 Criteria for issuing severe weather warnings   186
10.2 Examples of environmental trigger points and
     potential responses   190
11.1 Haddon's Matrix applied to the risk factors for road traffic
     crash injuries among children   209
11.2 Summary of Abbreviated Injury Scale (AIS)   213
11.3 Extract from the New Zealand Incident Severity Scale   213
11.4 Injury risk factors in contact sports   215
11.5 Potential causes of accidents in outdoor pursuits   216
11.6 Data collection   217
11.7 Risk factors for exertional heat illnesses   219
11.8 Risk factors in hypothermia   219

Figures

1.1 Different uses of outdoor activities *page* 6
1.2 The three-legged risk management stool 8
1.3 Risk management process adapted from Standards Australia and Standards New Zealand (2009) 13
1.4 Examples of impacts upon an objective for a sporting event 18
2.1 A simple model of sustainability 27
2.2 Three-pillar model of sustainability 29
2.3 Planning for sustainability at the 2010 Olympic and Paralympic Winter Games 37
3.1 Risk management framework AS/NZ/ISO 31000 Clause 4 47
4.1 Strategic management 73
4.2 Accreditation and review pyramid 76
6.1 The dramaturgy wave 123
7.1 Three-stage experiential learning cycle and program evaluation cycle 134
7.2 Continuum of motivation for research in evaluation 136
9.1 A Personal Locator Beacon 166
9.2 Low to High technology spectrum 168
9.3 Overdependency on technology 172
9.4 Example of outdoor fatality involving equipment 175
9.5 Technology and footwear 177
10.1 Managing severe weather risks in the outdoors 188
10.2 Sample detailed severe thunderstorm warning 194
10.3 Sample river height plot 197
10.4 Sample bushfire trigger point and response plan 201
11.1 Injury Iceberg Model 210
11.2 Hierarchy of OHS hazard controls 214

Contributors

Lyn Ainsworth, BA, GradDipEd, LLB, GradDipMgt (Arts), MStratHRM, is a legal practitioner and has been involved in secondary and tertiary education in the areas of law, workplace safety and human resource management. She is currently a member of the Federal and State Councils of Australian Business Industrial and a member of a number of committees of National Disability Services. Lyn has extensive experience as an executive manager and company secretary, responsible for governance and risk management in the not-for-profit sector, including disability services and independent education. She has served on the Boards and Management Committees of local sporting and cultural organisations and is currently a Director of Oakhill College, a large independent Catholic College.

Eric Brymer, BSc (Hons), MSc, GradCertHEd, GradDipBA, PhD, DipOutdoorRec, is a lecturer in the School of Human Movement at Queensland University of Technology. He has worked as a facility manager and organisational consultant and has also designed and facilitated school, organisational, recreational, therapeutic and sport performance programs in the US, Europe, UK, Asia and Australia. He is a past executive officer of the Outdoor Recreation Industry Council and a founding member and chief executive officer of the Asian Adventure Advisory. He has a variety of recreational coaching qualifications.

Paul Colagiuri is the General Manager for Camp Somerset and Encompass Outdoors in Sydney and runs outdoor programs for over 10 000 school students every year, across a broad range of environments and conditions. Paul is an accreditation assessor for ORIC, he sits on the Board of the Australian Camps Association and is the Australian representative for the International Camping Fellowship.

Clare Dallat, BA (Hons), MSc (Risk mgmt), is Director of Programs and Risk Management at The Outdoor Education Group (OEG), based in Eildon, Victoria. She has been a practitioner of outdoor education for over 15 years.

Tracey J. Dickson, B Com, GradDipEd, MEd, MCom, PhD, DipOutdoorRec, is Associate Professor in tourism management at the University of Canberra. Her research interests in areas such as risk management, injury prevention, sport event volunteer management and alpine tourism have been influenced by her passion for alpine areas, working in outdoor education for more than 10 years and her involvement on voluntary boards in sport and recreation. Tracey has been a qualified instructor in a wide range of outdoor activities from archery to telemark skiing and is an assessor for the ORIC Accreditation program.

Tonia L. Gray, BEd (Distinction), MA, PhD, is Associate Professor in Outdoor, Health and Physical Education at the University of Wollongong. She is the past editor of the *Australian Journal of Outdoor Education* (AJOE) and currently a review board member for the *Journal of Experiential Education* (JEE). Tonia's research interests include experiential learning in a variety of educational settings, risk taking and management, understanding the motivations and personalities of extreme sports participants, facilitation and leadership in adventure education and ecopsychology. She has been a practitioner of outdoor education for nearly three decades.

Jon Heshka, BSc, BA, BEd, MEd, LLM, is Associate Professor specialising in sports law and adventure studies at Thompson Rivers University in Kamloops, British Columbia, and is a visiting lecturer at two universities in the UK. He has been a senior instructor with Outward Bound, a climbing guide, he trained and coordinated search and rescue for the Ministry of Attorney General/Justice Institute of BC, worked in senior management with Petzl America and has climbed and led expeditions around the world from Alaska to Argentina and many points in-between.

James T. Neill, BSc, BSc (Hons), PhD, is Assistant Professor at the Centre for Applied Psychology at the University of Canberra. His expertise and interests are in outdoor education, experiential learning, research methods and open academia. James previously worked as an instructor and research coordinator for Outward Bound Australia. James is a past editor and current reviewer of the *Australian Journal of Outdoor Education* (AJOE).

Anne Terwiel, PDP, GradDipBA, MBA, is Lecturer at Thompson Rivers University, specialising in sport event management, resort management, business operations, HR, leadership and marketing. Anne is an active participant in the Canadian ski industry and is involved with the Canadian Ski Instructors Alliance, the Canadian Ski Coaches Federation and as an official for Canadian Ski Racing. She recently volunteered at the 2010 Olympic and Paralympic Winter Games at the alpine ski racing venue.

Brian Weir, BSc, GradDipLegStud, MPA, is a doctoral candidate in the Management Studies Discipline at the University of Canberra and his thesis focuses on policy responses to climate change in the Canberra tourism industry. Previously, Brian worked in the Australian Capital Territory government on business development, tourism policy and leading the development of nature-based tourism and visitor services in the ACT parks service. Brian has served on the boards of a number of local, regional and national tourism organisations, including Ecotourism Australia.

Preface

Undeniably, risk is part of the human experience. Risk management is a ubiquitous concern for those involved in outdoor education, sport and recreation as typically the focus has been on physical dangers. Varying degrees of danger exist within the myriad of activities undertaken in the outdoors, whether they are high physical risk activities such as rock fishing, equestrian sports or adventure racing or the more leisurely and low physical risk activities such as bird watching, dragon boat racing or simple bushwalking along a marked trail. Whatever the motivation, risk in its many forms and activities in the outdoors are inextricably linked.

There is universal acceptance that we engage in risk-taking behaviours as either an innate personal reward, or as a conquest or even as a badge of peer acceptance. Risk management in the outdoors covers the broad spectrum, from high to low risk activities. This book stems from over seventeen years of Australian industry interest in the management of risks in outdoor activities documented in the local literature on the subject, drawing upon a wide array of insights and experiences from industry experts.

Building on that body of work, Chapter 1 conceptualises risk in terms of a 'whole-of-organisation' approach, moving the focus from just physical dangers, to anything that may impact on why and how people engage in outdoor activities. Individuals need places or outlets in which they can experiment with risk, to test their skill levels, to learn from their misfortunes or mistakes and to develop into confident and well-rounded human beings and participants in their communities. Outdoor activities in sport, outdoor education and recreation provide opportunities where this can be manifested.

In keeping with the 'whole-of-organisation' approach, Chapter 2 introduces sustainability, drawing upon the views of triple bottom line accounting, corporate social responsibility and social businesses. This provides a wider context within which organisations may situate themselves by discussing economic, social and environmental sustainability. The legal context, with particular emphasis on issues related to negligence, liability, occupational health and safety and civil liability legislation are introduced in Chapter 3. Chapter 4 considers the organisational context, discussing the role of organisational culture, insurance, finance and human resources and policies and procedures related to risk management. Chapter 5 presents data on the real physical risks, drawing on published and unpublished sources.

Later parts of the book, beginning with Chapter 6, move to more practical aspects of risk management in relation to maximising the positive outcomes and minimising the negative, where program design and activity selection are considered. An overview of program evaluation and how organisations, small and large, may be able to develop a system of evaluation that explore the effectiveness of their activities and the degree to which they are achieving their program or organisational objectives is provided in Chapter 7. Chapter 8 introduces the concept of risk communication and considers how all parties in the equation may be part of the risk management solution, from participants to the media. The use of technology in education and safety and how it may contribute to desired outcomes, as well as insights into its limitations, is discussed in Chapter 9. Chapter 10 introduces risk management in the face of severe weather, including prevention, management and recovery. Finally, Chapter 11 provides insights into injury surveillance, what data could be collected and how it might be analysed in order to determine if the chosen risk management efforts are having an impact. Further, examples of risk analyses using a variation of the risk matrix are provided in the Appendix.

An introduction to risk, adventure and risk management

Tracey J. Dickson

> Avoiding danger is no safer in the long run than outright exposure. Life is either a daring adventure, or nothing.
>
> Helen Keller, author, activist and lecturer, 1957

FOCUS QUESTIONS

1   How are the terms 'risk' and 'risk management' used in organisations that conduct activities, programs or events in the outdoors?
2   What is the role of risk in their activities?
3   Why do people participate in activities in the outdoors?
4   What is the role of adventure in today's society?
5   What facilitates or limits people's pursuit of adventure?

CASE STUDY

Over time, what we seek in adventure and what we find acceptable changes. For example it has been suggested that when Sir Ernest Shackleton was preparing for his 1914 expedition to the South Pole that he placed the following advertisement: 'Men wanted for hazardous journey. Low wages, bitter cold, long hours of complete darkness. Safe return doubtful. Honour and recognition in event of success'.

In contrast, a travel company in 2010 who were marketing an Antarctic trip to retrace Shackleton's journey, said 'A small band of adventurous souls will attempt to repeat Sir Ernest Shackleton crossing with favourable weather. "If you love nature, this trip will awake the senses like no other. Teeming with wildlife from elephant seals, humpback whales, and albatross, to literally millions of penguins, South Georgia and the Falklands are among the most precious wildlife oases on the planet."'

Introduction

At the time when this book was planned the world was facing one of the worst economic crises since the Great Depression of the early 20th century. After an unprecedented period of economic growth, increase in share values, growth in personal wealth and property ownership, this economic 'tsunami' hit all countries and all sectors of their economies. The epicentre of this event was in the finance sector, where risk management has been central to their operations for decades; in fact, risk management emerged in the insurance industry. Yet, in an industry that is highly regulated, supervised and closely monitored, these well-defined and developed systems have been ineffective in the changing environment.

What does this worldwide event have to offer those who conduct activities in the outdoors, where risk management has only been part of our discourse for a little over fifteen years? If a highly controlled financial sector can experience worldwide damage, what could occur in the outdoors, where the very fact that nature is not controllable can be part of the attraction? Reflecting upon these events as they have unfolded, some lessons that may be gleaned from current events include:

- people who have not experienced new and challenging events may not have the knowledge or skills to manage within a changing and unfamiliar environment
- models, and thus decisions, based upon past experience have limited value if they are not changed to model and incorporate changing circumstances
- all decisions about future strategies need to consider how organisations and people may have the capacity to respond to the unknowns of the future
- transferring the risks to others may merely spread the 'disease' not limit the downside of the problem.

The problem with risk is that if we voluntarily take risks in life, we may die, if we do not take risks, we may also die. It has only been through the taking of risks that we have learned new things, explored new arenas, found love and discovered ourselves. If we had not been willing to live this adventurous life, then we may never have lived the lives we have, or will do.

This book is not about avoiding risks, but it is focused on managing the desirable benefits of taking risks while minimising the potential damages if things go wrong. This will involve understanding why you are operating, what you hope to achieve, who you are working with, where you are working, the types of technologies that can support your endeavours, and assessing whether you have achieved what you hoped to achieve. Risk management is not a 'one size fits all' process, it has to be adapted, refined and varied according to the differences in people, places, programs, communities, societies and environments. Risk management is an iterative process within which all stakeholders, internal and external, should be able to play a part.

Risk, adventure and the outdoors

There are many articles that define risk as the potential to lose something (e.g. Beedie 1994; Dickson & Tugwell 2000; Priest & Gass 1997), but if we reflect on any area of our lives, the main reason we take a risk is that we might gain. Rarely will someone take a risk with the expectation that it will fail (Bernstein 1996). In fact, if we did take a risk in the expectation that it would fail, many may question our very sanity! Some examples of where risks are taken in the hope of gaining is in finance, investments, relationships or gambling.

This book builds on over seventeen years of Australian industry interest in the management of risks in outdoor activities which has been documented in earlier editions of the risk management document published by the Outdoor Recreation Industry Council of New South Wales (Dickson & Tugwell 2000; Jack 1994). As with this book, the earlier publications drew upon a wide array of insights and experiences from industry experts.

Here we adopt a whole-of-organisation approach to risk management, drawing upon the definitions of risk and risk management that are used in the international standard AS/NZS ISO 31000: 2009 Risk Management – Principles and Guidelines (ISO 31000) (SASNZ, 2009) which supersedes earlier risk management standards (Standards Australia and Standards New Zealand 1999, 2004). This latest standard defines risk as 'the effect of uncertainty on objectives' (SASNZ 2009, p. 4).

As noted in ISO 31000, every aspect of an organisation may have objectives, such as economic objectives, social objectives and environmental objectives, and these may occur across all levels of an organisation, from the strategic to services, projects and processes. In each of the areas and across all levels there is 'uncertainty, whether, when and the extent to which they will achieve or exceed their objectives' (SASNZ 2009, p. iv).

While there is uncertainty, it is not a reason for risk to be avoided, rather, the term risk is applied in this book in the sense that activities are taken in order that a person, a group, or an organisation may achieve their objectives, so that they may gain, grow, learn or benefit. In doing so, there will always be some degree of uncertainty about those activities: that is normal, that is the risk. Given this understanding of risk, risk management is about maximising the potential positive effects upon the objectives, while minimising the potential negative effects. Risk management is therefore defined within ISO 31000 as 'coordinated activities to direct and control an organization with regard to risk' (SASNZ 2009, p. 2).

Why adventure and the outdoors?

> I went to the woods because I wished to live deliberately, to front only the essential facts of life, and see if I could not learn what it had to teach, and not, when I came to die, discover that I had not lived. (Thoreau, 1854/1986, p. 135)

Adventure

Increasingly adventure is being 'commodified', packaged as a saleable product for any consumer with the available funds to buy (Cater 2006; Dickson 2004; Varley 2006). Even the summit of Mt Everest appears to be accessible if you have sufficient funds (Krakauer 1997). Yet this process of selling 'adventure' is at the risk of losing the essential nature and role of adventure in life and society.

Colin Mortlock, British adventurer, author and academic suggests that adventure and the outdoors are an essential part of a person's growth:

> To adventure in the natural environment is consciously to take up a challenge that will demand the best of our capabilities – physically, mentally and emotionally. It is a state of mind that will initially accept unpleasant feelings of fear, uncertainty and discomfort, and the need for luck, because we instinctively know that if we are successful, these will be counterbalanced by opposite feelings of exhilaration and joy. (Mortlock 1984, p. 19)

Further, Mortlock wrote of the feelings and pleasure one may have in facing challenges in the outdoors, whether achieving one's goal or not:

> In all cases you, the person in the situation, are being challenged to the best of your abilities. If you have given of your genuine best, and either overcome the challenge or retreated with dignity through skill and experience rather than luck alone, then you have had one of the greatest experiences of your life. You have had a 'peak experience' with feelings almost indescribable and beyond those common to normal or routine living. Ultimately life is about feelings, those that are concerned with the joy of living, rather than the anxieties of modern existence. (Mortlock 1984, p. 19)

Kurt Hahn, the founder of Outward Bound quoted his friend when he suggested that there is an important role for the future of societies in the having of adventures: 'Without the instinct of adventure in young men (sic), any civilization, however enlightened, any State, however well ordered, must wilt and wither' (Trevelyan quoted in Hahn 1947, p. 2).

Varley (2006) in a review of available literature on adventure, suggested that there are some core qualities of adventure, including risk, uncertainty, participant responsibility, participants' use of skills, emotional engagement and authenticity. These may be reduced to three key conditions: responsibility (self determination), risk-uncertainty, and transcendence as a result of an ecstatic or marginal experience. If uncertainty is an essential component of adventure, then to offer to sell an activity, an event or a program that has a guaranteed outcome may be in contradiction to what an adventure really is (Dickson 2004). While *real* adventures with their attendant uncertainty and potential for danger may be desirable for individuals and societies, they may not actually be a commercially saleable product, but they may be important for an individual's lifelong education and development.

The outdoors

At a time when we are more disconnected from nature and nature's rhythms than at any other time, adventure and reconnection with the outdoors in a way that encourages freedom, relaxation and engagement is an ever-increasing challenge. Nature and the outdoors have been drawcards for personal development, growth and reflection for millennia. Across cultures, religions, eras and countries, outdoor environments, including deserts and wilderness areas, have been central to our beings as humans.

Louv (2006) coined the term 'nature deficit disorder' which is used to describe the costs associated with our alienation from nature. This 'disorder' is the result of a lack of contact with the natural world, with dirt and trees and insects and animals and birds and may be manifested in 'diminished use of the senses, attention difficulties, and higher rates of physical and emotional illnesses' (Louv 2006, p. 34). For Louv, connection with nature is essential for healthy development of children and adults, a view reflected in a wide range of recent research highlighting the health and community benefits of physical activity in the outdoors (e.g. Aldous 2006; Biddle, Gorely, Marshall & Cameron 2005; Dickson, Gray & Mann 2008; Mallar, Townsend, Brown & St Leger 2002; Pretty, Peacock, Hine, Sellens, South & Griffin 2007; Surridge 2004).

The outdoors may be used in a variety of ways depending upon the person's use of their time, the location with respect to where they reside, the activity focus or purpose, and the level of activity of the participant (Figure 1.1). Yet even these distinctions are not so simple, for example climbing at an indoor gym will have some similar concerns relating to personal protective

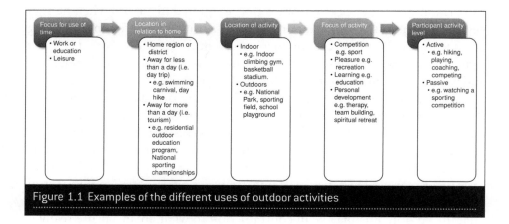

Figure 1.1 Examples of the different uses of outdoor activities

equipment as in climbing outdoors in a natural environment, while a local canoe club will have similar issues related to weather and personal safety as would competitors in a national canoe championships. Thus, from a risk management perspective, many of the issues discussed in this book will have application across sport, recreation and education where they use activities that are conducted primarily in the outdoors.

Perceived and real risk and safety

Another discussion that exists in the literature is the use of the terms perceived and real risk. Haddock defined real risk as 'the amount of risk which actually exists at a given moment in time (absolute risk adjusted by safety controls)' and perceived risk as 'an individual's subjective assessment of the real risk present at any time' (1993, p. 20). Regardless of whether the risk is 'real' or 'perceived', the reality is that the participant will respond to how serious they perceive the risk to be and how they evaluate the benefits or costs associated with taking the risks. Regardless of any objective measure by 'experts', people will perceive things differently and will feel and behave accordingly.

What may be deemed unsafe by one person, may be more to do with their lack of familiarity with the activity, while what is deemed too safe, may be due to too much familiarity. For example, for a new participant, abseiling may be considered as a 'high risk' activity, yet statistically may have less injuries than other activities in the outdoors (Dickson, Chapman & Hurrell 2000). In contrast, for an instructor, coach or guide, being too familiar with an activity may render them complacent and make them susceptible to not being conscious of relevant safety issues (Lange 2007).

Commensurate with these definitions of risk and risk management is the reiteration that an adventure is where the outcomes are uncertain. Risk is desirable. As noted by Walle, 'the absence of risk may decrease the satisfaction the participant receives from a would-be adventure' (1997, p. 266). If we can predict the outcome is it really an adventure (Dickson 2004)? In the context of classroom-based education, personal exploration and adventure are also important, as Eleanor Duckworth, Harvard Professor of Education, suggests:

> The virtues involved in not knowing are the ones that really count in the long run. What you do about what you don't know is, in the final analysis, what determines what you will ultimately know (Duckworth 2006, p. 68).

For Duckworth these virtues reflect the process of the adventure of learning that includes 'sitting alone, noticing something new, wondering about it, framing questions for oneself to answer, and sensing some contradiction in one's own ideas' (Duckworth 2006, p. 67).

What has not been addressed so far in this discusson about risk and risk management is the topic of safety. Risk and risk management is *not* about safety, though safety may be one aspect of risk management. We cannot guarantee safety, but we can manage the risks to maximise the potential outcomes, such as learning and growth, while limiting adverse effects, such as environmental damage or threats to physical wellbeing. As Willi Unsoeld (cited in Hunt 1991, p. 123) is quoted as saying,

> We used to tell them in Outward Bound, when a parent would come and ask us 'Can you *guarantee* the safety of our son, Johnny?' And we finally decided to meet it head on. We would say, 'No. We certainly can't Ma'am. We guarantee you the genuine chance of his death. And if we could guarantee his safety, the program would not be worth running. We do make one guarantee, as one parent to another. If you succeed in protecting your boy, as you are doing now, and as it's your motherly duty to do, you know, we applaud your watchdog tenacity. You should be protecting him. But if you succeed, we guarantee you the death of his soul'.

A whole-of-organisation approach to risk management

In the context of this book the term 'whole-of-organisation' is used to highlight the fact that risk management is the responsibility of everyone in an organisation, including clients and participants, not just the 'risk manager' or the risk and safety committee. To this end, risk management needs to be imbedded in all areas such as corporate governance, the human resource function, organisational culture, occupational health and safety, finance and in the familiar domain of standard operating procedures. Risk management is a proactive process and not a reactive process, in that the planning needs to happen before and throughout an event, so that plans are in place to deal

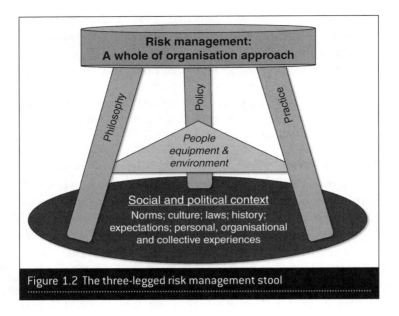

Figure 1.2 The three-legged risk management stool

with the situation before, during and after. (For further discussion of this in relation to severe weather, please refer to Chapter 10.)

First aid training is one example of reactive risk management in that the skills are in place to deal with a first aid situation should it occur. To make this a proactive approach, the first aid training may be supported by sessions exploring what first aid scenarios have arisen in the past or could happen in the future, what the contributing factors may be, and to plan what may be done to prevent these occurring. As an example, slips, trips and falls are frequent causes of injuries. The chance that a slip, trip or fall may occur will be exacerbated by fatigue, and fatigue can be exacerbated by poor hydration (Casa, Clarkson & Roberts 2005). Thus, a proactive risk management strategy would involve designing programs, activities or work processes to ensure that there is sufficient time for all to be adequately hydrated. This may also mean looking at the equipment used, in that hydration may be facilitated by the use of hydration packs which may be used 'on the go' instead of stopping and having to pull out drink bottles from packs or bags (Waddington, Dickson, Trathen & Adams 2010). Thus the 'solution' to managing the risk of slips, trips and falls may be a combination of hydration, program design and equipment choice that is supported by first aid training.

This book seeks to integrate previous views of risk management into one model or metaphor. A metaphor likens one thing to another. In this case, we are using the metaphor of a three-legged stool. Anyone who has ever used a tripod on uneven ground will know that it is very stable. The three legs of our structure are philosophy, policy and practice (Figure 1.2). These 'legs' are connected by the people, equipment and environment, while the stool itself is situated within a particular social, political, legal and historical context that may change over time or place. These will be discussed later in the chapter.

Philosophy

For any organisation, it is possible that a program or event that has operated for some time may not have a clear philosophy, but it is important to go back and clearly understand what this philosophy is in order that you may be sure that what you are doing and how you are doing it is consistent with what you say that you do. Other terms that may be used to refer to a philosophy include raison d'être, mission or vision. Essentially, though, your philosophy is articulating why you exist. This may include a social or community focus, an educational focus and an environmental focus. The philosophy underpins your organisation and must then be reflected in the policies of the organisation and ultimately the practice. The philosophy will inform 'how you do things around here' and thus the culture. Value statements may also support philosophies, visions and missions. A common value statement for many organisations that provides services to people are that their people are important part of the organisation, yet at a time of economic crisis, these value statements are put to the test with many organisations downsizing, rightsizing or more simply put, firing people.

People, equipment and environment

For risk management in the outdoors, Haddock (2004) introduces the importance of the interaction of the three key areas of people, equipment and environment as contributing factors in risk management. These areas fit within a broader framework known as human factors engineering that focuses upon the design of tools, machines, task, jobs and environments for the safe, comfortable and effective human use. Thus human factors is about the interactions and relationships between the people, i.e. the users, the tools or equipment they use and the environments in which they live and operate.

Social and political context

The context in which we operate will influence what is deemed to be acceptable or desirable risks. Changes in society have seen increased expectations that 'safety' will be assured with discussions of the 'nanny state', while generational changes impact the sills and experiences that participants bring to activities and programs. Each country with its various levels of government, will have their own legal frameworks and case histories that will also influence what may be deemed acceptable or appropriate at that time (this is explored in Chapter 3).

Child protection and the nanny state

If you obey all the rules, you miss all the fun. (Katharine Hepburn)

In the latter part of the 20th century and into the 21st century terms such as the 'nanny state' and 'helicopter parents' emerged as ways of expressing the increasing supervision and control over an individual's actions, potentially restricting the chance to venture, explore and discover. As society changes, the real adventures that children have, let alone the adventures adults have, have diminished to what can be offered by a commercial operator, seen on a screen or in the imaginations of the game designer. While there is little empirical evidence to support the views that the paranoia of parents is rising (Jenkins 2006), there are other reports highlighting the lack of engagement with the natural world that emerge as a result of increasing limits on a child's adventuring, exploring and playing in the outdoors (Charles, Louv, Bodner & Guns 2008; Louv 2006; Mallar et al 2002). Playing in the cubby house down the backyard, watching the tadpoles grow in the local creek and the riding of bikes until the sun goes down, have been replaced by supervised play dates, personal video game players, DVD players in cars and structured and supervised games and lessons. The time and place for children to play, dream, explore and learn from their trial and error have been managed out and replaced by programs, controls and the loss of adventure and the exploration of the unknown.

In place of having real personal adventures we have commodified adventure into packages bought over the internet. If we have lost the ability to have adventures, what are the implications for the future for us as individuals, organisations and nations? In May 2010, 16 year-old Australian Jessica Watson returned from a 210 day unassisted solo sailing trip. A spectator, who was a parent of a 16 year-old girl herself, while watching Jessica's return, reflected that if you bring children up to have dreams, you have to also give them wings to fly. To this may be added: and then let them fly.

An internet search using the term 'adventure tourism' reveals offerings of bungy jumping, tandem skydiving, white water rafting and jet boating. Each of these are provided and supervised by commercial organisations and resemble 'thrill seeking' activities which are more closely related to theme parks, than to 'real' personal adventures. As these 'packaged' adventures replace real adventures in the outdoors, the children may be physically safer,

Table 1.1 Generational characteristics

	Birth dates	Age in 2006	Proportion of population in 2006	Non-school qualifications	Born overseas	Christian affiliation	Employed at 15–19 yrs
Oldest generation	1891–1926	80 +	4%	23%	31%	79%	N/A
Lucky generation	1926–1946	60–79	15%	37%	36%	78%	est 73%
Baby boomers	1946–1966	40–59	28%	53%	32%	67%	62%
Generation X and Y	1966–1986	20–39	28%	57%	24%	63%	42%
iGeneration	1986–2006	0–19	27%	N/A	N/A	N/A	46%

Source: ABS (2009).

but there may be greater concerns as they become increasingly detached and disconnected from the healing properties of nature (Charles et al 2008; Louv 2006) and the risk that they may not be able to manage uncertainties and change in their own lives.

Concerns about the future of our young people are not new. Kurt Hahn said in 1936: 'It is our duty to equip this growing generation, irrespective of class, with willing bodies. It is our duty also to train them in self-discipline. Freedom and discipline are not enemies, they are friends' (Hahn 1936, p. 3).

Then 23 years later, Hahn reflected on the state of the young, comments that could easily apply more 50 years later:

> Our young are today surrounded by five decays – the decay of fitness due to our modern methods of locomotion, the decay of self discipline helped by stimulants and tranquilisers, the decay of enterprise due to the widespread disease of *spectatoritis*, the decay of skill and care helped by the decline in craftsmanship and above all the decay of compassion which William Temple called spiritual death (Hahn 1959, p. 4).

The changing generations

In designing, planning, delivering and evaluating programs and activities, it is important to understand who your target market or clients may be. One way of gaining some understanding of them is through the lens of the generations such as baby boomers, Gen X, Gen Y, etc. The Australian Bureau of Statistics in their analysis of the 2006 census (Australian Bureau of Statistics 2000) have sought to provide a summary of the current generations, and in doing so have blended the Generation X and Y into one group to enable better comparison with the other generations, most of which have a 20 year time span (Table 1.1). What may be seen is that later generations are more highly educated, less likely to be born overseas, less likely to be affiliated with the Christian faith and less likely to be employed at a young age. In combination with the fact that many young people are living at home longer, Generations X and Y are not achieving the traditional markers of being an 'adult', such as finishing their education, starting work, leaving home and starting a family (Furstenberg, Rumbaut & Settersten 2004).

While the transition to adulthood may appear delayed, the impact of technology on these later generations has increased communication and access to information to the point where individuals through mobile phones, PDAs, tablets and other emerging technologies may broadcast events around the world within minutes. These generations may not be 'moving up and moving out' in the same way that their parents and grandparents did, but they can be part of a world-wide network, sharing information through their personal blogs and wikis, creating short videos to entertain the world via websites such as Google and YouTube. Given the chance that Generations X and Y and the iGenerations are innovators, creators and thinkers, seeking adventure through their technology, the problem is that they may not be as familiar with adventure in the uncontrolled context of outdoor environments as their parents' or grandparents' generations where there is no 'undo' command if things go wrong. These generational and individual differences may have implications for the type of programs and activities offered, the equipment used, the level of supervision, the time required to achieve competence and the physical challenges faced. For example, individuals who have grown up in urban environments, with numerous communication devices, eating and drinking processed foods, may be highly challenged if walking on uneven dirt tracks in a national park, out of contact with friends, eating fresh salad and drinking water, and may feel stressed and uncomfortable. Equally, young persons from a farming background who have completed their schooling via correspondence might find that doing an urban challenge program with a team of people they do not know and which involves navigating public transport, dealing with large crowds and busy traffic may also be put outside their comfort zones.

To this end, the underlying philosophy of this book reflects that of the Royal Society for Prevention of Accidents (RoSPA), which is not about avoiding the risks to safety, but rather preparing people to make informed decisions in their own lives. Thus, RoSPA promotes 'the idea of "as safe as necessary, not as safe as possible" and places an emphasis on equipping people with the skills to ensure informed choices of behaviour. It is important that society becomes risk aware, not risk averse, and this begins with safety and risk education in schools' (Royal Society for Prevention of Accidents 2010).

To achieve this, it is proposed that the risk management process outlined in ISO 31000 will be of assistance as it provides a much broader approach

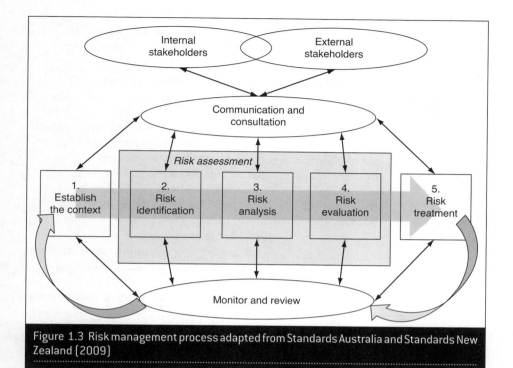

Figure 1.3 Risk management process adapted from Standards Australia and Standards New Zealand (2009)

to risk and risk management than the 'old school' version of risk where the focus was on the potential for loss. To reiterate, it is the belief of the authors of this book that no one takes a risk in the belief that it will fail, rather, the purpose of risk, is that there is some benefit or positive outcome related to the objectives of the individual, activity, program and/or event.

The risk management process

ISO 31000 (SASNZ, 2009) provides an outline of the process necessary to manage the risks (Figure 1.3 and Table 1.2). The five key steps, that are discussed in detail later, are:

1 Establish the context
2 Identify the risks
3 Analyse the risks
4 Evaluate the risks
5 Treat the risks.

Throughout this process it is essential to communicate and consult with both internal and external stakeholders about the risk management process

Table 1.2 Steps in the risk management process

Steps	Definitions from ISO 31000	Examples
Communicate and consult	'Communication and consultation with internal and external stakeholders should take place during all stages of the risk management process' (p. 14).	Listen to the concerns of external stakeholders about the risks and the risk management process. Communicate with external stakeholders about the risk management process and their role in the process. Involve internal stakeholders in the risk management process from risk identification through to monitoring and review. Provide ongoing communication strategies for both internal and external stakeholders to provide continuous feedback. Engage internal and external stakeholders as key partners in the risk management process.
1 Establish the context	'The organization articulates its objectives, defines the external and internal parameters to be taken into account when managing risk, and sets the scope and risk criteria for the remaining process' (p. 15).	What are the current regulations and standards related to your operations? Who are the internal/external stakeholders? What are their expectations in relation to risk? What is the philosophy or purpose of your operations? How does this relate to your risk management activities? What is the current risk management culture? What systems are in place? How is risk management managed across your organisation? What is an acceptable level of risk for your organisation or activity?
2 Risk identification	'The organization should identify sources or risk, areas of impacts, events (including changes in circumstances) and their causes and their potential consequences' (p. 17).	Human resources: insufficient volunteers to run the event, staff illness impacting upon service delivery, effective staff management ensures that experienced staff return each season, retirement of the core senior staff who established the organisation. Finance and the economy: insufficient cash flow to meet obligations, economic crisis reducing demand for your services, worsening exchange rate leading to an increased demand for domestic recreation opportunities.

Table 1.2 (*cont.*)

Steps	Definitions from ISO 31000	Examples
		Organisational success: the organisation is growing faster than you are able to adapt your systems or recruit staff. An incident in another organisation raises concerns from your clients about their 'safety' and they threaten to cancel. Insurance: failure of a large insurance agency reduces the availability of suitable insurance for your operations. Fire or flood closes normal areas of operation. Poor weather or challenging terrain renders GPSs and EPIRBs inoperable. Extremely fit and healthy participants complete all activities under time resulting in long periods of free time during the program.
3 Risk analysis	'involves consideration of the causes and sources of risk, their positive and negative consequences, and the likelihood that those consequences can occur' (p. 18).	Potential controls: policies and procedures in place and applied, risk management culture, staff experience, staff training, staff morale, knowledge management, risk communication. The level of risk is a function of the likelihood of the event and the potential consequences which may include financial, environmental, social, physical injury, educational outcomes.
4 Risk evaluation	'the purpose of risk evaluation is to assist in making decisions, based on the outcomes of risk analysis, about which risks need treatment and the priority for treatment implementation' (p. 18).	Compare the level of risk from Step 3 with the risk criteria established in Step 1 from which a decision will be made as to whether: • further analysis is required • the level of risk is tolerable • the level of risk is not tolerable and the risk requires some level of treatment

(*cont.*)

Table 1.2 (*cont.*)

Steps	Definitions from ISO 31000	Examples

5 Risk treatment	'Risk treatment involves selecting one or more options for modifying risks, and implementing those options' (p. 18).	For risks with positive outcomes this may include:
		Choose to take on the risk in order to attain the positive outcomes and/or
		• Find ways to enhance the positive outcomes, such as increasing:
		
		  the reflection processes around an activity
		  the time allocated to activities
		  staff training to enhance their abilities to facilitate activities.
		
		For risks with potential adverse outcomes, treatments may include:
		• Do not do the activity.
		• Reduce the likelihood through reducing the exposure to the risk, e.g.:
		
		  varying the activity or route taken
		  changing the timing of the activity to operate in different weather conditions
		  employing skilled staff who may be more capable of foreseeing problems
		  have backup technology in case batteries fail or where poor satellite coverage which renders GPSs, Satellite phones and EPIRBs inoperable
		  screen participants for pre-existing medical conditions
		  reduce the potential consequences through training staff to manage emergency situations
		  conducting activities closer to emergency services.

Monitor and review	'Both monitoring and review should be a planned part of the risk management process and involve regular checking or surveillance' (p.20).	Review the risk management process regularly to ensure the assumptions made about the context, risks and treatments remain valid and current. Review any key events to identify new learnings. Seek external review and feedback on the risk management process.

in order to engage them as partners in the process. Equally important is the ongoing monitoring and reviewing of the process to ensure that it is current and has been adapted for changing circumstances and learnings from reviews of the management of the risks.

To demonstrate the application of this process, the example of volunteers is used. Volunteers are essential for the conduct of many outdoor activities and programs, including the local guide and scout groups, bushwalking groups, coaching and managing of sporting teams, and running sporting events from local clubs to the Olympics, Paralympics and FIFA World Cups.

Expanding the steps in the risk management process

1 Establish the context

Understanding the context will influence how the risk management process is applied. Risk and risk management may differ in different social, legal, political and environmental processes. Each context is different from the frequency scale and level of public awareness, yet there may also be some overlap. For example the local guide or scout group and the Olympic and Paralympic Summer Games are dependent on volunteers for their operations, and they may also conduct similar activities such as canoeing, sailing and archery, but the scale of activity, the financial resources and media interest are significantly different.

Using a focus on the role of volunteers in conducting activities in the outdoors, questions that may be considered to explore the context include:

- What is the previous volunteering experience of the organisation/ staff?
- What is the culture of volunteering in the broader community?
- Who is likely to be a volunteer? Demographics, interests, skills, qualifications, previous paid and volunteer experience.
- What other demands (regular and irregular) are there for the volunteers' time from other groups in the community, sporting and charitable arenas?
- What encourages/discourages people to volunteer?
- What do the volunteers want from the experience?
- Who *isn't* volunteering and why?

2 Identify risks

As indicated earlier, the objectives of an organisation may be economic, environmental and social. As a result, what may impact upon these diverse objectives may also be equally diverse. Continuing with the focus on

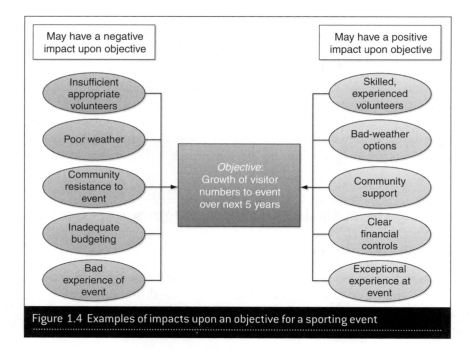

May have a negative impact upon objective		May have a positive impact upon objective
Insufficient appropriate volunteers		Skilled, experienced volunteers
Poor weather		Bad-weather options
Community resistance to event	Objective: Growth of visitor numbers to event over next 5 years	Community support
Inadequate budgeting		Clear financial controls
Bad experience of event		Exceptional experience at event

Figure 1.4 Examples of impacts upon an objective for a sporting event

volunteers, of the diverse things that may impact upon the supply of volunteers. During September 2009, the UK's Home Office's Vetting and Barring Scheme was expanded to include parents who drive children to sporting events or social clubs which organisations that depend upon volunteers fear the policy will reduce the number of people volunteering (BBC News 2009). In contrast, on the same day it was reported that Michelle Obama, wife of the President of the United States of America, promised to deliver a university commencement address if the students completed 100 000 hours of community service that year (Byers 2009).

Factors that may impact on an objective may be the 'two-sides of the one coin', where a risk that is not managed well may have a negative impact, while if it is managed well it may well have a positive impact upon the objective (Figure 1.4). In the example in Figure 1.4 the objective to grow a program that is dependent upon volunteer commitment will be negatively impacted if there are insufficient volunteers and equally may be positively impacted if there is a sufficient supply of appropriately skilled and experienced volunteers.

When considering the role of volunteers what may need to be considered includes:

- insufficient supply of volunteers from the target community
- insufficient demand for volunteers from within the organisation or event
- inappropriate management of volunteers impacting upon their willingness to volunteer again

Table 1.3 Risk analysis matrix

Likelihood	Consequences				
	Insignificant 1	Minor 2	Moderate 3	Major 4	Catastrophic 5
A (Almost certain)	A1 High	A2 High	A3 Extreme	A4 Extreme	A5 Extreme
B (Likely)	B1 Moderate	B2 High	B3 High	B4 Extreme	B5 Extreme
C (Possible)	C1 Low	C2 Moderate	C3 High	C4 Extreme	C5 Extreme
D (Unlikely)	D1 Low	D2 Low	D3 Moderate	D4 High	D5 Extreme
E (Rare)	E1 Low	E2 Low	E3 Moderate	E4 High	E5 High

- bad volunteering experiences elsewhere impacting upon volunteers' willingness to volunteer
- legislative changes such as with Child Protection, Occupational Health and Safety or Food Safety that makes using employees more difficult
- public transport changes that make it difficult for volunteers to travel to the event or activity
- government policies that promote the role of volunteers and increase the supply of volunteers.

3 Analyse risks

Many organisations or programs will already have some existing controls in place, some may be formalised in policies and procedures, while others may be less formal and dependent on word of mouth. In order to be able to effectively manage any risks, it is essential to understand the 'level' of risk, which is a result of the interrelationship between the likelihood that the event could occur, and the resultant consequences should it occur. Together this will give a risk score (Table 1.3) that then provides an indication of the level of intervention required:

- extreme risk: immediate preventative action required
- high risk: senior management attention needed
- moderate risk: management responsibility must be specified
- low risk: manage by routine procedures.

In relation to the supply of volunteers, questions that could be considered include:

- How do you ensure that there are sufficient appropriately skilled volunteers available when the work demands?
- How likely is it that there will be *insufficient* volunteers available?
- Would the event and/or organisation survive without volunteers?

Table 1.4 Risk analysis matrix: examples of acceptable and unacceptable levels of risk

Likelihood	Consequences				
	Insignificant 1	Minor 2	Moderate 3	Major 4	Catastrophic 5
A (Almost certain)		Not			
B (Likely)		Acceptable			
C (Possible)					
D (Unlikely)		Acceptable			
E (Rare)					

While questions in relation to the demand for volunteers include:
- What internal marketing is there to promote the contribution of volunteers and hence the internal demand for volunteers?
- Is there sufficient meaningful and challenging work available for volunteers that draws upon their skills and qualifications as well as development opportunities?

4 Evaluate risks

Depending on the risk criteria set in Step 1, the risk matrix will help clarify those areas of risk that are acceptable (such as low or moderate risks) or unacceptable (such as high and extreme) for the organisation, event or activity within a particular time and place (Table 1.4).

Considering what may or may not motivate volunteers (Vining 1998), it is also important to consider what may happen in the following instances:
- If there is an excess of volunteers for the work available how do you encourage the individual to be motivated to offer to volunteer again in the future?
- If there were insufficient volunteers, what would it cost to recruit, train and pay for qualified staff?
- What is the legacy of volunteering that you are leaving for other organisations, activities or the broader community?
- Do volunteers feel that they are not valued and that they are not making a meaningful contribution and are therefore leaving early or not returning in the future?
- Do paid staff have the skills to manage a flexible, volunteer workforce?

5 Treat risks

The risk management strategies may impact on the likelihood, the consequence, or both, of the identified risks and thus the resultant risk score.

Further examples of risk management strategies that may be relevant to the management of volunteers include:

- internal marketing of the benefits that volunteers bring and to further identify volunteer opportunities
- analysis of the skills of volunteers to ensure appropriate task allocation
- training of permanent staff to work with volunteers to maximise the opportunities for both groups
- job descriptions for volunteers to ensure clarity of expectations
- rewards and remuneration for volunteers, e.g. badges for service recognition, celebration events for volunteer contribution, articles in newsletters recognising the role of volunteers.

Communicate and consult and monitor and review

The final two phases discussed in ISO 31000 are essential for continuous improvement and to ensure that the risk management process reflects and adapts to any changing circumstances. Communication will assist with developing effective risk management strategies that have support of key stakeholders, while the monitoring and reviewing aid learning from the process and contribute to the continuous improvement of the risk management process.

Conclusion

All people, especially young people, need places where they can take acceptable risks to test their knowledge and skills, to learn from their mistakes and to grow into well-developed, confident and contributing human beings. Outdoor activities in sport, outdoor education and recreation are places and spaces where this may occur. The greater risk to our future generations is not the risk to their physical safety that may be a result of trying, but that we may not have helped them obtain the necessary skills to live and learn from their own adventures throughout their lives.

This book seeks to present a view of participation in the outdoors that supports people being able to go out, to have a go, to learn and grow and to have the skills and confidence to create and pursue their own adventures throughout their lives so that they may live happy, healthy and engaging lives.

References

Aldous, D 2006. 'The benefits of green space: greening our cities and surrounds'. *Australasian Parks and Leisure*, Summer, pp. 6–8.

Australian Bureau of Statistics 2000. *A Picture of the Nation: the Statistician's Report on the 2006 Census, 2006 (Cat. no. 207.0).* Canberra, ACT.

BBC News 2009. 'NSPCC criticises volunteer checks'. Retrieved from <http://news.bbc.co.uk/2/hi/uk_news/8253099.stm>.

Beedie, P 1994. 'Risk taking: the consensus view'. *The Journal of Adventure Education and Outdoor Leadership*, vol. 11, no. 2, pp. 13-7.

Bernstein, PL 1996. *Against the Gods: The Remarkable Story of Risk.* John Wiley and Sons, New York.

Biddle, S, Gorely, T, Marshall, S & Cameron, N 2005. 'Sport and exercise participation and time spent outside: differences between groups varying in sedentary behaviour.' (Part V: Psychology). *Journal of Sports Sciences*, vol. 23, no. 11-2, 1239 (1232).

Byers, A 2009. 'First Lady promises commencement address if George Washington University students volunteer'. Retrieved from <http://www.foxnews.com/politics/2009/09/11/lady-promises-commencement-address-george-washington-university-students/>.

Casa, DJ, Clarkson, PM & Roberts, WO 2005. American College of Sports Medicine roundtable on hydration and physical activity: consensus statements. *Current Sports Medicine Reports*, vol. 4, no. 3, pp. 115-27.

Cater, CI 2006. 'Playing with risk? Participant perceptions of risk and management implications in adventure tourism'. *Tourism Management*, vol. 27, no. 2, pp. 317-25.

Charles, C, Louv, R, Bodner, L & Guns, B 2008. Children and Nature 2008: A Report on the Movement to Reconnect Children to the Natural World. Children and Nature Network, Santa Fe.

Dickson, TJ 2004. 'If the outcome is predictable, is it an adventure? Being in, not barricaded from, the outdoors'. *World Leisure Journal*, vol. 46, no. 4, pp. 48-8.

Dickson, TJ, Chapman, J & Hurrell, M 2000. 'Risk in outdoor activities: the perception, the appeal, the reality'. *Australian Journal of Outdoor Education*, vol. 4, no. 2, pp. 10-7.

Dickson, TJ, Gray, T & Mann, K 2008. *Australian Outdoor Adventure Activity Benefits Catalogue*, available from <http://outdoorcouncil.asn.au/doc/Outdoor-ActivityBenefitsCatalogueFinal270808.pdf>

Dickson, TJ, & Tugwell, M (eds) 2000. *The Risk Management Document: Strategies in Risk Management for Outdoor and Experiential Learning.* Outdoor Recreation Industry Council, Sydney (NSW).

Duckworth, ER 2006. *'The Having of Wonderful Ideas': And Other Essays on Teaching and Learning*, 3rd edition. Teachers College Press, New York.

Furstenberg, FF, Jr, Rumbaut, RG & Settersten, RA, Jr 2004. 'On the frontier of adulthood: emerging themes and new directions'. *Network on Transitions to Adulthood: Policy Brief*, vol. 1, MacArthur Foundation Research Network on Transitions to Adulthood and Public Policy, Philadelphia.

Haddock, C 1993. *Managing Risks in Outdoor Activities.* New Zealand Mountain Safety Council, Wellington NZ.

Haddock, C 2004. *Outdoor Safety: Risk Management for Outdoor Leaders.* New Zealand Mountain Safety Council, Wellington, NZ.

Hahn, K 1936. 'Education and peace: the foundations of modern society'. Reprinted from the *Inverness Courier*, 24 March 1936. Retrieved from <www.kurthahn.org>.

Hahn, K 1947. 'Training for and through the sea'. Address given to the Honourable Mariners' Company in Glasgow, 14 February 1947. Retrieved from <http://www.kurthahn.org/writings/train.pdf>.

Hahn, K 1959. Speech Dr Kurt Hahn at the Forty-Eighth Annual Dinner of Old Centralians. *The Central: The Journal of Old Centralians*, February, no. 119, pp. 3–8.

Hunt, JS 1991. 'Philosophy of adventure education' in JC Miles & S Priest (eds), *Adventure Education*, Venture Publishing Inc, State College PA, pp. 119–28.

Jack, M 1994. *Strategies for Risk Management in Outdoor and Experiential Learning: A Manual Identifying Risk Management Issues, Creation of an Operations Manual, Common Practices and Standards.* The Outdoor Professionals, Brookvale, NSW.

Jenkins, NE 2006. 'You can't wrap them up in cotton wool! Constructing risk in young people's access to outdoor play'. *Health, Risk & Society*, vol. 8, no. 4, pp. 379–93.

Krakauer, J 1997. *Into Thin Air: A Personal Account of the Everest Disaster.* Macmillan, London.

Lange, C 2007. 'Entering unforgiving territory'. *Occupational Health and Safety*, vol. 10, pp. 44–5. Retrieved from <http://ohsonline.com/articles/2007/10/entering-unforgiving-territory.aspx>.

Louv, R 2006. *Last Child in the Woods.* Algonquin Books of Chapel Hill.

Mallar, C, Townsend, M, Brown, P & St Leger, L 2002. *Healthy Parks Healthy People: the Health Benefits of Contact with Nature in a Park Context. A Review of Current Literature*, vol. 1, Deakin University and Parks Victoria, Melbourne.

Mortlock, C 1984. *The Adventure Alternative.* Cicerone Press, Milnthorpe, Cumbria.

Pretty, J, Peacock, J, Hine, R, Sellens, M, South, N & Griffin, M 2007. 'Green exercise in the UK countryside: effects on health and psychological well-being, and implications for policy and planning'. *Journal of Environmental Planning and Management*, vol. 50, no. 2, pp. 211–31.

Priest, S & Gass, MA 1997. *Effective Leadership in Adventure Programming.* Human Kinetics, Champaign, IL.

Royal Society for Prevention of Accidents 2010. 'The Royal Society for the Prevention of Accidents'. Retrieved 28 April 2010 from <http://www.rospa.com>.

Standards Australia and Standards New Zealand 1999. *AS/NZS 4360: 1999 Risk Management.* Standards Association of Australia, Strathfield, NSW.

Standards Australia and Standards New Zealand 2004. *AS/NZS 4360: 2004 Australian/New Zealand Standard: Risk Management.* Standards Association of Australia, Strathfield NSW.

Standards Australia and Standards New Zealand 2009. *AS/NZS ISO 31000 Risk Management – Principles and Guidelines.* Standards Australia and Standards New Zealand, Sydney, NSW.

Surridge, J 2004. 'Wild at heart: tapping into the restorative power of the great outdoors'. *Mental Health Practice*, vol. 7, no. 7, pp. 20–4.

Thoreau, HD 1854/1986. Walden in HD Thoreau (ed), *Walden and Civil Disobedience.* Penguin Books, New York, pp. 43–382.

Varley, P 2006. 'Confecting adventure and playing with meaning: the Adventure Commodification Continuum'. *Journal of Sport and Tourism*, vol. 11, no. 2, pp. 173–94.

Vining, L 1998. *Working with Volunteers in Schools: Understand Volunteers and Reap the Benefits for Your School*. Lenross Publications, Carlingford NSW.

Waddington, GS, Dickson, TJ, Trathen, SD & Adams, RD 2010. 'Hydration packs modify professional skiers hydration levels in all day skiing: a randomised controlled trial'. *Journal of ASTM International*, vol. 7, no. 10. Retrieved from <http://www.astm.org/DIGITAL_LIBRARY/JOURNALS/JAI/PAGES/JAI102818.htm>.

Walle, AH 1997. 'Pursuing risk or insight: marketing adventures'. *Annals of Tourism Research*, vol. 24, no. 2, pp. 265-82.

Organisational sustainability and risk management

Brian Weir and Tracey J. Dickson

Wake up, this is serious.

Fyffe 2005, quoted in Gossling & Hall (2006, p. 305)

FOCUS QUESTIONS

1. What is sustainability?
2. What is sustainability in an organisational sense?
3. How will managers know their organisation is sustainable?
4. How will organisational sustainability assist managers of outdoor organisations, events or programs with risk management?

Introduction: what is sustainability?

Sustainability is more than the environment. As this chapter explains, sustainability is a concept and the basis for a business approach that will assist education, sport and recreation practitioners and organisations make their operations more financially/economically, socially *and* environmentally successful and beneficial to their stakeholders, communities and staff in the short term and into the future.

Background

When we think of sustainability, we may think of iconic old growth forests, magnificent wetlands with endless flocks of migratory birds, saving the whales, oil spills or degraded coral reefs. This is not unexpected, given that 'sustainability' originated in work on the environmental impacts of development, particularly in the Third World and previously underdeveloped areas. As Spenceley (2008) notes, 'development', was originally intended to improve human welfare through growth and extension of economic activity. However, by the 1970s development was also being seen to create environmental problems, including degradation of the natural environment. It was this idea, that development was good, but needed to be pursued in tandem with a commitment to maintaining the environment in which the development was being undertaken, that led to the idea of 'sustainable development' (Basiano 1995 in Spenceley 2008, p. 1).

The 1987 UN World Commission on Environment and Development (UNWCED) *Our Common Future Report* (often called the *Brundtland Report* after the Commission's chair) defined 'sustainable development' as development that 'meets the needs of the present generation without compromising the ability of future generations to meet their own needs' (UNWCED 1987, p. 43).

Further work on this concept over the following decade (including at the 1992 Rio Earth Summit) led to the realisation that not only environmental but also economic and social development needed to be included to ensure all elements of 'development' were considered (e.g. World Travel and Tourism Council, World Tourism Organisation and the Earth Council 1997). Elkington further developed this approach to define the 'Triple Bottom Line' of sustainable development as the simultaneous drive to achieve economic prosperity, environmental quality and social equity (Elkington 1997, cited in Spenceley 2008); this notion is discussed later in more detail.

The United Nations Commission on Sustainable Development (UNCSD) promoted this idea, defining sustainable development as development that ensures 'meeting the needs of present and future generations for goods and services in ways that are economically, socially and environmentally sustainable' (UNCSD 1999 cited in Spenceley 2008, p. 2).

Different organisations have taken slightly different terms for very similar ideas. The World Tourism Organisation, for example, suggests that sustainable tourism is a form of economic development that is designed to:
- improve the quality of life of the host community
- provide a high quality of experience for the visitor, and
- maintain the quality of the environment on which both the host community and the visitor depend (cited in Flagestad & Hope 2001, p. 445).

A sport example from the Canadian Green and Gold organisation suggests that sport is sustainable when 'it meets the needs of today's sports community while contributing to the improvement of future sports opportunities for all and the integrity of the natural environment on which it depends' (Green and Gold Inc., 2010).

So, how can we visualise 'sustainability'? A simple model is shown in Figure 2.1.

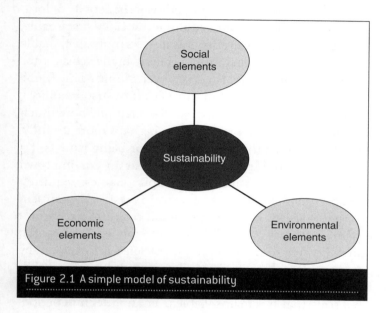

Figure 2.1 A simple model of sustainability

This model emphasises the interconnectedness of the three dimensions of sustainability: environmental, social and economic. Of course, this model applies not just to 'development', but to 'operations' as well. It is not just in the planning and development stage of an activity, event or attraction that sustainability needs to be considered, but during the life before and beyond.

Temporal and spatial dimensions of sustainability

Time and space are also issues in sustainability. The Brundtland Report focuses on the time or temporal dimension of sustainability principally through the idea of 'intergenerational equity', that activities today should not compromise the ability of future generations to meet their needs in their time (UNWCED 1987). However, more broadly this notion can be extended to considering the issue of the time frame of sustainability. The temporal or time elements of sustainability could be envisaged as: short term (e.g. measured in days to months), medium term (e.g. months to years) and long term (e.g. decades).

Of course, the idea of short, medium and long-term will vary with the sustainability issue under consideration. For example, from an economic perspective, the time frame for assessing economic sustainability may be year-on-year profit growth, while the time frame for assessing environmental sustainability may be three to five years, yet the time frame for social sustainability may be even longer, or vice versa. Thus, a short-term financially successful event or business may be achieved at the expense of the medium to long-term environment and/or the social sustainability of the activity or location. Alternatively, in seeking to be environmentally and socially sustainable, an organisation may struggle in its initial efforts as it seeks more sustainable equipment, resources and modes of operation, often at higher costs, thus jeopardising the economic sustainability. However, over a longer time frame they may be assessed as being viable across all three facets of sustainability.

A second dimension to consider is the spatial, for example, how much space does an activity or event take up or affect? Or, perhaps more usefully, what scale of development or operations is envisaged or being run? Is it a small, perhaps local, event; maybe a soccer match held at an existing town football field? Or is it a major event like an Olympics Games, requiring developments over many square kilometres of space? Is it a small tourism development, say a modest visitor kiosk in a regional recreation area, or a large, five-star hotel in a national park? This idea of scale and the spatial dimension of sustainability in a tourism development sense are explored by Butler (1999) who sees sustainable tourism development as 'tourism which is developed and maintained in an area (community environment) in such a manner and at such a scale that it remains viable over an indefinite period' (Butler 1999, p. 23).

In a similar way to the temporal dimension outlined above, the spatial elements or scale of development or operations issues may be envisaged as: micro level (e.g. measured in metres), meso level (e.g. kilometres) and macro scale (e.g. kilometres up to perhaps a planetary scale).

Thus, the three elements of sustainability, not only need to be considered collectively, but also within the context of both the temporal and spatial elements of the activity.

Organisational sustainability and risk management

How does risk management link to sustainability?

If your activity is not sustainable then you put at risk your reputation, your financial position and the very livelihoods of yourself and your staff, and thus your organisational objectives. Traditionally the main measure of success has been economic measure or financial returns such as profits, or return on shareholder funds. In this context, the risk is that the business will not be successful, and so much effort has gone into ensuring business success, using measures such as staff turnover, cost of goods sold, return on shareholder funds, and return on investment.

To illustrate the points made above, the risk analyses in the Appendix provides a sample risk analysis, which could be used for an organisation considering the risks it may face in a range of areas, including planning and implementing sustainability measures in its operations (see also Chapter 1 for more details).

What is sustainability in an organisational sense?

What does this mean for education, sport and recreation practitioners, and managers and staff of organisations operating in this field?

For organisations, programs and events, sustainability is an essential consideration. Figure 2.1 presented sustainability as an inter-relationship between economic, environmental and social elements. A more useful model might present your activity or organisation as being supported by these three pillars of environmental, social and economic sustainability (Figure 2.2).

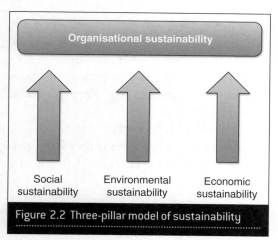

Figure 2.2 Three-pillar model of sustainability

Recalling the simple model of sustainability presented in Figure 2.1, sustainability may be seen as the resultant of the social, environmental and economic elements within an organisation's internal and external milieu. That is, any organisation operates within a social, environmental and economic context. Figure 2.2 reframes the simple model of Figure 2.1 to emphasise each element of sustainability as a 'pillar' supporting the organisation.

As is suggested in this figure, the strength of each pillar contributes to, or detracts from, the sustainability of the organisation. If one pillar is weak, then the sustainability of your operation is at risk. Your business may be financially sound, and thus financially sustainable into the future. However, if it is not socially and environmentally sustainable, it will run into difficulties, perhaps with the community in which it operates, with community groups, government regulators, land managers and perhaps also with its own stakeholders or shareholders. To explore this further, it is important to consider in more detail the components of these three pillars of sustainability within the context of risk management.

Environmental sustainability

As discussed earlier, 'sustainability' began with a focus on the environment: can we, and how can we, achieve our desired economic and social outcomes without damaging our environment?

Over the last fifty years, there has been ongoing discussion, and often heated debate, about environmental sustainability, and its importance to business and indeed society. Perhaps beginning with Rachel Carson's iconic book *Silent Spring* in the early 1960s, there has been a steady rise in awareness of, research into, and community concern about environmental sustainability. This has led to increasing regulation, but also community and business action, including in relation to:

- pollution – water, air and soil, including through clean water and clean air legislation, as well as restrictions on the storage and disposal of hazardous materials
- waste management – such as reducing, reusing and recycling of materials, but also on simple issues such as littering (e.g. Keep Australia Beautiful and Clean Up Australia campaigns)
- reducing or eliminating threats to species biodiversity
- reducing the carbon footprint of our lifestyles, communities and business operations (see Glossary at the end of the chapter for definition of terms).

In recent years, this focus has become more sophisticated, as seen with an interest in 'Food Miles' (the environmental, social and economic costs of transporting foods from producers to consumers). Small local groceries, for example, may be able to provide fresher, locally produced foodstuffs more easily than large, national supermarket chains.

Another part of this focus considers the environment as a background or setting for community or commercial operations or activities. That is, for activities conducted in an outdoor environment, the environment may be both the attraction as well as the setting for activities. Outdoor sports such as hockey and football are subject to the vagaries of the weather. They are often played on fields requiring water from limited potable water resources. In a country such as Australia where repeated and prolonged drought periods can reduce the amount of water available for watering sporting fields, sporting clubs may have their activities reduced or event cancelled if fields become too hard and bare to play on. White water rafting activities on natural rivers require sufficient water flow, but not too much, and hiking in alpine areas can be challenging in poor weather with low clouds.

Climate change

There has also been growing concern about climate change in recent years. Climate is critical to the world we experience; the landscape, and the plants and animals in it are all determined to a large extent by climate acting over long intervals of time. Over long periods of geological time climate shapes mountains, builds up soil and changes the course of rivers and landscapes. Note the difference between 'weather' and climate – as one commentator has noted, 'weather is what we get, climate is what we expect' (Burroughs 2007, p. 2). Beginning with the establishment of the Intergovernmental Panel on Climate Change (IPCC) by the United Nations in 1992, a more concerted international effort has been underway to study greenhouse gas levels, their sources and impacts. The IPCC and its associated bodies have issued a number of reports which with increasing confidence show the continuing rise of greenhouse gas levels due to human activities (in particular fossil fuels consumption) is impacting on the world's climate, driving up atmospheric temperatures, with significant environmental, social and economic impacts (IPCC 2007).

Climate change and its expected impacts are likely to affect many, if not all, areas of human activity over time. While there have been some suggestions that there are ideal climate-related conditions for recreational activities (e.g. Hall & Higham, 2005), the reality is that people or organisations cannot control the climate. All that can be controlled is how we respond to the weather that is present at that time in that place. For example, that response can be a change in clothing, a change in behaviour or a change in attitude or expectations: as one of the authors in this book, and a ski instructor, opined to one of the authors of this chapter, 'There is no bad weather, just bad clothing choices!'.

Social sustainability

As alluded to in the definitions of sustainability, social sustainability refers to the manner in which an organisation or event creates or induces change in the quality of life, lifestyle, behaviour or perhaps even value systems of its host community (adapted from Hall 2008). Organisations should be aware of these impacts. As Steiner noted,

> Business is and must remain fundamentally an economic institution, but it does have responsibilities to help society achieve its basic goals and does, therefore, have social responsibilities . . . It is a philosophy that looks at the social interest and the enlightened self-interest of business over the long run as compared with the old, narrow, unrestrained short-run self-interest. (Steiner 1971, p. 164)

Such impacts may be beneficial or conversely have negative impacts.
Possible positive impacts:
- provide additional sporting, recreational and educational opportunities for residents and visitors
- improve quality of life for local residents and
- foster pride and confidence in participants and the local community.

Possible negative impacts could do the following:
- adversely impact on local culture and values
- impact on the pace or quality of life of the community and
- lead to the 'commodification' of local (especially Indigenous) culture.

Of course, there is a greater likelihood of adverse impacts where the activity or operation introduces a new and discordant element into a community. For example, the building of a motor racing circuit in a suburban neighbourhood, holding a loud rock concert in a community venue previously used for more conservative musical events or taking large groups into areas considered as wilderness.

A frequently underestimated element of social sustainability is the organisation's staff. Any organisation is itself a small ecosystem and its social sustainability is one of its most important elements in terms of its own performance and future viability. Un-engaged or disinterested staff, or worse, dissatisfied staff, may not perform well, or even leave, with often severe impacts on turnover, morale and business performance (Robbins, Judge, Millett and Waters-Marsh 2008). As with all aspects of risk management, a crucial element for implementing a stronger commitment to social sustainability is to ensure that it is embedded in the organisation's culture, as well as in the operations of your organisation or activities (see Chapter 4 for more discussion on culture). As Carroll notes:

> For Corporate Social Responsibility to be accepted by the conscientious business person, it should be framed in such a way that the entire range of business responsibilities is embraced. (Carroll 1991, cited in Carroll 1999, p. 289)

For an organisation or activity, questions on social sustainability might include:

1 What benefits does my organisation or event bring to my community, city or region?
2 Do I make sure my staff (including volunteers) understand the 'big picture' of what we are doing and why?
3 Are we operating in ways that supports the work–life balance of our staff?
4 Do I acknowledge the values and culture of my local community (including Indigenous culture, if appropriate)?

Economic and financial sustainability

In some senses economic or financial sustainability may be the easiest element of sustainability to understand. With respect to financial sustainability, if an organisation or operation does not earn enough to pay its way, it will fail. However, operations may have much broader benefits or impacts on employees, their families, the surrounding community and even further afield. These may include both positive and negative impacts.

Possible positive impacts:
- providing jobs for local residents, perhaps even acting as an attractor to bring skilled workers to a local area
- creating increased demand for existing businesses, which may attract additional businesses to the area
- generating local investment, including infrastructure
- benefiting local communities through the collection of taxes and other government charges.

Possible negative impacts:
- drawing employees from existing businesses
- crowding out other possible developments
- increasing demand on public services and infrastructure.

For an organisation or event, questions on economic/financial sustainability could include:

1 How is the financial bottom line? Is the organisation financially viable in the short to medium term or do we continually look for sponsorship, grants and other support?
2 Do my staff (and volunteers) understand and appreciate the importance of organisational financial viability? Do they share in the planning required to achieve financial viability in the 'big picture' of what we're doing and why?
3 Does my organisation or event bring benefits to the local community? Do I ensure that my organisation or event makes sure of appropriate local products, services and workers?

How will we know our organisation is sustainable?

Understanding what sustainability is, why it is important and some of the possible positive and negative sustainability impacts of your operation is useful, but how will you know if your organisation or event is sustainable?

Indicators of sustainability

The most common means of assessing sustainability is the use of indicators. Often termed Key Performance Indicators, or KPIs, these provide straight-forward measures of performance. They are often mandated through government legislation or regulation, although they may come from industry groups in more self-regulating industry sectors, or from an organisation itself.

One of the benefits of an indicator approach is the ability of organisations to choose measures that are most appropriate for their organisation, to track the indicators that will allow effective testing and control of operations to ensure good outcomes. The choice of indicators needs to reflect the vision and mission of the organisation in order to provide feedback on specific aspects of the organisation's or event's performance. Such indicators can be used to track organisational performance over time. They can also be used to evaluate the effectiveness of particular strategies as well as to compare, or benchmark, to similar organisations using the same or similar indicators.

Indicators are often used as part of licensing or accreditation schemes, run by government or industry bodies. An example of the latter is the New South Wales Caravan and Camping Industry Association 'Gumnuts' accreditation program, which aims to certify particularly environmental performance by measuring a number of environmental indicators. A particular feature of this scheme is that it was developed by the Association in a bottom up approach – industry consultation, as well as work with regulators, led to the development of a scheme that 'fitted' the industry. Indicators used in measuring performance for accreditation were also designed to fit the industry, and to measure organisational performance in ways that the industry, operators and (hopefully) consumers will value. However chosen, it is useful to have indicators that are 'SMART': Specific, Measureable, Attainable, Relevant and Time specific (Doran 1981), to ensure what you are measuring is appropriate to what you are trying to achieve in your organisation.

A further challenge with the indicator approach is to ensure indicators are part of the practice of an organisation's culture, and are not simply 'added on'. If indicators are not integrated, they will simply become just one more thing to do, rather than a means of assisting the organisation to continuously monitor and improve its sustainability, economically, socially and environmentally.

Table 2.1 Examples of economic, social and environmental sustainability indicators

Economic	**Financial performance** Net cash flow Return on investment Current asset ratio Dividend per share Number of full time-equivalent staff	**Economic performance** Economic impacts on host community	
Social	**Labour practices and decent work** Work/life-balance of staff Diversity in and across the workforce Training and development of staff, permanent and casual Staff turnover rates and staff retention Safe and ethical work practices	**Society** Impact on host communities such as noise, social impacts or use of scarce resources Support of social programs in host communities such as health, education, environmental Volunteering legacy of events for the host communities Enhanced levels of physical activity as a result of programs or activities	**Human rights** Degree to which activities or programs are accessible for clients and staff with access requirements such as permanent or temporary disabilities Measures of discrimination Measures of the degree to which purchasing policies that promote the use of ethical organisations
Environmental	**Energy** Energy consumption Use of renewable energies Energy savings due to conservation and efficiency programs	**Water** Water consumption Water recycling	**Waste management** Carbon footprint Zero net emissions Measures of waste recycling Landfill usage

There are many such indicators, and Table 2.1 provides an illustrative sample of those available.

How would this work in practice? Figure 2.3 provides a brief case study, based work undertaken by the organisation planning and preparing for the 2010 Olympic and Paralympic Winter Games in Canada in 2010.

Bringing it all together: triple bottom line accounting

How can we bring all these elements together? A simple approach is to use the triple bottom line (TBL) accounting approach. The term was first coined by Elkington in the 1990s (Elkington 1997). TBL calls for an expansion of the traditional financial reporting framework for organisations to include social and environmental performance. This broadening of focus calls for managers and staff of organisations to concern themselves with a broader range of values – social and environmental – than the usual financial values organisations have often focused on. It also calls on managers and staff of organisations to look beyond their own organisational boundaries to neighbouring bodies, organisations and communities. Under this approach, these need to be seen as important 'stakeholders' of the organisation – those affected, either directly or indirectly, by the organisation or its activities. In private sector organisations, there is a parallel development towards 'corporate social responsibility', which also implies a broader focus than simply financial returns (e.g. Carroll 1999).

While there are criticisms of TBL (e.g. Robin 2006), this approach has achieved national and international standing as best practice for bringing together accounting for performance on the three pillars of sustainability. Crucially, the TBL approach has been adopted by many businesses and other organisations not as an additional burden, but as a model that ensures the maximising of success and thus sustainability, delivered within a framework which is integrated into the overall culture, planning, operations and evaluation of an organisation or activity.

Some strategies to assist

How can practitioners and managers pursue stronger sustainability? A number of strategies are outlined below (see also Chapter 4 on the organisational context).

Reviewing your own operation

The most obvious strategy is to start at home. By reviewing your own operation or event you will learn more about its strengths and weaknesses in

Background

For the organisers of the 2010 Olympic and Paralympic Winter Games held in Vancouver, Canada, sustainability meant managing the social, economic and environmental impacts and opportunities of these Games to produce lasting benefits, locally and globally.

The challenge

The organisers realised that sustainability touched just about everything they did in planning for the Games, the running of the event and what happened afterwards. That is, there were environmental issues, social issues and economic or financial issues for the Games site and operations, for the host community and for businesses and other organisations involved in the Games. This in turn meant the organisers had to consider the environmental, social and economic benefits and impacts of the Games, from the planning stages all the way through to post-Games community legacies.

In response to this challenge, the Vancouver Organising Committee for the 2010 Winter Olympic and Paralympic Games (VANOC) developed a planning, management and reporting process to ensure it did cover each of these elements.

VANOC's response

Some elements of VANOC's responses to this challenge included:

Taking the heat

Waste heat from ice-making refrigeration unit used at the Games venues was used to help warm the rest of the venue, saving money and reducing Green House Gas (GHG) production from heat generation. Heat from municipal wastewater and sewer water services was also used to help warm the Olympic and Paralympic Villages in Whistler and Vancouver, saving money and reducing GHG production.

Low footprint and saving local biodiversity

Through careful planning and innovation in venue and site design and layout, the overall footprint of the Whistler Olympic Park venue was 30 per cent smaller than originally planned in the bid phase, meaning fewer trees were cut and there were fewer streams to cross with roads and trails.

At the Whistler Creekside Alpine Ski venue, VANOC, working with the local community and environmental agencies, ensured that steps were taken so that the locally endangered Boyd Creek's Tailed Frogs were protected during site preparation and running of the Games. Additionally, significant plants at the Games' Cypress Bowl site were transplanted to allow a win–win for the operation and the environment: both the installation of a required new snowmaking reservoir and to provide for the protection of these important plants.

Reusing and recycling

Zero-waste to landfill goal meant striving to reduce, reuse and recycle materials to minimise waste being deposited in local landfills. Over two hectares of pine beetle wood was salvaged and used for aesthetic treatments in the Richmond Olympic Oval roof. All waste wood from site clearing at Whistler Olympic/Paralympic Park, The Whistler Sliding Centre and Olympic/Paralympic Village was chipped and re-integrated on site.

Ensuring the benefit for local businesses

VANOC targeted local employment, purchasing and contracting opportunities for the design and construction of venues, as well as providing products and services associated with the convening and running of the Games. This maximised the financial and business benefits to local businesses and communities. VANOC also ensured ethical sourcing of licensed merchandise was created and implemented locally and globally. That meant VANOC helped ensure merchandise was made in a way that respected local laws and workers' rights.

Figure 2.3 Planning for sustainability at the 2010 Olympic and Paralympic Winter Games

sustainability terms and probably discover means to increase the operation's social, environmental and financial/economic sustainability.

Referring again to the section above on indicators, you will need measures that make sense to you and to your operation to test your organisation's sustainability. Joining or using a quality benchmarking or assessing body will provide useful and practical measures for you to measure your operation against. A number of web-based sources of information and advice are listed at the end of this chapter to assist.

Of course, reviewing, measuring and benchmarking are only a beginning. Once issues are identified, action must follow to put in place appropriate sustainable practices. This may include enhancing environmental sustainability via reducing energy use, switching to renewable or green energy sources, such as solar, increasing recycling initiatives, reducing water use and considering the use of low emissions vehicles.

Developing appropriate policies

Reviewing your operation may show you that your organisation or event needs further work to develop policies that set out the organisation's commitment to sustainability. While consultants may assist this development, there may be considerable value in having staff and stakeholders work together to draft such policy statements. The engagement and discussion that arise in developing, benchmarking against other similar organisations or seeking advice from industry bodies (see below) may actively increase your organisation's own internal social sustainability by encouraging staff (and volunteers') understanding of and commitment to their employer.

Training and staff development

A further means of enhancing sustainability, as well as raising staff awareness and engagement is through training and development. Whether through more formalised vocational or tertiary training, or through participation in local environmental programs, or simply environmental and conservation activities, staff will be encouraged to learn more about the issues. Perhaps as importantly, staff and volunteers may feel encouraged to engage more with your operation or event and to more actively participate in enhancing its sustainability.

Industry-led sustainability

Industry associations can be leaders in modelling and supporting sustainability, as well as providing practical information for members on appropriate strategies to enhance sustainability. Bodies such as Ecotourism Australia provide certification schemes to support enhanced environmental sustainability (such as through their Ecotourism Accreditation and Climate Action Certification programs), and social sustainability (through their Respecting Our Culture Indigenous cultural tourism accreditation program).

A further method is through the provision and promotion of awards programs that recognise high quality sustainable practices (such as the Australian Banksia Awards).

Points for action for practitioners

- How well do you know your own operation? How well do your organisational strategies and performance measures align with your understanding of social, environmental and financial/economic sustainability?
- What are the benefits and/or impacts of your operation in spatial terms? Does it bring positive benefits to a wide area around your event or organisation, such as your whole town, region or country, or does it perhaps have significant negative impacts over a large or small geographical area?
- How can you enhance these to provide a more balanced and sustainable operating model for your organisation?
- How can you use your sustainable strategies to engage, inform and gain support from your staff, clients and other key stakeholders?

Further questions and activities

Economic and financial sustainability

There are many sources of theory and practice for developing the profitability or financial sustainability of your organisation. However, two approaches worth mentioning in this brief review include ensuring a strategic approach to developing your business plan (e.g. Hill, Jones, Galvin & Haidar, 2007) and considering the Balanced Scorecard as a strategic approach to planning and operating your organisation (e.g. Kaplan and Norton 2001, see also <www.balancedscorecard.org>).

Thinking about a local outdoor or sporting organisation, what do you know about their financial viability? Is this organisation able to adequately finance its current operations? Is it growing to keep pace with demand for its activities or services? Does the organisation contribute to the local economy? Does it have negative economic impacts on your local community?

Environmental sustainability

Over a week measure your operation's energy, water and waste, then consider the following:

1 What could you do to reduce energy and water use?

2 How could you cut down on waste production? How much of the packaging used in your operation is from recyclable materials? How much of the recyclable material is actually placed in recycling facilities?

3 What strategies could you use to engage the members of your household to improve environmental sustainability of your operation?

Social sustainability

There are many possible sources of suggestions in this field, including the UN *Global Compact* (UN 2001), the United Nations Intergovernmental Working Group of Experts on International Standards of Accounting and Reporting (UN 2008) and the International Standard Organisation's *Social Responsibility* ISO 26000 standard (ISO 2010).

If you are thinking about establishing local outdoor education, sport association or event, consider the following:

1 To what extent are you aware that social factors can form part of your organisational strategy?

2 How are the social aspects imbedded into your mission/objectives/strategies?

3 How do you evaluate the effectiveness of your efforts?

If not aware of the items listed above:

1 What information sources do you use to learn about ways to develop your business/activity?

2 What information would you need in order to introduce social aspects into your organisational strategies?

References and further resources

References

Australian Standards/New Zealand Standards 2009. *Risk Management – Principles and Guidelines. AS / NZS ISO 31000:2009*. Standards Australia, Sydney.

Burroughs, WJ 2007. *Climate Change: A Multidisciplinary Approach* (2nd edition). Cambridge University Press, Cambridge.

Butler, RW 1999. 'Problems and issues of integrating tourism development' in DG Pearce and RW Butler (eds) *Contemporary Issues in Tourism Development*. Routledge, London, pp. 65–80.

Carroll, A 1999. 'Corporate social responsibility: evolution of a definitional Construct. *Business Society*, vol. 38, no. 3, pp. 268–95.

Doran, GT 1981. 'There's a S.M.A.R.T. way to write management goals and objectives'. *Management Review*, vol. 70, no. 11, pp. 35–7.

Elkington, J 1997. *Cannibals with Forks: the Triple Bottom Line of 21st Century Business*. Oxford University Press, Oxford.

Flagestad, A & Hope, CA 2001. 'Strategic success in winter sports destinations: a sustainable value creation perspective'. *Tourism Management*, vol. 22, pp. 445–61.

Gossling, S & Hall, CM 2006. *Tourism and Global Environmental Change*. Routledge, Abingdon, UK.

Green and Gold Inc. 2010. 'The sustainable sport source'. Retrieved 16 November 2010 from http://www.greengold.on.ca.

Hall, CM 2008. *Tourism Planning: Policies, Processes and Relationships*. Longman, London.

Hall, CM & Higham, J 2005. 'Introduction: tourism, recreation and climate change' in CM Hall & J Higham (eds), *Tourism, Recreation and Climate Change*, Channel View Publishing, Clevedon, UK, pp. 3–28.

Hill, CWL, Jones, GR, Galvin, P & Haidar, A 2007. *Strategic Management*. Wiley, Milton.

Intergovernmental Panel on Climate Change 2007. *Summary for Policymakers of the Synthesis Report of the IPCC Fourth Assessment report*. Retrieved 24 November 2010 from <http://www.ipcc.ch/pdf/assessment-report/AR4/SYR/AR4_SYR_SPM.pdf>

International Standards Organisation 2010. *Social Responsibility ISO 26000*. Retrieved 23 November 2010 from <http://www.iso.org>.

Kaplan, RS, Norton, DP 2001. *The Strategy-Focussed Organisation*. Harvard University Press, Boston.

Robbins, SR, Judge, TA, Millet, B & Waters-Marsh, T 2008. *Organisational Behaviour*, 5th edition, Pearson, Sydney.

Robin, F 2006. 'The challenge of TBL: a responsibility to whom?', *Business and Society Review*, vol. 111, no. 1, pp. 1–14.

Spenceley, A 2008. 'Sustainable and responsible tourism' in A Spenceley (ed) *Responsible Tourism: Critical Issues for Conservation and Development*, Earthscan, London, pp 1–26.

Steiner, GA 1971. *Business and Society*, New York: Random House.

United Nations 2008. *Guidance on Corporate Responsibility*. Retrieved 24 November 2010 <from http://unctad.org>.

United Nations 2010. *Global Compact*. Retrieved 24 November 2010 from <http://unglobalcompact.org>.

United Nations World Commission on Environment and Development 1987. *Our Common Future*, Oxford University Press, Oxford.

World Travel and Tourism Council, World Tourism Organisation and the Earth Council 1997. *Agenda 21 for the Travel and Tourism Industry: Towards Environmentally Sustainable Development*, World Tourism Organisation, Madrid.

Further resources

Web resources on sustainability:

Balanced Scorecard <http://balancedscorecard.org>
BEST Environment Network <http://www.besteducationnetwork.org>
Green Globe <http://www.greenglobeint.com/>
Sustainable Sport and Event Toolkit Centre <http://sustainable-sport.org/>
Sustainable Tourism Cooperative Research Centre <http://crctourism.com.au/>
Sustainable Tourism Online <http://www.sustainabletourismonline.com/>

United Nations Environment Program <http://www.unep.org/>

Web resources on carbon footprint reduction:

Carbon Footprint Calculator <http://www.carbonfootprint.com/
    calculator.aspx>
Global Footprint Network <www.footprintnetwork.org>
Global Reporting Initiative <www.globalreporting.org>
Open Carbon World <www.opencarbonworld.com>
WWF Carbon Footprint Calculator <www.wwf.org.au/footprint/
    calculator/>

The legal context for outdoor activities and programs

Lyn Ainsworth and Jon Heshka

Many forms of outdoor recreation involve a risk of physical injury. In some cases, while the risk of injury is small, the consequences may be severe. . . . A general prohibition in a given locality may be a gross and inappropriate interference with the public's right to enjoy healthy recreation.

Chief Justice Gleeson, *Vairy v Wyong Shire Council*, (2005) 223 CLR 422

FOCUS QUESTIONS

1 What are the key legal areas that an organisation conducting outdoor activities needs to consider?
2 What can constitute a workplace in the context of outdoor activities?
3 Are an employer's obligations to an employee different to the obligations to a visitor to the workplace?
4 What would be considered 'reasonable' under the law?
5 Can duty of care be reduced?

CASE STUDY

In March 2007, a 13 year-old boy attended his first Army Cadet camp, a three day training camp, as part of his Melbourne school's cadet program. The camp was primarily run by staff of the school. On the first day he was given an army ration pack containing beef satay, despite his parents having given written warning to the school and camp organisers that he was allergic to peanuts. Two others with peanut allergies also received similar ration packs. The young boy, an Army Cadet, died from an allergic reaction to the peanuts. The Australian Defence Force (ADF) was found guilty in 2009 under Section 16 (1) of the *Occupational Health and Safety Act 1991* (C'th), where an employer must take all reasonably practicable steps to protect the health and safety of its employees. Under the Act, Army Cadets undertaking cadet activities are deemed to be employees of the ADF. The ADF was fined over $200 000. (<http://www.austlii.edu.au/au/cases/cth/FCA/2009/700.html>)

Introduction

There has been an increasing tendency to consider the 'law' as a constraint to an organisation's capacity to provide challenging, quality, experiential and recreational opportunities. However, the above quote by Chief Justice Gleeson in the High Court of Australia in *Vairy v Wyong Shire Council* took a more balanced look at the issue of civil liability in this context with important implications for providers that will be explored in some detail in this chapter.

The legal context in which such activities take place is important to understand because:

1 It identifies an area of risk that clearly needs to be managed; no organisation wants to find itself embroiled in litigation. Defending a lawsuit is costly, time-consuming and can have devastating effects for all, including volunteers, who may have to give evidence before the injured person or the family of a person who has been severely injured or killed.

2 As the law emerges, it provides clarity around what community expectations are of service providers and helps to define and improve our practice.

3 It provides clear indicators as to how we can optimise the opportunities as well as minimise risks.

So rather than being considered a constraint, the law becomes an enabler – a support and guide for better practice and a protection when things go wrong, a way of achieving objectives rather than an obstacle to be overcome. This is the perspective from which we are considering the law in the context of outdoor recreational activities. Hence, it is vital that those who are involved in the provision of outdoor recreation activities have a sound knowledge of the legal context in which they are operating.

That is not to say that a thorough understanding of the law is not a vital risk management tool for other areas of an organisation's operations.

For example, for many organisations to operate there are compliance, registration or accreditation requirements. Those organisations need to understand those regulatory obligations to eliminate the risk of being deregistered or losing accreditation. Failing to effectively manage risks, particularly legal risks, can also have an adverse impact on an organisation's reputation in the community, undermining its capacity to achieve its strategic objectives.

In this chapter, we will consider the two areas of the law that have the potential to impact most significantly, both positively and negatively, laws relating to safety and laws related to duty of care. These will be considered by drawing upon examples from Australia and Canada. Along with the principles of risk management, both of these areas are evolving, as every situation is a 'stand alone' one, requiring consideration on its merits. They are also areas where recent developments have led to a more common sense approach, which can only be an improvement for those providing outdoor recreational activities.

Although each area will be considered separately, it is important to remember that these are commonly concurrent areas of liability. That is, any given set of circumstances may give rise to liability under either or both of these areas, as well as others (e.g. employment law, consumers law, child protection, privacy and the criminal law). It is also important to note that, while they are separate heads of liability, with different consequences, non-compliance in one area may be evidence of a breach of the other obligation. For example, in a claim in negligence, a failure to adhere to occupational, health and safety requirements could be evidence of a breach of duty of care.

The concept of 'reasonableness'

There is a tension in the law between reasonableness and adventure. Risk, and thus uncertainty, is inherent to adventure, and it is the reason why some people are attracted to adventure. In some circumstances the attraction is highest when the risk is greatest – like rafting class five white water or climbing a Himalayan peak or even abseiling down a 50-metre waterfall. How can we reconcile reasonableness with adventure when no 'reasonable' person may wish to be there in the first place! The answer, in short, lies in mitigating the risk (i.e. the degree of uncertainty) without eliminating that which is essential to the adventure experience for those people at that time in that place.

The law, both civil and common, is littered with references to 'reasonableness' and the 'reasonable man' (which we should assume also includes the reasonable woman!). The areas of law that we are going to consider in some detail are no exception. The concept is rarely defined in any concrete way. Ultimately, it is about making judgments, in the expectation that those judgments will be made on consideration of appropriate evidence – much like the courts themselves. In essence, the following question may be asked: 'Have I undertaken reasonable steps to effectively manage the risks in my activity?' There is no ambiguity about the fact that effective risk management would be considered a minimum standard of 'reasonableness', so it is essential to understand it and implement it well. It is also important to remember that risk management is situational. While we can have access to guidelines and other resources for information and assistance, the risks and how we control them will be very specific to the circumstances in which we are operating. Of course, the extent to which the risks will be controlled (and controllable) will vary according to degree of adventure associated with the activity, the experience of the participant and their willingness to accept the risks. Adventure, by definition, involves intentionally placing people in situations that involve uncertainty.

Risk management standard AS/NZS/ISO 31000: 2009

The recent adoption by Australia of the new international standard provides us with an opportunity to reframe perspectives on risk. Even the definition of risk as: 'The effect of uncertainty on objectives' (AS/NZS/ISO 31000, 2009, Clause 2.1) diminishes the sense of adversity that has so long been a part of risk management.

While strictly speaking not a law, the standard provides a benchmark against which the laws in this area will be interpreted. When considering what is reasonable, the courts will have reference to the standard. Failure to meet the expectations of the standard will, at first glance, be evidence of a failure to meet the minimum expectations of 'reasonableness' required under the law.

The enhancement of our understanding of risk management through the standard is a welcome development. The key parameters of the standard that will assist in our risk management practice include the clear articulation of the principles of risk management (see Chapter 4), the establishment of an organisational framework within which the process of risk management can operate and the creation of key performance indicators which provide a guide to good practice (Figure 3.1).

The focus is on integration of risk management into the organisation's overall management system: 'Risk management is not a stand alone activity that is separate from the main activities and processes of the organisation', it is 'an integral part of all organisational processes' (AS/NZS/ ISO 31000, 2009, Clause 3(b)).

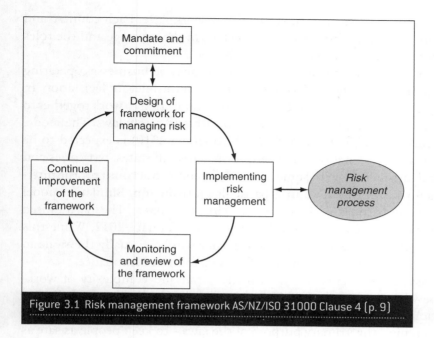

Figure 3.1 Risk management framework AS/NZ/ISO 31000 Clause 4 (p. 9)

The key performance indicators in the standard reflect the minimum expectations of an organisation's risk management system to satisfy governance obligations and its duty of care:

- emphasis on continual improvement
- comprehensive, fully defined and fully accepted accountability for risks, controls and treatments
- staff appropriately skilled with adequate resources
- effective communication about risks and their management to external and internal stakeholders
- all organisational decision-making involves explicit consideration of risk and application of risk management to an appropriate degree
- comprehensive and frequent reporting of risk management as part of good governance
- risk management viewed as central to the organisation's management processes
- effective risk management is regarded by managers as essential for the achievement of an organisation's objectives.

Work health and safety: statutory liability

Workplace injuries can be a major cost and imposition to an individual and the organisation. Many countries have Occupational Health and Safety (OHS) laws that seek to protect employees from injury while at work and, in some circumstances, also those visiting a workplace. Each country and jurisdiction will have differences in the extent of the coverage and the roles and responsibilities of employers and employees.

In Australia, a major challenge for organisations and businesses operating across a number of states has been the diversity of the relevant legislation. In 2008, the Council of Australian Governments committed to work together to develop and implement consistent work health and safety laws. The model Work Health and Safety Act (Safe Work Australia 2010) is expected to be enacted in a predominantly consistent form across all states, territories and the federal jurisdiction, with some minor differences to account for the inter-relationship with other laws in a particular jurisdiction. Similarly, model regulations and Codes of Practice are being developed. The harmonised work health and safety regime will commence 1 January 2012. While this still means that the laws are state-based, they will be virtually the same in terms of the obligations and the ramifications for non-compliance.

It is easy to get overwhelmed with the detail and complexity of work-place safety laws with their variation across jurisdictions both nationally and internationally. They can also seem bureaucratic and pedantic. However, if we keep in mind the primary purpose of the laws – to keep people as safe as reasonably practicable in their work environments by minimising exposure to unnecessary risk – we cannot underestimate their value. From a risk management perspective, the laws support the intention of outdoor recreational organisations to:

- operate in a best practice governance environment
- manage risks that may give rise to injury to participants
- manage risks that will impact on their organisational sustainability including financial and reputational risks.

The primary duty under work health and safety laws for providers of outdoor recreation activities and services is: 'To ensure, so far as is reasonably practicable, the health and safety' of:

- workers engaged by the provider (employees and possibly volunteers, as unpaid workers)
- workers whose activities are influenced or directed by the provider, while at work at the business (contractors and potentially sub-contractors).

There is also an obligation on a provider 'to ensure, so far as is reasonably practicable, that the health and safety of other persons is not put at risk' (Model Work Health and Safety Act 2010, Sections 19 and 20) from any work carried out. This will capture participants in outdoor recreation activities, volunteers and potential onlookers or bystanders.

In the context of outdoor recreational activities, this sets a very high benchmark and one that potentially undermines the nature and value of the activity. There is often a tension between the regulations governing workplace health and safety and standards that are considered appropriate for the outdoor recreational industry. Invariably, this is only considered after an incident occurs. In this context, it is important to consider the intersection between work health and safety legislation and the state-based civil liability legislation (see below) that enables participants in recreation to voluntarily assume some risk. In these circumstances, a provider could be expected to provide information to participants based on a thorough risk assessment process, as well as fulfilling obligations in relation to instruction, equipment and safe systems of work.

The focus on 'carrying out work' is a variation on the 'place of work' that features in most current legislation. It will encourage (and in fact obligate) us to think more not only about the physical environment but also about the way we do things.

While the critical question for providers may seem to be 'What do we need to do to fulfil the obligations under the legislation?', the real question should be 'What do we need to do to ensure, as far as reasonably practicable, that our clients are not unnecessarily exposed to unreasonable risks that are not essential to the experience?'. There are three dimensions to this question:

- What are the key areas of the operations and activities that I need to manage?
- What do I need to do in relation to those areas?
- What is 'reasonably practicable'?

Key operational areas of responsibility

In considering key areas of responsibility, a question needs to be asked: 'What does this mean for me?' The list below offers some clues.

The model legislation does not significantly change the responsibility of providers to take into account the following points:

1 A work environment without unreasonable risks to health and safety: consider the diverse contexts in which outdoor recreation activities are provided, many of which are uncontrolled, subject to the elements or subject to change.

2 Safe plant and structures: ensuring that structures, plant and equipment are of the right quality, are appropriate for the purpose (and the likely participants) and are adequately maintained (including inspection, storage, set up and servicing, supported by documentation). The responsibility may be greater if the organisation designs, manufactures, imports or supplies equipment, substances or structures, or if they install or commission plant and structures.

3 Safe systems of work: such as safe use, handling, storage and transport of plant, substances and structures.

4 The qualifications and training needs of employees, contractors and volunteers, as well as participants: this would include how to cope in circumstances of high risk or changing conditions.

5 Access to facilities and amenities: this would certainly include first aid, but may also extend to communication and protection from the weather. The scope and nature of the amenities will be dependant on the type of activity. For example, water-based activities may be governed by legislation that requires the use of PFDs and signalling devices whereas backcountry skiing may not be governed by legislation, but have standards or best practices that involve carrying transceivers, probes and shovels. Factored here would also be the level of required training (first aid qualifications, determined in part by an assessment of proximity to paramedics, exposure to risk, nature of the client group, etc.) and emergency response procedures which would identify such considerations as helicopter landing zones, communications coverage and mutual aid resources.

The regulations under the model legislation are likely to deal with each of these issues in detail but, as noted above, will continue to require interpretation according to the activity. Current state-based regulations and codes of practice reflect most of these elements.

Special characteristics of participants

If we start with the assumption that outdoor recreational activities can have a positive impact on those involved and hence be available to all, it is critical, when considering risk, to take into account both the general and specific characteristics of those participating. However, it is worth reflecting on the needs and expectations of different client groups as they will impact on the legal obligations, expectations, behaviours and abilities, and thus the way that we manage risks, such as:

* age: children and young people, adults, elderly
* abilities: existing physical and psychological conditions.

A person's age or capacity should not be considered an impediment to opportunity. While it may require a different approach to risk management, we also have ethical and legal responsibilities under human rights and state and federal anti-discrimination legislation. This legislation makes it illegal to discriminate, directly or indirectly, against a person because of age or disability in areas of life that include provision of goods and services, access to premises and activities of clubs and sport. The provider has a responsibility to make reasonable adjustments to accommodate a person's disability or other conditions that may limit their ability to participate. Matters that would be considered in determining what is reasonable include the reason why the limitation was imposed, the effect of the restriction on the individual, the financial burden of making reasonable accommodations and the availability of alternatives. This is an objective test and it is determined on the circumstances. However, the positioning of the provider may be significant. For example, a Scout group organising a camp would be expected to cater for a young person with a disability who was part of that group in the planning of the activity. By contrast, a caving club offering activities may be able to reasonably exclude an obese person from membership or participation if their physical condition would put them and/or others at risk of harm, if it is not possible to make reasonable accommodation by way of equipment or site selection for the activity. This would reflect the provider's expert knowledge of, for example, the site, the physical capacity of the person to manoeuvre through passages and the degree of physical fitness required for the activity. An accommodation may be providing the opportunity to walk through cave chambers or abseil down a rock wall.

This is in no way a full statement of the law in this area. It is important to be mindful of the issues and seek appropriate advice if uncertain.

Obligations

The legislation imposes duties on a range of people who may have different roles:

1 A person conducting a business or undertaking, including a 'corporate' person: a company or incorporated association, whether for profit or not, as well as an individual.

2 Officers of 'persons' conducting a business or undertaking: this clearly includes formally appointed officers of incorporated and unincorporated bodies (it may not be as far reaching as some state OHS legislation which imposes obligations on managers and supervisors).

3 Employees ('workers') including volunteers.

4 Other persons.

The scope of the duties is determined by the relationship to the organisation. However, an individual may have multiple relationships simultaneously. For example, a person who may be an officer of an incorporated not-for-profit association may also be an employee, volunteer or participant. Also, more than one person may have the same duties. However, the duties are not transferable. The person must discharge those duties to the extent that they have the capacity to 'influence and control' the matter. To illustrate this, the following draws upon the Australian Model Work Health and Safety Act 2010 (Safe Work Australia, 2010):

1 A 'person' conducting a business or undertaking must:
- eliminate risks to health and safety, so far as is reasonably practicable and
- if it is not reasonably practicable to eliminate, to minimise those risks so far as is reasonably practicable.

This is a critical consideration in the context of the provision of outdoor recreational activity where some level of risk is integral to the very nature of the activity and the experience. It is fundamental to the purpose of a participant in an activity that there is a degree of risk. So the question becomes, in the context of an activity, what is a *reasonable* level of risk in order to maintain the authenticity of the experience. This does not detract from the employer's primary duty to the employee.

2 'Officers' of persons conducting a business or undertaking must:
- exercise *due diligence* to ensure that the person is complying with its duties.

Due diligence includes:
- maintaining knowledge of work health and safety matters
- understanding the hazards and risks associated with the operations
- ensuring appropriate resources are available and applied to eliminate or minimise risks
- ensuring that appropriate processes are implemented for compliance with the duties
- verifying the provision and use of appropriate resources and processes.

3 'Workers' must:
- take reasonable care for their own health and safety
- take reasonable care that things they do (or fail to do) do not adversely impact on the health and safety of others.

You will note that the requirement of 'reasonable care' is echoed in the expectations under the law of negligence. Through good risk management practices, the obligations under both areas of liability should be covered, such as:
- complying with reasonable instructions about work health and safety matters
- cooperating with reasonable policies and procedures that may be in place relating to work health and safety (obviously, these need to have been made known to the worker).

4 'Other persons' must:
- take reasonable care for their own health and safety

- take reasonable care that things they do (or fail to do) do not adversely impact on the health and safety of others
- comply with reasonable instructions about work health and safety matters.

While the respective obligations and duties appear to be largely common sense, the challenge is for organisations to translate them into practical policies, procedures, guidelines and practices that manage risk, while still providing the experience sought by participants. The goal is to manage the risks or uncertainties, given that it is not possible to completely eliminate them.

Ways in which organisations would be expected to respond to these duties include the following:

1 Having a systematic and comprehensive risk management program covering responsibilities at all levels as well as programs for managing specific aspects of risk.

2 Consulting with workers: employees are most likely to be able to identify hazards and risks and come up with practical and effective ways to control them in the context of the work they do. The more potentially serious the issue, the more extensive the consultation needs to be. Both the Model Work Health and Safety Act and the draft regulations deal extensively with the mechanisms for consultation with staff and others. Consultation is the best way of building a positive and collaborative culture of health and safety in a work environment.

3 Ensuring that workers are adequately trained, according to the type of work they are undertaking and their relative responsibility. (This includes training about job-specific work health and safety issues, as well as about the regulatory context. Ongoing refresher training also needs to be considered. Even if a well-qualified and experienced person is engaged, an induction into the specifics of the work environment is essential.)

4 Monitoring, analysing and reviewing incident and hazard reports, and acting in response to these. (Refer also to Chapter 10)

5 Having well documented processes and safe operating procedures which are readily accessible and in which employees and volunteers are well versed.

6 Ensuring that all activities are adequately supervised.

7 Planning, planning, planning: although conditions may change suddenly and significantly in the outdoors, a thorough risk assessment can only be undertaken through a site visit and consideration of contingencies, both controlled and uncontrolled.

8 Ensuring that equipment is used and maintained as per manufacturers' guidelines, and by people who have been appropriately trained in its use. This would include equipment designed for emergencies.

9 Expecting the unexpected and being prepared.

10 Incorporating the management of safety as an integral part of the outdoor recreation experience for participants.

Reasonably practicable

The words 'reasonably practicable' appear in multiple contexts in the legislation. A number of jurisdictions in Australia have had the concept of 'reasonably practicable' in previous OHS legislation. It is often a challenge to ascertain what is reasonably practicable in advance. The Model Work Health and Safety Act (Safe Work Australia 2010) defines 'reasonably practicable' as: 'That which is, or was at a particular time, reasonably able to be done in relation to ensuring health or safety, taking into account and weighing up all relevant matters including' (Section 18):

- the likelihood of the hazard occurring
- the seriousness of the risk
- what was known, or ought to have been known, about the risk, and ways of eliminating or minimising the risk
- the availability and suitability of ways to eliminate or minimise the risk, including the cost or other burden to eliminate or mitigate the risk (this means that if the cost of eliminating the risk is unreasonably excessive, then it would not be reasonably practicable to do it: for example, the cost of cleaning, such as sweeping and shovelling, a climbing crag of all loose rock to eliminate the possibility of someone being struck by rock fall, may not be reasonably practicable).

To adequately address all of the relevant matters requires a rigorous risk management approach across all aspects of operations. It could be argued that the analysis of these matters is subjective. However, there are available objective benchmarks, such as adherence to any relevant codes or best practice guidelines and the expectation that the risk management process has been undertaken competently and comprehensively by persons who have the appropriate skills and expertise to 'weigh up' the relevant matters.

Only after consideration of these matters can the costs be taken into account. It would only be in circumstances where the cost of eliminating or minimising the risk is 'grossly disproportionate' to the risk that it would contribute to the determination about whether it is reasonably practicable.

Invariably, it is only with hindsight and the assistance of the courts that what is, or was, reasonably practicable in a given set of circumstances becomes evident. A number of decided cases have thrown light on this, and they are considered later in the chapter. The implications for those involved in conducting outdoor recreation activities is that they must keep up with advancements in the law, particularly case law relevant to the interpretation of statutes.

Penalties

While we need to focus on the positive benefits of effectively managing health and safety, we also need to be aware that Work Health and Safety is a quasi-criminal jurisdiction with the potential for significant fines for corporate entities and individuals and for imprisonment of individuals. In many jurisdictions, including Australia and Canada, specific legislation has been enacted imposing criminal liability for deaths in the workplace, often referred to as 'industrial manslaughter'. The liability extends to the entity, directors and managers. Similar UK legislation was used in the 1993 Lyme Bay canoeing tragedy in which four students were drowned, resulting in the conviction of the managing director for manslaughter and a custodial sentence (Geary 1996).

Relationship with civil liability

Whilst, from a legal perspective, we are considering different areas of the law, with different considerations and consequences, at a practical level, there is a strong inter-relationship. For example, a failure to meet the duties of work health and safety laws would be an indicator of negligence. Similarly, many of the things that a provider would be expected to do in order to meet their duty of care will support good work health and safety practice. It is worth keeping this in mind as we review the next section of this chapter.

Law of negligence: breach of duty of care

The law of negligence has been evolving over centuries. In essence, it determines who, if anybody, is responsible when something goes wrong. The basic principles continue to be applied to a diverse range of new and emerging contexts with the overall impact that the net of responsibility is being cast wider. Fortunately, for those involved in outdoor recreation, there has been a realisation that the law of negligence has the potential to limit experiences and opportunities for participation and so the legislature has, fortunately, provided a framework for circumscribing liability in some circumstances. This will be discussed in detail in the next section. However, an overview of the common law of negligence is essential to understanding the operation of relevant legislation. It is also important to recognise that situations that fall outside the scope of the civil liabilities legislation will be dealt with according to the common law of negligence.

Common law, as opposed to statute, is law that is made and developed by decisions made by the courts. Each decision is made based on the specific facts of that case so that, unless the facts are identical (which is rare) the law may not be applied in precisely the same way. This can create a degree of uncertainty in the application of legal principles, especially in a new situation or environment, which is so often the case with outdoor recreational activities.

In spite of this ambiguity, some clear principles have developed, most notably the concept of duty of care. In its simplest formulation, duty of care means the responsibility one person (including a corporate 'person') owes to another to take *reasonable* care to avoid *foreseeable* harm to that other person through the person's act or omissions. The relationship with risk management should be immediately obvious:

1 Foreseeability implies that the person has thought about what might reasonably happen: this is risk identification.
2 Reasonable care implies that the person has thought about what they might do to avoid or minimise the consequences: this is risk analysis and control.

Whether a duty of care is owed by one person to another will depend on a number of circumstances including:

- the nature of the relationship of the parties
- the extent to which they relied on the expertise of the person
- whether other circumstances (such as contractual terms or repre-sentations made in marketing materials) impact on the existence of the duty.

It would be rare to find a situation where a provider of outdoor recreation activities (whether for profit, not for profit or voluntary) did not owe a duty of care to participants in those activities. By offering to provide those activities, the provider is saying: 'We will take reasonable care to avoid any potential harm to you in the context of this activity'. That is often implied in the advertising and promotion of activities (it is important to note that a failure to live up to those advertised expectations could also constitute a breach of consumers legislation and work health and safety legislation). By way of example, the only way to avoid the chance of dying in an avalanche on a backcountry skiing trip would be to stay at home. In this light, Taylor J. of the Court of Appeal for British Columbia in *Scurfield v Cariboo Helicopter Skiing Ltd* (1993, 74 B.C.L.R. 225) stated: 'It is not contended that the defendants had a duty to ensure that their guests were kept away from all places where avalanches could occur – in the context of helicopter skiing that would be impossible'. In effect, the provider promises to take reasonable care to avoid harm, but cannot guarantee a client's safety, thus it comes down to what is reasonable in the circumstances.

For liability in negligence, it is necessary to establish:

1 That a duty of care was owed.
2 That the duty was breached, in that an appropriate standard of care was not provided.
3 That, as a consequence of that breach, harm was suffered by another person.

We have considered above when a duty of care will be owed. Once we have established that, the critical questions are:

1 What does an organisation (or individual) need to do to fulfil the duty?
2 What is the standard of care required in the given circumstances?

The answer will bring us back to risk management. The responsibility is to identify what a reasonable person would do (or not do) in the circumstances, taking into account:

• the seriousness of the potential harm (the risk)
• the likelihood of the risk eventuating
• what measures could and should have been implemented to prevent the harm
• any special characteristics of the person, i.e. age, disability, previous experience. (When dealing with young children, the courts have clearly stated that the service provider is *in loco parentis* and so the standard of care is the same as a careful parent would take of their own children; judgments by the courts would suggest that in fact while the standard of care continues to be articulated in this way, the practical expectations, by the community and the courts, of what is required to meet this standard are increasing as our society, especially in relation to risks to young people, becomes increasingly risk averse.)

It is worth remembering that the decisions by the courts are made with the benefit of hindsight. Careful foresight, through effective risk management practices, should ensure that there are no surprises if you find yourself defending a claim of negligence.

Liability in negligence will not be established if:

1 The risk in question was not reasonably foreseeable (and therefore would not have arisen during the risk identification process).
2 The exposure to risk was insignificant (and therefore would have been identified as a very low risk rating based on an assessment of likelihood and consequences).
3 Given the risk rating, the steps taken to control the risk were reasonable.

In considering liability, the courts will also take into account the relative burden of controlling the risk, and the social value of the activity.

Another element to be aware of is what constitutes 'harm' for the purposes of liability. Physical injury (or even death) is obvious. However, it will also include financial or economic loss (such as loss of future earning capacity) and psychological injury. In evaluating the persons to whom a duty of care is owed, it is important to be mindful of those who may suffer an indirect harm. For example, participants in an outdoor activity who observe a significant injury to another person, or who are close family members of an injured person, may also have a claim for breach of duty of care.

Some other legal issues to consider

Occupier's liability

A long established specialised area of the law of negligence defines the duty owed by an occupier or controller of 'premises' to a person entering the premises, in relation to hazards resulting from the state of the premises. The law has recognised that an occupier may have varying degrees of responsibility to take reasonable care that a person does not suffer injury or damage as a result of any such hazards. Increasingly, the general law of negligence has impacted to raise the standard of care expected by an occupier. A number of jurisdictions (including UK, New Zealand, Victoria, Western Australia and South Australia) have responded by enacting legislation to clarify the expectations of occupiers. Key elements of the legislation include:

1 The capacity of an occupier to limit or restrict liability by way of contract.
2 Exclusion of risks willingly assumed by the person. (This assumes that they were aware of the risks and able to appreciate the danger.)
3 Specific things to be considered in determining if the duty of care has been discharged. These are largely derived from established common law principles and take into account:
   • the nature of the land or structures on the land
   • activities that are undertaken on the land
   • the degree of control over the land that a party has (this could be impacted by the terms of a lease or licence agreement)
   • the capacity of the person who is injured on the property (a higher standard of care is owed to persons who would be expected to be using the property for a particular purpose, as opposed to a trespasser coming on to the land)
   • any special characteristics of the user of the premises or land (a higher standard of care will be owed to children and persons with impaired capacity).

It is worth noting that effective workplace health and safety risk management practices should identify hazards that may give rise to occupier's liability and a risk control measure may include providing appropriate advice to persons coming on to the premises, ensuring public liability insurance is in place and framing contracts to limit liability. The concept of 'premises' includes all land that is controlled (owned, leased and licensed) but is narrower than the concept of a 'workplace' under workplace health and safety laws.

Contributory negligence

As a defence to a claim of negligence, a service provider may claim that a person's injury was not solely the fault of the provider and that the person contributed to the cause of their loss or injury. The amount of damages they can claim is reduced to the extent they are found to have contributed. To establish 'contributory negligence' the provider would need to prove:

- that the plaintiff failed to take reasonable care and
- that failure contributed or added to the act which caused the loss or injury.

The same principles are applied by the court to determine the failure to take reasonable care. The civil liabilities legislation in most jurisdictions enable a court to determine that the person contributed to his/her own injury to such an extent that it effectively cancels out the liability of the provider. The legislation also includes specific provisions in relation to the contribution of a person who is intoxicated. Courts have been reluctant to reach a finding of contributory negligence by students who have acted foolishly or misbehaved, especially if there is evidence of a lack of appropriate supervision.

The analysis above is intended to serve as a starting point only. The intricacies of the law vary from jurisdiction to jurisdiction, posing a real challenge for providers who operate across a number of jurisdictions. Good risk management practice would include a requirement to investigate the specific legal and regulatory environment in which the provider is operating.

Using the law to mitigate risk: civil liabilities legislation

Consider the following statement by the High Court of Australia in the context of activities such as horse riding, abseiling, high ropes, snow skiing and sky diving.

> People who pursue recreational activities regarded as sports often do so in hazardous circumstances; the element of danger may add to the enjoyment of the activity. Accepting risk, sometimes to a high degree, is part of many sports. A great deal of public and private effort and funding is devoted to providing facilities for people to engage in individual or team sport. This

reflects a view, not merely of the importance of individual autonomy, but also of the public benefit of sport. Sporting activities of a kind that sometimes result in physical injury are not only permitted, they are encouraged. (*Agar v Hyde* 2000 201 CLR 552)

In response to this philosophy, in the early years of the 21st century, jurisdictions across Australia have adopted legislation that may operate to limit the liability of a provider in some circumstances. Another way of looking at it might be to say that the legislation defines the standard of care required in some situations.

The specific types of risk that are dealt with by the legislation and the impact of the legislation on what would otherwise be the position in relation to liability are obvious risks and risks relating to dangerous recreational activities.

Obvious risks

An obvious risk is one that is obvious to a reasonable person in the position of the individual and will include risks that
- are of a matter of common knowledge
- have a low likelihood of occurring
- may not be prominent, conspicuous or physically observable.

There is no duty of care to warn of an obvious risk unless:
- a person has specifically requested advice or information and/or
- there is a specific statutory requirement.

While this appears straightforward, you will note that the legislation talks about a reasonable person in the position of the individual. The implication is that the extent to which something is obvious may be a subjective test, taking into account particular attributes of a person. For example, a risk may be obvious to most people because it is physically observable, but this will not be the case if the person has a vision impairment, just as a risk that is obvious to an instructor or guide may not be obvious to their client.

Recreational activities and dangerous recreational activities

The legislation defines recreational activities to include sports, pursuits and activities engaged in for enjoyment, relaxation or leisure or at a place where people engage in such activities. It then describes dangerous recreational activities as those that involve significant risk of physical harm. It is essential for a provider to identify activities that may be defined as dangerous recreational activities. A significant risk of physical harm is defined as more than trivial, and less than likely – it considers the likelihood and consequences. A significant risk of insignificant harm (for example, something that requires simple first aid) does not make the activity dangerous. That does not mean that it should not be identified and managed, it simply means that it is not the type of activity that is subject to the legislative provisions and protections.

Impact of the legislation

The legislation effectively excludes a finding of negligence against a provider in circumstances where the harm arises from an obvious risk of a dangerous recreational activity, whether or not the participant was aware of the risk.

In relation to other recreational activities, the legislation also impacts to limit liability in certain circumstances:

- where a warning of the risk(s) was provided
- either orally or in writing
- in a way that is reasonably likely to result in people being warned beforehand (this includes advice to a parent or companion of a child or person with an incapacity)
- that warns of the general nature of a particular risk
- that is not contradicted by actions, documentation or processes.

It is clear that it is still essential for a provider to undertake a comprehensive risk assessment in order to be able to provide the appropriate risk warning.

It is also possible for a provider of recreational services to exclude, restrict or modify potential civil liability contractually by including a term in the contract for the provision of services that the person engages in the activity at their own risk. However, it must be clear and unambiguous. The general law of contract would require that the term be disclosed prior to the person participating, with sufficient time for them to make an informed decision about whether to proceed. However there are situations when there is limited time for a participant to consider a contract, such as a commercial rafting trip. In those circumstances the operator must ensure that any communication, signage, marketing materials and/or website provide consistent messages as one would expect in a risk warning. An exclusion or limitation does not minimise the requirement of the provider to provide the services with due care and skill. It will not afford protection to a provider who operates in contravention of a law, particularly where the law establishes practices or procedures for protecting safety. This would include any circumstances in which work health and safety laws are applicable. It does not exclude other potential statutory liabilities. It would not provide protection in respect of a breach of duty of care in relation to other aspects of the provider's operations that are not directly related to the recreational activity, e.g. an injury resulting from a slip in the office of the provider due to pooling of water on the floor.

From a risk management perspective, the various pieces of legislation that have the potential to limit civil liability require a provider to:

- identify, through a risk identification process, what activities might be considered 'dangerous recreational activities'
- include as part of the documented risk management plan the need for appropriate warnings in relation to other recreational activities
- ensure that other 'non-recreational' aspects of the provider's operations are appropriately risk managed.

Risk management when something goes wrong

Incidents do occur even with the best practices and care. A comprehensive risk management framework for an organisation will include consideration of how the organisation will respond in the event of an incident occurring. While it is not possible to explore this in detail, organisations should have in place a critical incident management plan that identifies responsibilities and actions in the event of a serious incident occurring. The plan would include aspects such as:

- immediate responses to ensure safety, and to stabilise the situation (including assessing the medical condition of all participants)
- contingency and evacuation
- communication strategies (including radio frequencies, repeater station locations, need for SAT phones)
- critical incident response (including debriefing and trauma counselling and support arrangements)
- business continuity arrangements (including contacts for lawyers and insurers)
- incident investigations and strategies for dealing with the media (the media plan should identify who is authorised to speak to the media, training for staff in dealing with media requests and enquiries and training for those charged with the responsibility of dealing with the media).

This plan will be supported by a well-documented set of policies, procedures and programs, including training needs analysis and registers of training for staff and volunteers that have been implemented and reviewed. These will be an evidentiary mainstay in the event that a claim is made.

Recent cases

In recent years, many Australian and international jurisdictions have had to consider the issue of liability of providers of outdoor recreational activities. The providers include corporate providers, not-for-profit organisations, voluntary groups, local government authorities and schools. Following is a short, representative list of relevant cases. In no way is it intended to be exhaustive, but it serves to reinforce the fact that no two cases are alike and that there is a high expectation on service providers to conduct their operations with due regard to their duty of care to participants. The cases also provide insight into the ongoing evolution of the law, especially in relation to limitations of liability in relation to inherently dangerous activities.

Australia

Finding by the Australian Consumer Complaints Commission (ACCC) against Contiki Holidays that it had misrepresented safety information in its promotional material and failed to adequately investigate the safety of a tour operator promoted. Twenty people died in a canyoning incident on the Saxetenbach River canyon in Switzerland. (<http://www.accc.gov.au/content/item.phtml?itemId=331712&nodeId=6b77fc6d12f6f95a7fd94963b8179c09&fn=d02_64643.pdf>)

Seven suppliers of down sleeping bags were required to give undertakings to ACCC as a result of misrepresenting their thermal qualities and hence potentially putting people at risk if they relied on those representations. (<http://www.accc.gov.au/content/index.phtml/itemId/711720/fromItemId/232>)

Agar v Hyde (2000) 201 CLR 552: an action against directors of the International Football Board by two players who suffered spinal injuries in NSW on the basis that they had not adequately monitored the rules of the game relating to scrums, resulting in risk of serious injury. The applications were dismissed by the High Court who noted the applicants were 'freely consenting adult participants' who chose to play a game which had an obvious element of danger.

Mikronos v Adams (2004) 1 DCLR (NSW) 369: considered the NSW Civil Liability Act 2002 and noted that horse riding was a recreational activity, but that trail riding was not a dangerous activity. While the risk of falling off a horse is obvious, the risk of the saddle slipping (due to the straps not being properly tightened) was not.

Falvo v Australian Oztag Sports Association [2006] NSWCA 17: action against the association and local council for injury resulting from a fall during the game due to the condition of the ground. Oztag was considered a dangerous recreational activity. However, the state of the ground was considered to be obvious and expected: 'If perfection were insisted upon, countless people in this country would be deprived of the opportunity to participate in sporting activities.'

Larner v Parks Victoria [2008] VCC 827: parks authority was found liable for a camper's injuries resulting from a falling tree limb. The authority had identified the risk, but failed to act on its own risk assessment and failed to advise campers.

Woods v Multisport Holdings (2002) 186 ALR 145: the court held that failing to provide a helmet with a face guard to an indoor cricket player was not a breach of duty of care. The risk was so obvious that there was no duty to warn.

Canada

Crocker v Sundance Northwest Resorts Ltd, [1988] 1 S.C.R. 1186: majority decision of Supreme Court of Canada on appeal, determined that the plaintiff was responsible for own injuries suffered in a snow tubing accident as a result of his intoxication even though the resort owed a duty of care.

Ochoa v Canadian Mountain Holidays Inc, 1996 CanLII 378 (BCSC): British Columbia Supreme Court held that a provider of heli-skiing services would only be liable for the death of a skier as a result of an avalanche fatality if negligence was 'criminal' – that is, it was conducted in a dangerous manner.

Murao v Richmond School District No. 38, 2005 BCCA 43: Court of Appeal for British Columbia confirmed that in relation to a skiing excursion the standard of care owed by a teacher to students is that of a careful parent.

Wong v Lok's Martial Arts Centre Inc, 2009 BCSC 1385: British Columbia Supreme Court found that a parent could not waive their child's right to sue in negligence for an injury resulting from a sparring match.

Myers v Peel County Board of Education, [1981] 2 S.C.R. 21: Supreme Court of Canada noted that the standard of care to be applied by school authorities is that of a prudent parent, but will depend on a number of circumstances in a particular case.

New Zealand

Andersen v R [2004] NZCA 238: at first instance (but overturned on appeal) the organiser of a cycling road race was convicted of criminal nuisance when a cyclist was killed during the race, even though she had not followed event rules. The key issue was whether the information sheet given to participants before the event was clear.

Queenstown Lakes District Council v Palmer [1999] 1 NZLR 549: the Council and rafting operation were held liable for the psychological injuries suffered by a man who witnessed his wife drown in a rafting accident. (http://www.voxy.co.nz/national/adventure-centre-ordered-pay-480000-following-tragedy/5/10663)

Following the 2008 Mangatepopo Gorge tragedy in which six students and a teacher were killed, the Sir Edmund Hillary Outdoor Pursuits Centre was fined $40 000 and ordered to pay $480 000 in reparations in Auckland District Court after admitting two charges under the Health and Safety in Employment Act.

United Kingdom

Watson v British Boxing Board of Control [2001] 2WLR 1256: failure to provide adequate emergency first aid facilities was negligent.

Blake v Galloway [2004] EWCA Civ 814: compared 'horseplay' with organised games and noted that recklessness or a high degree of carelessness would be required to constitute a breach of duty of care.

Poppleton v Trustees of the Portsmouth Youth Activities Committee [2008] EWCA Civ 646: the inherent and obvious risks of 'bouldering', indoor climbing without safety ropes, together with the waiver signed by the adult participant negated any duty of care by the climbing centre.

Orchard v Lee [2009] EWCA Civ 295: held that a 13-year-old boy did not breach a duty of care in playing tag in the playground in a way the resulted in a supervisor being injured because it was not out of the norm of behaviour of a 13 year-old.

Woodroffe-Hedley v Cuthbertson, QBD transcript, 20 June 1997: a climbing guide found negligent in death of client on Mont Blanc Massif. The court noted that a mountain climber consents to the ordinary dangers of climbing but is entitled to rely on the expertise of a paid guide.

Learnings

In deciding cases, the courts are mostly considering the facts retrospectively. Not only do they have the benefit of hindsight, they are considering a very specific set of circumstances. Our challenge in managing risk in the current legal environment is to take those 'learnings' and apply them prospectively, that is going forward, but in a way that enhances our lives rather than restraining and restricting.

> Properly planned outdoor recreation programs are, in my view, one of the best ways to develop these essential attributes [self-worth and self-reliance] in people of all ages, and they should be encouraged. Virtue J. in *Bain v Board of Education* (Calgary) (1993), 146 A.R. 321 (Q.B.)

Points for action for practitioners

- For all aspects of your work, where would be considered a workplace?
- How have you assessed the level of risk to your employees and those visiting your workplaces?
- To what extent are you complying with the civil liabilities and occupational health and safety legislation that you operate under with respect to:
  - the different locations/places in which you work

- the different activities you undertake (e.g. recreational versus dangerous recreational activities versus non-recreational activities)
- the different client groups you work with (e.g. children, adults, elderly, people with different access requirements such as physical needs or cognitive impairments)
- the various people who work with you: employees, volunteers, interns, work experience students.
- How does your advertising material and documentation that goes to clients support your risk management and any risk warnings you issue?
- How does your staff recruitment, induction and training support your risk management in relation to occupational health and safety and civil liabilities?

Questions for further discussion

- To whom do you owe a duty of care when you are running a program, event or activity with under 18 year-olds or over 18 year-olds?
- What are the key environmental factors in your operations and activities that you need to consider in managing risks?
- How do they impact on the duty of care owed to your customers/client group?
- Are there any characteristics of your client group that may require particular attention to ensure that risks are well managed?
- Develop a risk register for a specific area of your operations and activities (Appendix). Based on that analysis, how well do you think you are managing risks at the moment? How can you improve your organisation's risk management performance?
- How can you keep up to date in relation to developments in the law that may impact on your activities?
- What documentation do you currently maintain? Is it adequate? Why or why not?

References and further resources

References

Geary, R 1996. 'The Lyme Bay sea kayaking tragedy and the criminal law'. *The Sea Canoeist Newsletter*, vol. 65, pp. 4–6.

Safe Work Australia 2010. Model work health and safety. Act Retrieved 15 December 2010 from <http://www.safeworkaustralia.gov.au/Legislation/ModelWHSAct/Pages/ModelWHSAct.aspx>.

Further resources

Canadian Centre for Occupational Health and Safety (CCOHS).

'From Lyme Bay to licensing: past, present and future – the development of current regulation of outdoor adventure activities,' <http://www.aals.org.uk/lymebay01. html>.

Fulbrook, J 2005. *Outdoor Activities, Negligence and the Law*. Ashgate Publishing, Hampshire, UK.

Healey, D 2009. *Sport and the Law*, 4th edn. UNSW Press, Kensington, NSW.

Heshka, J 2006. 'Canada's legal standard of care for outdoor education'. *Canadian Association for the Practical Study of Law in Education 2005 Conference Proceedings*, Georgetown, ON, pp. 221–42.

International Labour Organisation Programme on Safety and Health at Work and the Environment (SafeWork) <http://www.ilo.org/safework/>.

Lines, K & Heshka, J 2008. 'Falling in line with the law – should adults who are injured after deliberately putting themselves at risk expect to be compensated?'. *New Law Journal*, London, pp. 1026–7.

Lynch, P, Jonson, P & Dibben, M 2007. 'Exploring relationships of trust in "adventure" recreation'. *Leisure Studies*, vol. 26, no. 1, pp. 47–64.

Work-related injuries, Australia 2005–06 <http://www.abs.gov.au/AUSSTATS/ abs@.nsf/DetailsPage/6324.02005–06?OpenDocument>.

Relevant legislation

Occupational Health and Safety Legislation:

Table 3.1 Occupational Health and Safety (OHS) and safety legislation

Jurisdiction	Occupational health and safety legislation	Civil liabilities legislation
Australian Model legislation	Work Health & Safety Act 2010	
Commonwealth	Occupational Health & Safety Act 1991 Australian Workplace Safety Standards Act 2005	
Australian Capital Territory	Occupational Health & Safety Act 1989 Occupational Health & Safety Regulations 1991	Civil Law (Wrongs) Act 2002
New South Wales	Work Health & Safety Act 2011 Occupational Health & Safety Regulations 2001	Civil Liability Act 2002

(cont.)

Table 3.1 (*cont.*)

Northern Territory	Workplace Health & Safety Act 2007 Workplace Health & Safety Regulations 2007	
Queensland	Workplace Health & Safety Act 1995 Workplace Health & safety Regulations 2008	Civil Liability Act 2003
South Australia	Occupational Health, Safety & Welfare Act 1986 Occupational Health, Safety & Welfare Regulations 1995	Civil Liability Act 1936
Tasmania	Workplace Health & Safety Act 1995 Workplace Health & Safety Regulations 1998	Civil Liability Act 2002
Victoria	Occupational Health & Safety Act 2004 Various regulations under the Act	Wrongs Act 1958
Western Australia	Occupational Health & Safety Act 1984 Occupational Health & Safety Regulations 1996	Civil Liability Act 2002
New Zealand	Health & Safety in Employment Act 1992	

Other legislation

Trade Practices Act 1974 (C'th)
Australian Consumer Law 2011 (C'th)
Fair Work Act 2009 (C'th)
Disability Discrimination Act 1992 (C'th)
Age Discrimination Act 2004 (C'th)
Discrimination Act 1991, ACT
Anti-Discrimination Acts in states of Australia: NSW (1977), Tasmania (1998), Queensland (1991), Northern Territory
Occupiers Liability Act 1962, New Zealand
Occupiers Liability Act 1985, Western Australia
Occupiers Liability Act 1983, Victoria

The organisational context of risk management

Tracey J. Dickson and Anne Terwiel

> One of the many reasons for the bewildering and tragic character of human existence is the fact that social organisation is at once necessary and fatal. Men are forever creating such organisations for their own convenience and forever finding themselves the victims of their home-made monsters.
>
> Aldous Huxley

FOCUS QUESTIONS

1   In what ways is risk management embedded into an organisation's culture?
2   How do an organisation's management, structures and/or policies support the desired risk management culture?
3   Who is the best person to 'champion' risk management in an organisation or program?
4   How can stories, images or activities support or undermine the achievement of the desired risk management culture?
5   What is the role of safety audits or organisational accreditations?

CASE STUDY

While Olympic and Paralympic Games are held every four years, host cities are named seven years prior to the Games they will be hosting. This long lead time allows the organising committee the opportunity for adequate planning, thereby maximising opportunities and minimising uncertainty. For the 2010 Winter Games in Vancouver, the workforce grew from the few committed individuals who were part of the bid process, to up to 50 000 workers, 19 000 of whom were volunteers. These volunteers needed to be recruited, trained, equipped, tasked, supervised, fed, rewarded and released for an event that ran for just 17 days for the Olympics and 10 days for the Paralympics. At the macro level the cultural ideals of 'Olympism' underpinned the event, but at the micro level, buses needed to run on time, people needed to be fed, and event schedules needed to be maintained. The 2010 Vancouver/Whistler Olympic and Paralympic Winter Games provide examples of both excellent planning that minimised exposure to risk and gaps in planning that contributed to dissatisfaction.

Some volunteers found that the training promised to them when they signed up to volunteer was not delivered in a manner that was efficient or effective, thereby leading to a measure of dissatisfaction with the training process. For a few this led to an inability to do their jobs properly, for some it was an annoyance in their otherwise positive volunteer experience. The risk in providing training that is less than adequate is that it may lead to an impact on the potential volunteer legacy for the host communities that had been intended as an outcome of the Games.

In contrast, an example of effective planning was provided by the Vancouver Organising Committee (VANOC) at the Cypress Mountain venue where the freestyle skiing and snowboarding events were conducted. Due to unseasonably warm temperatures there was very little natural snow on the ground just days before the events were to begin. Proper planning minimised the chance of cancelled events as contingencies were in place to bring snow to the mountain in case the mountain did not have enough snow. These plans included snow farming, helicoptering in snow from storage sites and trucking in snow from other areas. This, combined with innovative uses of refrigeration and dry ice systems, ensured that the freestyle events ran as scheduled.

Introduction

Risk is present in organisations in many ways and organisations must be aware of various forms of risk. On the surface, the most obvious form of risk is physical risk: the risk of injury to patrons, employees or the public. But from the standpoint of the overall health of an organisation there are many other forms of risk, including but not limited to: economic and financial risk, political risk, the risk of damage to public image, the risk to the organisation of labour shortages or labour unrest, the risk of complacency and falling behind. Risk management strategies that address a myriad of issues must be put in place in order to ensure successful long-term operation.

In most circumstances sport, outdoor activities and events occur within the context of one or more organisations, which may be public or private, large or small, which include individuals and groups of interested people or stakeholders. In the case study above, the delivery of an Olympic and Paralympic Games is the culmination of the co-ordination of stakeholders over many years by an organising committee, such as VANOC. Other participating stakeholders include the International Olympic Committee, the International Paralympic Committee, national, state and local governments, athletes, corporate sponsors, sport organisations, media and finally the viewing public. For each stakeholder their expectations, involvement, commitment and length of time connected to the event will vary, yet from a risk management perspective, each is important. ISO 31000 defines risk management as 'coordinated activities to direct and control an organisation with regard to risk' (Standards Australia and Standards New Zealand, 2009, p. 2). One step in the risk management process involves establishing the context where the 'organisation articulates its objectives, defines the external and internal parameters to be taken into account when managing risk, and sets the scope and risk criteria for the remaining process' (Standards Australia and Standards New Zealand 2009, p. 15).

The external context relates to the environment in which the organisation operates and includes aspects such as the social, cultural, economic, environmental, legal and political contexts, as well as competitor's strategies, trends in society and relationships with key stakeholders. The risk management process also needs to align with the internal context such as the organisation's mission, culture, structure, size, policies, processes and strategy (Standards Australia and Standards New Zealand, 2009). Risk management strategies must cross both the internal and the external contexts.

As the case highlights, any scenario is situated within a broader context, be that an activity, an event, a program, an organisation, a community or a society. Understanding that context and being proactive is essential for effective risk management. The key parameters of the Standard that will assist in our risk management practice as set out in the Standard include the clear articulation of the principles of risk management, which are that it:

- creates and protects value
- is an integral part of all organisational processes
- is part of decision-making
- explicitly addresses uncertainty
- is systematic, structured and timely
- is based on the best available information
- is tailored
- takes human and cultural factors into account
- is transparent and inclusive

- is dynamic, iterative and responsive to change
- facilitates continual improvement of the organisation.

To this end this chapter focuses upon the organisational context of risk management and in so doing draws upon insights from areas such as strategic management, leadership and human resource management in relation to how they support the desired risk management culture and process.

Strategic management: an overview

Strategic management is defined as:

> The process of identifying, choosing and implementing activities that will enhance the long-term performance of an organisation by setting direction, and by creating compatibility between internal skills and resources of the organisation, and the changing external environment within which it operates. (Viljoen & Dann 2003, p. xi).

The first part of this definition bares close resemblance to the definition of risk management used throughout this book in that it focuses upon a process that supports the ongoing successful operation of an entity. The changing external environment that is referred to in the definition involves the environment within which the organisation operates and includes such things as other organisations, competitors, licensing bodies (both industrial and governmental), the natural environment, the social/political environment, etc. Strong strategic management involves keeping one eye on one's organisation and the other eye on the external environment. The main elements of strategic management that are discussed below are: strategic analysis, strategic direction, strategy formulation, strategy implementation and strategy evaluation.

Strategic analysis

In order to develop a relevant strategy, it is imperative to conduct a strategic analysis, a thorough analysis of the organisational situation, in order to develop an understanding that will allow one to devise a plan to achieve some end. The analysis should focus on the things that influence an organisation, primarily externally, but internally as well. There are many tools available for this, such as SWOT analysis, Porter's Five Forces analysis and PEST analysis (Tribe 2005), which can help an organisation look at the range of forces acting upon it in order to identify issues and implement solutions and review.

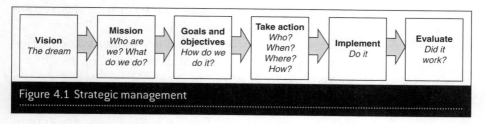

Figure 4.1 Strategic management

Strategic direction

The key elements of the strategic direction, as indicated in Figure 4.1, are the mission and vision statements and the goals and objectives. These elements emphasise the strategic direction of an organisation, allowing the public and stakeholders to be knowledgeable about why the organisation exists, what it does and the direction it is heading in the future. This knowledge reduces the risk of misunderstanding and misdirection, and increases the possibility that stakeholders of the organisation, within and without, are clearly informed and in tune with the business.

1 Vision statements

A vision statement answers the question 'what do we want to become'. Vision statements are broad and visionary and look ahead to the future. Some examples from the sport and outdoor world include:

- To inspire character development and self-discovery in people of all ages and walks of life through challenge and adventure, and to impel them to achieve more than they ever thought possible, to show compassion for others and to actively engage in creating a better world. (Outward Bound)
- To enable Paralympic Athletes to achieve sporting excellence and inspire and excite the world. (Paralympic Organisation)
- For the Game. For the World. (Fédération Internationale de Football Association, FIFA)

2 Mission statements

A mission statement outlines the reason an organisation or entity exists and explains some of the products or services it will deliver, indicating that this is who we are and what we do. Some examples are:

- To touch the soul of the nation and inspire the world by creating and delivering an extraordinary Olympic and Paralympic experience with lasting legacies. (Vancouver 2010 Olympic and Paralympic Winter Games)
- To help people discover their potential to care for themselves, others and the world around them through challenging experiences in unfamiliar settings. (Outward Bound International)

- Develop the game, touch the world, build a better future. (Fédération Internationale de Football Association, FIFA)
- RDA NSW is a volunteer organisation providing equine assisted activities for people with disabilities to develop and enhance abilities. (Riding for the Disabled Association, NSW)

Who we are is, in part, the products and the processes, but it also incorporates the culture of an organisation, which is discussed later. Where an organisation is going will be impacted not only by its culture, but also the application of creativity and innovation in and through the organisation, which is also explored further below.

3 Goals and objectives

Goals are broad statements identifying desired outcomes. Objectives provide specific targets for the steps that contribute to achieving those outcomes. Objectives need to be SMART (specific, measurable, attainable, realistic and timely) and may be specific to different operational areas, such as finance, human resources and marketing. For example:
- business goal: to increase market share
  - objective: to obtain 30 per cent of the market share within 24 months
- financial goal: to increase profitability
  - objective: to increase net profit by 40 per cent within 36 months through reducing wastage, implementing a social networking marketing strategy and reducing staff turnover
- human resource goal: to increase staff retention
  - objective: to reduce staff turnover to less than 25 per cent within 12 months through enhanced work–life balance strategies
- marketing goal: increased e-marketing presence
  - objective: to implement cost-neutral social networking marketing strategy within six months.

Strategy formulation: plan of action

The plan of action needs to translate the vision, mission, goals and objectives into specific activities. To be effective it needs to be supported by appropriate organisational structures, human resource plans, financial plans, review processes and ultimately communicated, along with the vision and mission statements, to all key stakeholders.

Strategy implementation

An implementation plan is critical to achieving organisational goals and objectives. The plan should contain action items related to each objective and identify the key people responsible for undertaking those actions.

The risk matrix in the Appendix provides a small example of these. Part of the plan of action and implementation strategy will be supporting documents such as policies and procedures that support the practice in the field.

Policies, procedures and practice

In order to achieve organisational goals and objectives, many organisations will use a mixture of policies and procedures to support and inform their practice. These need to be consistent with the mission and vision of the organisation and also the desired organisational cultures, including the risk management culture.

A policy is a deliberate plan of action to guide decisions and achieve outcomes. A procedure is a specified series of actions or operations that have to be executed in the same manner in order to obtain the same result. Policies and procedures must be living documents brought to the attention of leaders and staff during training and development in order for them to support organisational goals.

Examples are:

- anti-bullying policy: every employee and volunteer of Company ABC has the right to work in an environment free from harassment and bullying
- business ethics policy: Company ABC aims to develop ethical relationships with all its business partners built through honesty, openness and fair play.

Practices are what is seen in the field. From how things are done, observers will have a sense of what is important to an organisation and to some degree, what the philosophy of an organisation is. For example, an organisation that espouses careful management of risk but demonstrates wasteful or inefficient practices will have observers believing they are sloppy, regardless of how loudly the organisation trumpets their philosophy of managing risk. An organisation that demonstrates care and attention at every step of the way, talking to clients about risk and showing them the proper way to operate in a risk-filled environment, will have clients/observers who believe the organisation has a philosophy and practice of risk reduction. Practice may be supported by documents such as standard operating procedures (SOPs), which should be informed by policies and philosophies. As such, policies, procedures and practices should be linked, each informing the other and growing and changing as is necessary for the growth of the organisation and the changing milieu in which the organisation operates.

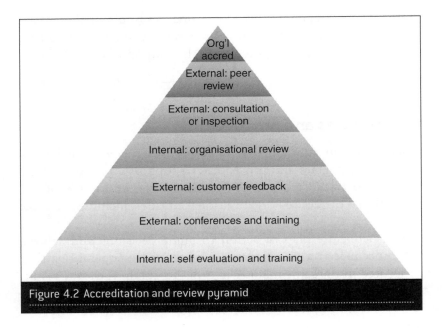

Figure 4.2 Accreditation and review pyramid

Strategy evaluation

Consistent with the monitoring and evaluation steps within the risk management process, evaluation of the overall strategic direction and individual elements of the strategy should be undertaken during and after implementation, that is formative and summative evaluation respectively. Formative evaluation allows for changes to be made during implementation in order to improve the process. Summative evaluation provides a summary at the end of the process, indicating the success or failure of the strategy and informing those responsible for the overall strategy of improvements that can be made next time.

Accreditations and reviews

Examples of organisational evaluations are internal reviews and external peer reviews and accreditations. These provide opportunities to explore the progress of the organisation or program against the stated objectives in the context of the current and expected social, economic and natural environment. The pyramid in Figure 4.2 shows the range of review, benchmarking and accreditation opportunities that are available in many outdoor or sporting contexts. At the base are those things that are able to be done regularly such as staff evaluation and training and attending conferences where current practices may be benchmarked. At the top of the pyramid are opportunities that are less frequent but very important, and that require significant investment of time and money to maximise the benefits.

Accreditation programs are not new and their worth has been discussed internationally for some time (Carlsen 2000; Chisholm & Shaw 2004; Gass & Williamson 1995; Harris & Jago 2001). But as evidenced by the tragedy at Mangatepopo Gorge in New Zealand (see Chapter 11), where the organisation was undergoing an accreditation review at the time of the incident, accreditations are no guarantee of safety. What these processes will do is provide opportunities to learn from within and from those outside an organisation in order that changes, improvements and adaptations may be made to be in the best position to respond to all the risks an organisation faces on a daily basis.

An external organisational accreditation should be supported by a range of other strategies to achieve organisational improvement. These may include attending internal and external staff training programs, obtaining external feedback from customers or consultation (such as a Challenge Ropes Course Inspection), a peer review process where industry peers are invited in to review particular aspects of an organisation's work and finally an externally conducted accreditation program conducted by a relevant industry body. The importance of all of these is not the end result of accreditation, but rather how the organisation willingly learns from the process and the information obtained to continually improve their products, processes and services beyond the accreditation cycle.

Different industry groups have a range of accreditation models, such as for training organisations, activity providers and campsites (see Further Resources for examples). Some may be mandatory, while others may be voluntary. Each program seeks to provide feedback on how the organisation operates, however, each accreditation program will differ in relation to the mix of self-assessments, external reviews of paperwork site and/or program visits. With this diversity comes diversity in the cost of the programs. While each accreditation program seeks to provide the consumer with some assessment of the 'quality' of the program or activity, what accreditations cannot do is indicate what is happening on a particular day and time. All accreditations, even those with extensive program observations will only ever provide a snapshot of operations, they cannot provide any guarantee that what was observed in the review process is still happening.

Having conducted a review, evaluation or accreditation it is important to use and manage that information, to learn from it and transfer it to other contexts as would be considered normal when applying the experiential learning cycle (Kolb 1984). This then raises the concepts of knowledge management and knowledge transfer.

Knowledge management and knowledge transfer

From the perspective of strategic management it is essential to be able to maximise the resources (e.g. financial, human and capital) available within the organisation or activity. Argote and Ingram suggest that it is the 'knowledge embedded in the interactions of people, tools and tasks [that] provides a basis for competitive advantage in firms' (2000, p. 150). If this is the case, then methods need to be developed to both manage knowledge as well as transfer knowledge, both tacit and intuitive knowledge, within an organisation to enhance that competitive advantage.

Experiential knowing is a combination of tacit knowledge and intuitive knowledge, where tacit knowledge is defined as 'that which people cannot say' (Sandercock 1998). The Oxford Dictionary defines tacit as 'understood without being put into words' (Crowther 1995, p. 1214). The concept of tacit knowing draws on the work of the philosopher Michael Polanyi who suggests that we know more than we can say (Nisbett & Wilson 1977). Intuitive knowledge is more like informed guesswork where a process is applied in a situation' of 'using our senses to interpret signs' (Sandercock 1998, p. 76). What is needed are policies, processes and a culture of learning that supports the sharing of ideas and the questioning of how things are done in order that in the future uncertainty may be managed, positive outcomes supported and negative outcomes avoided.

Moving beyond strategic management

One risk associated with discussions of strategic management is that those discussions may be perceived as being a high-level process that is removed from the front lines, but in reality it is an important aspect of managing an organisation. Yet the steps previously discussed do not occur in isolation. They are affected by a range of other aspects within an organisation that may impact across many of the steps outlined above. The aspects to consider include: culture, innovation and creativity, leadership, knowledge management and policies and procedures.

Culture

A limiting factor in any risk management discussion to date is the broader impact of the organisation on people, equipment and environment, in particular the role of the organisation's culture on how people act, the decisions they make, the equipment they use and the environment in which they work. Culture can include national cultures, organisational cultures and sub-group cultures and may be defined as the 'shared values and beliefs which are seen to characterise particular organisations' (Dawson 1996, p. 141). Hofstede more broadly defines culture as 'the collective programming of the mind which distinguishes one group or category of people from another' (1993, p. 89). The latter definition focuses on culture at the national level while the former is at the organisational level where the following discussion will focus.

Organisational culture: stories, plots and heroes

Organisational culture or 'the way things are done around here' may be demonstrated in the stories being told about the organisation, the people within that organisation, the marketing images, the organisational structures (hierarchy), dress, language, humour, rules, policies and procedures (Linstead 1999). The stories told (and re-told) are a conduit through which an organisation's culture may be portrayed and/or preserved; they establish the norms for an organisation which enable people within the organisation to determine how to behave. Externally, culture made visible through the behaviours and stories that are retold and celebrated, helps clarify, for other organisations, whether there may be synergies that would allow the two organisations to do business effectively together.

For new staff the artefacts of culture, such as the structures, language, rituals and stories, may be one way to learn what behaviour is acceptable and what is not: How are the heroines/heroes portrayed? What are the preferred behaviours conveyed in those stories? What attitude is portrayed regarding compliance of safety policies?

Stories told by top managers and influential people within organisations can have a significant impact upon the perceptions of staff and clients. It will be these stories that influence perceptions, and it is perceptions that will determine organisational cultures and ultimately employee action, even more so than policies and procedures. For outdoor organisations there may be a challenge to manage the perception of adventure alongside of the need to limit uncertainty and risk.

A safety culture gap

While adventure, sport and recreation managers may express their desire to reduce injuries, there is a potential cultural gap between the desired 'safe' environment and the portrayed image of an activity, seen in marketing activities, brochures, advertisements, newspapers and online stories (Fluker & Turner 2000). Definitions of adventure include terms such as uncertainty, hazard and risk, yet not all participants, staff or leaders may actually be comfortable with this, especially where safety is a necessary outcome. Some examples of how this culture gap or mismatch may be created and also encouraged include:

- marketing a risky activity to a young risk-taking audience, predominantly male, through brochures and magazines that celebrate risk, but at the same time the organisation is required or expected to keep those clients 'safe'
- conducting events and providing areas that appeal to 'extreme' participants but needing to meet the often risk-adverse needs of land managers and insurers
- sport media outlets promoting 'plays of the week' that highlight big 'hits' in tackles where players experience concussions and injuries as 'entertainment' or amusement, where those hits may put the players at risk of long term brain damage and depression
- celebrating risk-taking behaviours of staff through the stories told to junior staff and clients about those personal adventures, to create a caché about themselves as bona fide adventurers
- the push from the clients to be taken to places where no one else goes
- sponsors wanting a sport event to be seen to be risky enough in order to be appealing to their target market but not desiring the cost of the reality of injury or death.

These examples demonstrate that while sport and outdoor organisations seek to provide a safe environment for clients, the mythology built around perceived risk may need to be maintained in order to attract targeted clients and be commercially successful. This raises the question as to why we need to maintain these stories when the reality of safety may be different. The maintenance of the stories cannot be at the expense of physical safety nor can the stories be used to encourage risk-taking behaviours by clients and staff. As the manager of an organisation I may want the client to be inspired by the guide's stories but I don't want them replicating the behaviour without the commensurate training and experience.

Organisational cultures model, monitor and modify behaviours of individuals. A risk-averse culture may not achieve the opportunities and/or changes desired of many sporting or recreation activities, just as much as a high-risk culture may inhibit the potential outcomes due to the participants and staff being under excessive stress. The organisation's culture must reflect and support the desired outcomes of the organisation, financially, strategically and in service and product delivery and development. One aspect of culture that will support organisational development is how innovation and creativity is encouraged, supported and rewarded within the organisation and across programs and activities.

Innovation and creativity

At a time when life has 'sped up' and the pace of change seems to be accelerating, there appears to be a need to assist people to be more effective in being creative and innovative in order to be able to adapt to and move beyond the demands of today. The risk for a business of not being innovative or creative is that it stagnates and in a market place of constant change stagnation may lead to extinction. Yet, can creativity be manufactured? Or is it a result of creating the 'space' for creativity to happen? Insights may be gleaned from diverse writings in psychology, science fiction and art.

In her writing, Buchholz reinforces Asimov's (1977) observations about the need to create 'space' for creativity and problem-solving to emerge: 'the natural creativity in all of us – the sudden and slow insights, bursts and gentle bubbles of imagination – is found as a result of alone time . . . Both creativity and curiosity are bred through contemplation' (Buchholz 1998, p. 82). It must also be remembered, however, that what works for one may not work for another. For example, Csikszentmihalyi noted that 'in many preliterate cultures solitude is thought to be so intolerable that a person makes a great effort never to be alone' (Csikszentimihalyi 1990, p. 165). As Asimov (1977) observes about creating space to solve problems:

> It helps to relax, deliberately, by subjecting your mind to material complicated enough to occupy the voluntary faculty of thought, but superficial enough not to engage the deeper involuntary one. In my case, it is an action movie, in your case, it might be something else (p. 98).

This concept of creating some form of mental space is not new. In 1977 Nisbett and Wilson recalled Ghiselin's work in 1952 on the creativity of people including Picasso, where Ghiselin concluded that 'the individual has no idea what factors prompted the solution; and even the fact that a process is taking place is sometimes unknown to the individual prior to the point that a solution appears in consciousness' (cited in Nisbett & Wilson 1977, p. 240). This raises the question of how organisations that are busy doing their core business can create the time and space for individuals and teams to be creative and innovative in order to support organisational growth and development, and also be balanced with the role of policies and procedures.

Within the context of outdoor education, beyond the operation of the business there is great benefit in creative and innovate solutions during high stress/high risk events, such as for a leader during a rescue, or when bad weather forces a change in plans. In these situations there is a balance between 'going by the book' in terms of accepted practice and the necessity for creativity or innovation because of situational demands. Careful training, through scenarios and case studies, and extensive experience in this area, will reduce the uncertainty associated with being either too rigid or too experimental in a high stress situation. An effective leader will know when a creative solution is required and when accepted practice must be followed and will be able to encourage the commitment of his or her followers. But is there a single model of leadership?

Leadership and power

In outdoor education, sport or adventure learning contexts leadership may occur from the group level through to the program, event, organisation and industry levels. As with other aspects of risk management and strategic management, the model of leadership needs to reflect the purpose, vision and mission of the activity or organisation. While there are numerous books and articles on leadership, possibly the most insightful comments come from two religious leaders who emphasise the centrality of the followers and not the leader. The first is from Lao-Tzu, 6th century BC, who is reputed to have said:

> A leader is best when people barely know he exists, not so good when people obey and acclaim him, worse when they despise him . . . But of a good leader who talks little when his work is done, his aim fulfilled, they will say, 'We did it ourselves'. (Lao-Tzu)

The second comment is from Jesus, c. 5 BC–c. 30 AD:

> Whoever wants to be a leader among you must be your servant, and whoever wants to be first among you must be the slave of everyone else. For even the Son of Man came not to be served but to serve others and to give his life as a ransom for many. (Mark 10: 42–45)

The responsibility of the leader to their 'followers' is further reflected in the words of former General Peter Cosgrove, Australian of the Year in 2001, who in the 2009 Boyer Lecture said this about leadership:

> Let's start therefore with a universal truth: leaders fundamentally are accountable. Whether it is the dad who by example becomes a leader of other dads at the soccer game when he starts to put out the witches hats and the goal nets on a shivering cold morning, he is a volunteer who has assumed responsibility. Continuing the family analogy, those mums who rally to the tuckshop assuming a leadership-by-example position, they have made themselves accountable (Cosgrove 2009).

Cosgrove went on to say 'Leaders who fail to appreciate this fundamental precept of accountability must also fail to muster the profound commitment true leadership demands' (Cosgrove 2009).

These ideas link to the concept of the servant leader, a term coined by Greenleaf who in an essay entitled *The Servant as Leader* (1970) said that

> the servant-leader *is* servant first . . . It begins with the natural feeling that one wants to serve, to serve *first*. Then conscious choice brings one to aspire to lead. . . . There is care taken by the servant-first leader to make sure that other people's highest priority needs are being served. The best test, and difficult to

administer, is: Do those served grow as persons? Do they, *while being served*, become healthier, wiser, freer, more autonomous, more likely themselves to become servants? (Greenleaf 1973)

For example, in terms of managing organisational risk, the servant leader ensures that employees are empowered to make decisions and share ideas, thus sharing the decision-making burden and adding to organisational knowledge in a way that increases the effectiveness of the organisation.

Leadership styles

Just as an organisation gets the behaviour that it rewards, power and leadership are inter-linked, and certain leadership styles create and support certain behaviours in their followers. In contrast to the servant leader, autocratic and authoritative leaders beget followers who grudgingly do their bidding, while charismatic and expert leaders encourage others to willingly and enthusiastically follow and who often do more than they are asked. Contrasting examples of charismatic leaders are Adolf Hitler, who highlights that effective leadership does not necessarily equate with positive outcomes and Winston Churchill as an example of an effective leader in war, if not in peace. By comparison, Mother Teresa led simply by touching human emotion and encouraging trust, and, importantly, led by example, thus creating a very positive social movement.

In the management of risk, leadership styles have costs or benefits that will impact the organisation, but also different leadership styles may be appropriate at different times. An authoritative leader may be appropriate in a high stress, high risk outdoor environment, such as a mountaineering situation, but the risk of this style is that if that leader is withdrawn from the situation one has to question whether the followers will have the knowledge and skills to continue. By contrast, a charismatic leadership style may inspire action beyond what people think is possible, but there is a real risk that their outward style may be masking a lack of skill that may be exposed in difficult and technical situations.

For most organisations, there is no one correct leadership style. As with the risk management process, the leadership style needs to adapt to reflect the needs of a range of factors, such as the environment, people, program, outcomes, the skills of the leader, program length and the stage of group development. For new groups in unfamiliar environments who are learning new skills, a more authoritative leader may be most effective, while for an intact work group going through a team development program a more facilitative style may be most effective (Table 4.1). In outdoor and experiential learning programs or sporting teams there is a need to balance the roles of the leader, instructor or coach who is facilitating the overall program, with

Table 4.1 Examples of different leadership scenarios

Scenarios: which leadership style/s would be most appropriate for the following:

1 A group is climbing a colour and an avalanche has been triggered above
2 A group of young adults paddling a river in fine weather with a couple of hours of daylight to go is searching for a campsite for the night
3 A professional football team has been playing poorly during the first half of their grand final and the coach wants to encourage them to do their best
4 An organisation is struggling due to a global financial crisis and change has to be made in the client base, shifting from working with underprivileged groups to corporate clients
5 Staff unrest is affecting the team's effectiveness, but the program/activity must continue

the needs of leaders within the group or team who are seeking to grow and develop their leadership skills. It may not always be possible to have a single leader who is able to adjust their style to the situation. What may be more effective is to recruit and develop a leadership team with individuals with a range of skills that are able to be applied in different situations.

In any discussion on leadership it is also worth considering how power may be sourced from different areas and how this impacts upon the behaviours and thus outcomes of those that follow.

Sources of power

Over 50 years ago French and Raven (1959) outlined five sources of power: coercive, reward, legitimate, referent and expert power. These sources of power are derived from either a 'position' occupied by the leader or by something 'personal' to the leader. It is important to be able to identify the source of a leader's power as followers will react in predictable ways to the assertion of that power.

Positional power

1 Legitimate power: this comes from the belief that a person has the right to make demands and expect compliance and obedience from others, and it depends upon the granting of an official position of authority.
2 Reward power: this results from one person's ability to compensate another for compliance. Rewards can be an effective tool when one keeps in mind that one will get the behaviour he or she rewards, when the reward is commensurate with the desired activity and when there

is an obvious connection between the employees' behaviour and the reward.

3 Coercive power: this comes from the belief that a person can punish others for non-compliance. These individuals rely upon physical strength, strong verbal skills and occasionally emotional manipulation and gamesmanship.

Personal power

1 Expert power: this is based on a person's superior skill and knowledge. Often expert power can only be utilised in the range of activities in which the power holder has expertise and cannot be generalised to other situations.

2 Referent power: this is the result of a person's perceived attractiveness, worthiness and right to respect from others. Group members gain a sense of personal satisfaction from identification with the power holder. A charismatic leader may have referent power.

Table 4.2 Potential responses of 'followers' to types of leadership power

Source of leader power	Most likely follower response
Coercive power	Resistance
Reward power	Compliance
Legitimate power	Compliance
Expert power	Commitment
Referent power	Commitment

From the perspective of organisational risk, an organisation must be clear on the type of follower behaviour that is desired and choose leaders accordingly, supported by appropriate organisational cultures, processes and practices. The high levels of commitment shown by followers of leaders exercising expert and referent power may be desirable in most contexts. Leaders relying on reward and legitimate power will get compliant followers, however those followers may not exhibit the desired behaviour when the reward is removed, or, indeed, when the leader is removed from the situation (Table 4.2).

One thing is certain when speaking about leadership, leadership style and the source of the leader's power: that leaders with a certain level of authority must balance that authority with a corresponding level of responsibility and accountability. Leaders with authority over a group of people who do not feel a sense of responsibility for those individuals may abuse their power.

Leaders with responsibility over individuals who are not given authority to make decisions may end up powerless. Along with choosing a leadership team with complementary styles, a balance of responsibility and authority must be encouraged by the structure and the culture of an organisation in order for strong, positive leaders to emerge.

Given the discussion on sources of power above, there is a challenge for a leader who may not have the industry background that others within the organisation may have. This lack of technical competence, the specialised knowledge or expertise that one develops when working within an industry, can be mitigated by interpersonal competence, the ability to work with, understand and motivate others. The ability to see the whole scenario, to analyse and diagnose problems and implement solutions (conceptual competence), is a critical skill for all leaders, particularly those arriving in a new industry or organisation. This in turn raises the questions of how knowledge is managed and transferred within and across groups and organisations and how frontline staff are trained and developed for supervisory and management positions. Regardless of whether a new leader is coming into an organisation from outside or a new leader is being groomed from within the organisation, a well planned, well executed training program will reduce the risk associated with a leader who is lacking the skills or knowledge to do their job well.

Training, development and education

Garavan, looking from within a human resource development or management context (HRD or HRM), considers the question of differences between training, development and education and reaches the conclusion that 'training, development and education are essentially concerned with learning' (Garavan 1997, p. 41). With respect to training and development, Garavan (1997) concurs with Smith who says that:

> training is most commonly associated with the development of job-related skills; education suggests a much broader activity based on the 'holistic' development of individuals; and development implies growth in a non-organisational context as well as in the workplace. (Smith 1998, p. 1)

This places the emphasis of training upon the achievement, in the short term, of specific skills and abilities that are relevant to the current work situation, while development is often focused upon future job needs. Training and development plans should be included as part of ongoing employee management programs, where both leaders and staff are monitored and evaluated to determine the status of current skills and knowledge and encouraged to increase skills and knowledge in areas important for the development of both the employees and the organisation.

Whether you know someone is 'trained' may not be clear. Kirkpatrick (1959, 1996) has suggested four levels of evaluating training, the first is the reaction of the participants to the learning process, the second is the learning gained, the third level is the behaviour change evidenced on the job and the fourth level is the results of the organisation that have been influenced by the training. In most circumstances, the only evaluation that is done within organisations is at level one, with little effort at the higher levels. Evaluation of levels two, three and four are important to the organisation as those levels have an impact on both the individual undergoing training and on the organisation itself. While a training program may be enjoyable for an individual, if there is no learning gained by the individual and commensurate benefit to the organisation, the training program should not be supported by the organisation. Another issue is training that is experienced on-the-job via formal training and informally through time and experience. For Michelson (1996), experience is the input and learning is the outcome. This type of experiential learning is valuable to organisations in that it is specific to the work of the organisation itself.

In comparison to training and development, education is a much broader term and usually relates to more general skills and knowledge rather than specific vocational outcomes, as may be expected in training and development (Garavan 1997). Organisational leaders familiar with the vision and direction of the organisation may wish to develop long term or overarching educational programs for employees who are committed to the organisation for the long haul. Training, development and education can come from within the organisation or outside of it, via universities and colleges, industry associations and accredited training bodies. Regardless of what the process is or who it is offered by, organisations reduce the risk of error, stagnation and complacency by encouraging the continual development of their staff and leaders and by linking formal education and training with field experience and practice.

Conclusion

To be effective, risk management needs to consider both the external and the internal contexts. As such, it will be part of all aspects of an organisation, imbedded into the culture, underpinned by policies and procedures, modelled by effective leaders and supported by relevant training, development and organisational evaluations and reviews. Risk management is not a once-off action, but is part of every aspect of the organisation on every day.

Points for action for practitioners

1 What other organisations (from any industry) do you know of that demonstrate effective risk management as defined in ISO 15031000? Arrange to meet with their key staff to discuss and share ideas.

2 Identify the current champions of risk management in your organisation. How can their efforts be supported by job redesign and/or training and development?

3 Identify a program of internal and external review processes that will support the development of risk management in your organisation.

4 Identify and attend a range of conferences or trainings that will support the development of all staff in your desired risk management culture.

5 Choose an outdoor recreation organisation for which you are able to find a website.
  • If they have a vision and/or mission statement identify it. If they do not, try to write one for them.
  • Based on information from the website, choose a goal for the organisation, then create some objectives that will help the organisation to meet the goal.
  • For one of the objectives, write a plan of action. Discuss how this plan will be implemented.
  • Describe how you will evaluate the success of the plan.

Further questions and activities

1 Search the internet for two similar sport or recreation organisations or events: one domestic, one international:
  • Compare and contrast their vision, mission and objectives.
  • To what extent are they focused on their own operations versus the broader role they may be able to have in the wider community or society?
  • For the activities or programs they offer, what challenges do you think they will face in maintaining sufficiently trained, qualified, experienced and motivated staff?

2 For each of the scenarios in Table 4.1 what differences might there be in the outcomes if the leader were to exercise an authoritative style, a charismatic style, expert style, etc.? How does the leadership style of a leader of an organisation contribute to or mitigate risks to the organisation?

3 Choose two sport or recreation organisations and compare their accreditation and review process. Are they using industry standard accreditations, national or worldwide accreditation (i.e. ISO) or institutional

accreditation? How do organisations use review and accreditation to differentiate themselves from other organisations?

References and further resources

References

Argote, L & Ingram, P 2000. 'Knowledge transfer: a basis for competitive advantage in firms'. *Organizational Behavior and Human Decision Processes*, vol. 82, no. 1, pp. 150–69.

Asimov, I 1977. 'The Eureka phenomenon' in AM Eastman (ed), *The Norton Reader: An Anthology of Expository Prose*, 4th edn. WW Norton and Company, New York, pp. 97–107.

Buchholz, E. (1998). The Call of Solitude. *Psychology Today*, vol. 31, no. 1, pp. 50–82.

Carlsen, J 2000. 'Events industry accreditation in Australia'. *Event Management*, vol. 6, pp. 117–121.

Chisholm, H & Shaw, S 2004. 'Prove it: the "tyranny" of audit and accreditation in the New Zealand outdoors industry'. *Leisure Studies*, vol. 23, no. 4, pp. 317–27.

Cosgrove, P 2009. 'Leading in Australia'. *Boyer Lectures*, Lecture 3. Retrieved 31 March 2010 from <http://www.abc.net.au/rn/boyerlectures/stories/2009/2725184.htm#transcript>.

Crowther, J (ed) 1995. *Oxford Advanced Learner's Dictionary*. Oxford University Press, Oxford.

Csikszentimihalyi, M 1990. *Flow: The Psychology of Optimal Experience*. Harper Perennial, New York.

Dawson, S 1996. *Analysing Organisations*, Macmillan, London, UK.

Fluker, MR & Turner, LW 2000. 'Needs, motivations, and expectations of a commercial whitewater rafting experience. *Journal of Travel Research*, vol. 38, pp. 380–9.

French, JRP & Raven, B 1959. 'The bases of social power' in D Cartwright & A Zander (eds), *Group Dynamics*. Harper & Row, New York, pp. 150–67.

Garavan, TN 1997. 'Training, development, education and learning: different or the same?'. *Journal of European Industrial Training*, vol. 21, no. 2, pp. 39–50.

Gass, MA & Williamson, J 1995. 'Accreditation for adventure programs'. *The Journal of Physical Education, Recreation & Dance*, vol. 66, no. 1, pp. 22–6.

Greenleaf, RK 1973. 'The servant as leader'. Retrieved from <http://www.greenleaf.org/catalog/The_Servant_as_Leader.html>.

Harris, R & Jago, L 2001. 'Professional accreditation in the Australian tourism industry; an uncertain future'. *Tourism Management*, vol. 22, pp. 383–90.

Hofstede, G 1993. 'Cultural constraints in management theories. *Academy of Management Executive*, vol. 7, no. 1, pp. 81–94.

Kirkpatrick, DL 1959. 'Techniques for evaluating training programs'. *Journal of the American Society of Training Directors*, vol. 13, pp. 3–26.

Kirkpatrick, DL 1996. 'Great ideas revisted: techniques for evaluating training programs and revisiting Kirkpatrick's four-level model'. *Training and Development*, January, pp. 54–9.

Kolb, DA 1984. *Experiential Learning: Experience as the Source of Learning and Development*. Prentice-Hall, Englewood Cliffs, NJ.

Linstead, S 1999. 'Managing culture' in L Fulop & S Linstead (eds), *Management: A Critical Text* (pp. 82–121). Macmillan Education, South Yarra, Victoria, pp. 82–121.

Michelson, E 1996. '"Auctoritee" and "experience": feminist epistemology and the assessment of experiential learning'. *Feminist Studies*, vol. 22, no. 3, pp. 627–55.

Nisbett, RE & Wilson, TD 1977. 'Telling more than we can know: verbal reports on mental processes'. *Psychological Review*, vol. 84, no. 3, pp. 231–59.

Sandercock, L 1998. *Towards Cosmopolis*. John Wiley and Sons, Chichester.

Smith, A 1998. *Training and Development in Australia*, 2nd edn. Butterworths, Sydney.

Tribe, J 2005. *The Economics of Recreation, Leisure and Tourism*, 3rd edn. Elsevier, London, UK.

Viljoen, J & Dann, S 2003. *Strategic Management*, 4th edn. Prentice Hall, Frenchs Forest, NSW.

Further resources

A sample of accreditation programs:

Adventure Activities Licensing Authority, UK <http://www.hse.gov.uk/aala/>

Association for Experiential Education Accreditation Program, US <http://www.aee.org/accreditation/>

Australian Campsite and Outdoor Activity Provider Accreditation Program (ACOP) <http://www.auscamps.asn.au/accreditation/accreditation.html>

Australian Registered Training Organisations <http://www.dest.gov.au/>

National Accommodation, Recreation & Tourism Accreditation <http://www.narta.org.au/>

New Zealand Qualifications Authority <http://www.nzqa.govt.nz/index.html>

ORIC Organisational Accreditation <http://www.oric.org.au/AccreditationRegistration/index.htm>

Project Adventure Accreditation Program, US <http://www.pa.org/credentialing/accreditation.php>

The real physical risks: putting it into perspective

Tracey J. Dickson

A ship is safe in harbour, but that's not what ships are for.

William Shedd (1820–1894), theologian and philosopher

FOCUS QUESTIONS

1 What are the real physical risks that people face when participating in outdoor activities?
2 Which activities do you consider most 'unsafe'?
3 What available data sources exist to inform you about the risks to physical safety?
4 What does it mean to be 'safe'? Do you *really* want to be safe or to minimise the physical risks?
5 What are the main mechanisms of injury in outdoor activities?

CASE STUDY

Australia's 'hidden dangers' take deadly toll on tourists or do they?

In 2007 a British newspaper reported that 'Australia is one of the most popular holiday destinations in the world, but its beaches, rainforests and deserts take a deadly toll on tourists. According to official statistics, 2433 overseas visitors, including 25 children, have died in the past seven years with causes of death ranging from drowning to heat stroke and even a jellyfish sting' (McMahon 2007). Yet, what was not reported was that of all reported deaths of visitors to Australia in the periods 1997–2000 and 2003–05, 76 per cent were a result of natural causes (Dickson & Hurrell 2008). Accidents accounted for 20 per cent of deaths, of which half were land transport accidents, i.e. motor vehicle accidents and around four per cent from accidental drownings and submersions. Further investigation of deaths reported to the coroner for the 2003–05 period indicated that the activity when most deaths occurred was while resting or sleeping (22 per cent), followed by general travel (19 per cent), being nursed or cared for in a formal health care setting (11 per cent) and informal sport and active recreation (eight per cent). Of all deaths that occurred while participating in sport and active recreation, swimming accounted for 37 per cent of the deaths, then scuba diving or snorkelling (25 per cent), walking (seven per cent) and hiking (six per cent).

The public does not usually see the *real* data, but they may see an article or TV news item that appears to misinterpret the situation without sufficient investigation of the issues. It is in this latter scenario that most organisations will find they are operating.

Introduction

As discussed previously, risk management is about maximising the positive outcomes and minimising the negatives effects, of which physical risk may be one negative. Yet, there is a balancing act between limiting the risks to one's physical wellbeing, while simultaneously maintaining the physical challenge necessary to achieve the aims and objectives of the activity. An activity such as a hike could be made 'safer' by having increased supervision, staying close to urban areas to improve access to emergency services and for food and water drops to be provided limiting the weights to be carried. However, the individuals or groups may miss the opportunity to develop skills in route planning, food planning and preparation, team building, leadership, problem-solving skills, communication, navigation, environmental appreciation and development in their self-confidence and efficacy, which raises the questions of why people go outdoors and what is that they achieve in doing so? These topics are explored further in Chapter 6 on program design and in Chapter 7 on program evaluation.

This chapter seeks to bring together available data on injuries and deaths in outdoor activities as a basis to discuss the systemic issues related to the completeness of the data. To this end, data is drawn from reports on outdoor activities, sport and recreation, adventure activities and mountaineering. Before proceeding with this discussion, four definitions are clarified:

- risk: in this book we are using the definition of risk as 'the effect of uncertainty on objectives' (International Organization for Standardization 2009)
- safe means 'not damaged, hurt or lost [or] not likely to cause or lead to damage, injury or loss' (Crowther 1995, p. 1035)
- accident is 'a random or chance event, and thus one that cannot be prevented . . . [it is] the primary event in a sequence that leads ultimately to injury if that event is genuinely not predictable' (Pless & Hagel 2005, p. 182)
- injury is the consequence of 'the transfer of one of the forms of physical energy (mechanical, chemical, thermal, etc.) in amounts or at rates that exceed the threshold of human tolerance' (Baker et al cited in Pless & Hagel 2005, p. 182). Injuries may be intentional such as assaults, homicides or suicides, or unintentional.

The physical wellbeing of participants, spectators and staff is a concern for managers, supervisors, teachers, parents and boards. However, it is unclear how people obtain information about what the real physical risks *actually* are in to order to inform their decisions given the lack of consistent and/or co-ordinated data collection for outdoor activities. One influencing factor upon people's perceptions may be media reports, both of the sport or activity itself, or any incidence that may occur. This latter point influences another potential impact on people's perceptions which is that many people may not be familiar with some of the activities and as a result assume a greater level of physical risk than may be the case, such as with abseiling or rock climbing. In the latest Australian report on participation in sport and recreation (Australian Sports Commission 2010) for people aged over 14 years demonstrates how activities that may be part of an outdoor education or recreation program, such as bushwalking, canoeing or rock climbing, often have much lower participation rates than other activities that may be more familiar and/or seen more frequently in the media such as Australian Rules football (AFL), soccer and aerobics (Table 5.1). For example, around 106 000 people over the age of 14 participated in rock climbing compared to nearly 900 000 in soccer/football.

In an essay on preventing childhood sporting injuries, van Mechelen and Verhagen (2005) suggested that any measure that aims to reduce injuries in young people 'should be based on knowledge of the incidence and likely severity of the particular injury, causal factors, and mechanisms that contribute to the risk of sustaining sport-related injuries' (p. 546). They highlight the impact of the social context upon injury prevalence as well as the individual's role in injury prevention when they suggest that many children's sport-related injuries are avoidable 'through changes to the behaviour and attitudes of children and the adults who influence them' (2005, p. 546).

Table 5.1 Exercise and recreation participation data for people aged 15 years and over in select activities (organised and non-organised) 2009

	Males	Females	Total 000	Participation rate
Activities used in outdoor education				
Walking (bush)	52.0%	48.0%	862.9	5.0%
Ice/snow sports	56.5%	43.5%	219.7	1.3%
Canoeing/kayaking	58.5%	41.5%	214	1.2%
Orienteering	49.7%	50.3%	118.7	0.7%
Sailing	75.3%	24.7%	104.2	0.6%
Rock climbing	73.1%	26.9%	105.7	0.6%
Popular sport and recreation activities				
Aerobics/fitness	37.5%	62.5%	3,932.4	22.9%
Soccer/football (outdoor)	74.7%	25.3%	879.8	5.1%
Netball	11.0%	89.0%	686.8	4.0%
Australian Rules football	90.4%	9.6%	486.9	2.8%
Surf sports	83.4%	16.6%	437.9	2.5%
Rugby league	95.2%	4.8%	258.2	1.5%

Source: Australian Sports Commission (2010), Table 14.

For activities conducted in the outdoors, the decreased involvement of today's society with the natural world will impact on a person's ability to move safely through it, as well as their emotional comfort within that environment and thus the individual's knowledge or ability to take a greater role in preventing injuries to themselves (e.g. Louv 2006). In order to ensure that physical safety is managed appropriately to support the ongoing participation in and enjoyment of the outdoors, it is essential to base our decisions upon relevant and valid data on the frequency, severity and causes of injuries.

In investigating injuries, another factor to consider is the changing societal context, both in terms of what is deemed an acceptable risk and also the changes in the legal frameworks. As people are able to communicate more effectively and access more information more quickly through devices such as computers, phones, personal digital assistants (PDAs) etc., there has been a commensurate increase in the expectation of being 'safe' at all times; and if not, then being able to call someone for help. This can be seen in the dependence on mobile phones as a risk management strategy and expectations from some parents that their children are contactable at all times. What is not always understood is that while most mobile phones will cover the majority of the population who live in urban areas, they do not cover the majority of non-urban and remote areas where many adventurous programs may occur. Also, when extreme weather events occur, even satellite phones, global positioning systems (GPSs) and emergency position-indicating radio beacons (EPIRBs) will be limited in their effectiveness or not operational at all. This is considered more in Chapter 6 on risk communication and Chapter 9 on technology in the outdoors.

Research on incidents in outdoor, adventure and sporting activities

To help provide an understanding of the real physical risks, the following is a summary of available data from Australia, New Zealand and North America on injuries and deaths in outdoor and sporting situations. What this review highlights is the lack of consistent and quality data upon which decisions may be based or comparisons made between activities or over time. In some cases there is complete data on the injuries or deaths, but no comparable participation data, or in contrast, there may be a reasonable sample of the injury and death data with estimates made of participation data, but it is not clear what proportion of the total population is represented in the data. The major limitations for most of these reports are: the lack of consistency of what is considered a reportable incident, the absence of participation or exposure data such as hours of participation in the activity in many circumstances and the lack of information about the contributing factors to the incident. These topics will be explored further in Chapter 11 when considering injury surveillance.

Australian data

The following Australian data draws mostly on a range of data sources including hospital admissions data, Australian Bureau of Statistics and the National Coroner's Information System. The reports cover hospitalisations because of injuries and deaths because of injuries. What is considered a reportable incident varies across the reports.

1 Serious injury and death during sport and recreation activities in Victoria 2001–03

Gabbe, Finch, Cameron & Williamson (2005) reported on sport and recreation-related serious injuries to people aged 15 years and over, including deaths, who presented to hospitals in the state of Victoria from July 2001 to June 2003. The research drew on the Victorian State Trauma Registry (VSTR) and the National Coroner's Information System (NCIS). The VSTR 'is a state-wide trauma registry which captures information about all major trauma patients in Victoria. Major trauma, as defined by the VSTR, includes death, admission to an intensive care unit, an injury severity score (ISS) >15, and urgent surgery' (Gabbe et al 2005, p. 573). The NCIS is 'a national centralised data storage and retrieval system for coronial information' (Gabbe et al 2005, p. 573). The injury severity was coded using the abbreviated injury scale (AIS).

A total of 150 serious injuries were reported along with 48 deaths. Motor sports had the highest level of incidents (32 per cent of cases), followed by horse riding (14 per cent), then Australian football and water skiing/power boating (nine per cent each). Snow skiing and rock climbing accounted for only two per cent of all incidents each. Most deaths were the result of drowning (69 per cent of the 48 cases).

When the number of serious injuries and deaths were compared to the available annual participation data, motor sports had the highest injury and death rate per 100 000 participants per year (113.3), followed by water skiing/power boating (31.5), horse riding (29.7), fishing (9.2), rock climbing (6.6), Australian football (5.5), snow skiing (2.2) and swimming (1.8). So while an activity such as fishing may be seen as relatively 'safe', the statistics suggest that the rate of serious injury and death is 1.4 times that of rock climbing, and horse riding has 13.5 times more serious injuries and deaths than snow skiing.

2 Injuries resulting in hospitalisations in Australia, 2002–03 and 2004–05

Two Australian reports on injuries that resulted in an admission to hospital were produced for the financial years of 2002–03 (Flood & Harrison 2006) and 2004–05 (Bradley & Harrison 2008). The reports drew on the National Hospital Morbidity Database which is compiled from data supplied by Australian state and territory health authorities on hospital care in public and private hospitals. The reports were coded by the Australian Modification of the International Classification of Diseases (ICD–10–AM) and included 'records containing codes from either Chapter XIX (injury, poisoning and certain other consequences of external causes) and/or Chapter XX (external causes of morbidity and mortality) of the ICD–10–AM' (Bradley & Harrison 2008, p. 1).

2.1 Hospitalised sports injury, 2002–03 In the financial year 2002–03, 45 452 people with sport and recreation related injuries were admitted to hospitals in Australia, accounting for 0.7 per cent of all hospitalisations, or 6.3 per cent of hospitalisations where there was an external cause (Flood & Harrison 2006). Of the 45 452, children aged 0–14 years accounted for 31 per cent followed by 15–24 year olds (28 per cent). Most hospitalisations were for males (74 per cent) (Table 5.2), even though males and females aged 15 years and

Table 5.2 Summary measures for sports- and recreation-related injury hospitalisations

Key indicators	0–14 yrs	15–24 yrs	25–34 yrs	35–44 yrs	45–54 yrs	55–64 yrs	65 yrs +	Male	Female	All
Sport-related injury cases	14 218 (31%)	12 810 (28%)	8 095 (18%)	4 618 (10%)	2 503 (6%)	1 304 (3%)	1 903 (4%)	33 590 (74%)	11 862 (26%)	45 452
Rate per 100000 population	543.2	469.7	299.2	155.2	86.6	54.6	57.0	344.4	120.0	231.4
Rate per 100000 participants	N/A	526.5	316.9	188.5	115.6	85.0	114.2	373.4	114.6	243.1

Source: Flood and Harrison (2006). Table 3.1 Summary measures for sports and recreation related injury hospitalisations, by age group at admission, Australia, 2002–2003, p. 6.

Table 5.3 Injury rates (hospitalised) per 100 000 participants across selected activities, 2002–03

	Males	Females	All
Wheeled motor sports, such as motor racing, go-karting, motorcycling	1102.9	373.7	942.7
Roller sports, including skateboarding and rollerblading	900.7	425.8	738.6
Australian Rules football	780.5	163.6	734.3
Equestrian activities	836.3	616.3	692.7
Rugby league	734.4	146.3	677.9
Ice and snow sports	423.5	519.4	459.5
Soccer	292.0	95.1	242.0
Basketball	203.0	99.9	161.6
Netball	173.3	147.1	150.2

over had a similar participation level in sport and recreation for that period (Australian Sports Commission 2004).

The combined results for all football codes (i.e. soccer, Australian Rules, Rugby League and Rugby Union) accounted for 28 per cent of hospitalisations. Those activities with the highest number of hospitalisations were:

- Australian Rules football (AFL) (n = 3944)
- soccer (n = 3270)
- water sports (n = 2799)
- cycling (n = 2725)
- rollers sports (n = 2265)
- wheeled motor sports (n = 2093)
- equestrian activities (n = 1816).

Flood and Harrison (2006) combined the hospitalisation data with sport and recreation participation data (Australian Sports Commission 2004) to estimate the injury rate per 100 000 participants aged 15 years and over. Those sport and recreation activities with the highest estimated injury rates for all participants are presented in Table 5.3. As with the research by Gabbe et al (2005) on deaths and serious injury in the state of Victoria, motor sports had the highest injury rate.

For men, the activities with the highest rate of hospitalisation per 100 000 population were Australian Rules football (39.7) and soccer (29.8) while for women it was for equestrian activities (11.7) and netball (10.0). However, when compared to the participation numbers for people 15 years and over, the highest rate of hospitalisation for men per 100 000 participants was wheeled motor sports (1012.9), followed by roller sports (900.7), while for women it was highest for equestrian activities (616.3) followed by ice and snow sports (519.4).

While this information is useful, it cannot be concluded what the most 'dangerous' activities are, given that the duration and intensity of participation is not known. As an example, an AFL player may have played for two hours on a flat, mown sports ground when he was injured, but a snowboarder may have participated for six hours or more on ungroomed steep terrain riding between the trees when she was injured.

2.2 Hospital separations due to injury and poisoning, 2004–05 A 'hospital separation' is the number of in-patients who leave hospital through discharge or death, and thus does not include those who are still in-patients or those who go to an emergency department but are not admitted as an in-patient. Of 356 000 community injuries that resulted in hospitalisation separations during 2004–05, most were deemed unintentional (86 per cent) with the remainder being from assaults and self-harm (Bradley & Harrison 2008). The main mechanism of injury was an unintentional fall (36 per cent). Women accounted for 55 per cent of all hospitalisation separations. Transport-related incidents, such as motor vehicle accidents, accounted for 14 per cent of all cases, with men most prevalent (68 per cent) in these.

Injuries that were incurred during sport accounted for only 10 per cent of cases. The total for all codes of football (Australian Rules, soccer, rugby league and rugby union) represented four per cent of all injuries, or 37 per cent of sports-related cases. Men represented 78 per cent of sport-related injury cases, with those aged 15–9 years having the highest injury rate per 100 000 population (849.9). The mean length of stay was 2.2 days (Table 5.4).

Table 5.4 Key indicators for sports-related hospitalisations 2004–05

Key indicators	Male	Female	All persons
Estimated number of sport-related injury case	28 977 (78%)	8275 (22%)	37 253
Cases per 100 000 population	288.3	81.4	184.3
Total patient-days due to sport-related injury	62 620	18 221	80 842
Mean patient-days per case	2.2	2.2	2.2

Source: Bradley & Harrison (2008). Table 6.1 Key indicators for hospitalised sport-related injury: males, females and persons, Australia 2004–05, p. 125.

The most common activity at the time of injury was team ball sports (44 per cent of sport-related cases), which included football codes, netball and basketball (Table 5.5). Injuries in all football codes were the main activity

Table 5.5 Frequency of injuries across selected sport and recreational activities 2004–05

	Males	Females	All
Football – all codes	12 690 (44%)	924 (11%)	13 614 (37%)
Cycling	2367 (8%)	526 (6%)	2893 (8%)
Wheeled motor sports	2578 (9%)	168 (2%)	2746 (7%)
Individual water sports	1839 (6%)	503 (6%)	2342 (6%)
Equestrian activities	564 (2%)	1132 (14%)	1696 (5%)
Basketball	989 (3%)	356 (4%)	1345 (4%)
Skateboarding	1,157 (4%)	83 (1%)	1,240 (3%)
Ice/snow sports	709 (2%)	477 (6%)	1186 (3%)
Netball	119 (<1%)	970 (12%)	1089 (3%)
Scooter riding	129 (<1%)	77 (<1%)	206 (<1%)
Adventure sports	113 (<1%)	71 (<1%)	184 (<1%)
Volleyball	104 (<1%)	42 (<1%)	146 (<1%)

Source: Bradley & Harrison (2008).

resulting in hospitalisations for men (44 per cent), while equestrian activities (14 per cent) and netball (11 per cent) were the leading activities for women. Adventure sports such as abseiling, bungy jumping and white water rafting had less hospitalisations (n = 184) than scooter riding (n = 206) and slightly more than volleyball (n =146). As noted previously, these figures need to be compared to participation data in order to allow a more meaningful comparison across activities.

Understanding what anatomical parts may be injured helps in developing strategies to prevent injuries and ensuring there are sufficient resources on hand to manage an injury to that body part as well as to develop plans should someone be injured. On this latter point, injuries to the lower extremities such as feet, ankles and knees may impact on someone's mobility and ability to self-evacuate from a remote area, while injuries to the upper body may mean that same person would still be able to walk out with some assistance with their equipment. Knowing the anatomical location and injury severity may also help determine the potential longer-term burden of injury. For example, a traumatic brain injury (TBI) or multiple TBIs, may have greater long term consequences than a wrist or leg fracture (Greenwald, Gwin, Chua, & Crisco 2008). In 2004–05 knees and lower legs had the highest rate of injury (25 per cent), followed by the elbows and forearms (19 per cent) and the head (17 per cent).

An indicator of the injury severity is the length of stay in a hospital. The activities with the longest average length of stay were aero sports (6.5 days per case) and adventure sports (6.0 days). The shortest stays were for team water sports (1.1), with team ball sports, including football codes, having an average length of stay of 1.7 days.

In seeking to understand the risks to physical wellbeing, it is also important to delve further to understand the contributing factors to injury. The most common cause of sport-related community injuries was 'other unintentional' external causes, such as a collision with another person or an inanimate object, such as in a tackle, (45 per cent), followed by falls (33 per cent), transport-related external causes (21 per cent) and drowning/submersion (<1 per cent). Of these, falls can provide an example of how further questions may help investigate the cause of the fall and thus inform future injury prevention strategies. Further questions include:

- Is there a pre-existing condition that affects the individual's strength and/or balance?
- What is their previous experience in the current environment? For example, if they are walking on uneven rocky ground, have they ever experienced that environment before?
- Is the equipment contributing to the individual's diminished balance, such as a pack changing the centre of gravity or shoes being too big causing a trip hazard?
- What other factors may be contributing to someone falling, such as lack of concentration, fatigue and dehydration?

3 Community injury-related deaths, Australia, 2003–04

In the period, 2003–04 9924 deaths occurred as a result of injury in Australia reported to the Australian Bureau of Statistics (ABS) mortality unit record (Henley, Kreisfled, & Harrison 2007). The data included those reports that had one or more of the ICD Chapter XIX diagnosis codes S00–S99, T00–T75, or T79 anywhere in the record. These so-called community injuries exclude complications from surgical and medical care which may be included in earlier reports. Community injuries include both intentional and unintentional injuries where self-harm (suicide) and assault (homicide) are categorised as intentional injury. These injuries may have occurred in the home, at work, in sport and recreation activities and/or in transport-related incidents.

Of all deaths as a result of a community injury, the most common causes of death were falls (30 per cent), suicide (22 per cent), transport accidents (17 per cent), poisoning (10 per cent), drowning (three per cent) and homicide (two per cent). There was no information to identify that deaths may have occurred during a sport or recreational activity.

4 Injury-related deaths among young Australians, 2005

A report from the Australian Institute of Health and Welfare (AIHW) on injuries among young Australians aged 12–24 years (Eldridge 2008) drew upon information contained in the AIHW National Hospital Morbidity Database, the AIHW National Mortality Database, the ABS 2004–05 National Health Survey (NHS) and National Aboriginal and Torres Strait Islander Health Survey (NATSIHS).

During 2005, 1401 deaths were recorded, with 954 being the result of an injury (68 per cent), or 26 deaths per 100 000 young people. The age group with the highest proportion of death by injury was the 18–24 years (71 per cent of all deaths), followed by 15–17 years (66 per cent) and 12–14 years (38 per cent).

The main causes of death by external causes were:
- transport accidents (44 per cent of injury-related deaths)
- suicide (31 per cent)
- accidental poisoning (six per cent)
- assault (three per cent).

5 Deaths of young people (under 25 years) while engaged in sporting/leisure activities in Australia: 1 July 2000–31 December 2008

In a report generated for this book, the Victorian Institute of Forensic Medicine searched the National Coroners Information System (NCIS). The NCIS is an electronic database of coronial information that contains case information from the coronial files of all Australian states and territories, except Queensland, dating back to 1 July 2000. Queensland data is contained from 1 January 2001. A limitation of this dataset is that it only includes those cases referred to the coroner for investigation. Additionally, it only includes cases where investigation has been completed by the coroner, for example, in October 2009, approximately 16 per cent of all deaths reported to a coroner between 1 July 2000 and 31 December 2008 were open on the database (National Coroners Information Service 2009). For further discussion about what is referred to the coroner, please refer to Chapter 11.

As of the report date of October 2009 there were 388 closed cases where an individual aged under 25 years died while undertaking a sport or leisure activity in Australia during the period 1 July 2000 to 31 December 2008, an average of 45.6 deaths per year. The top five activities at the time of the incident were swimming (recreational) (n = 114), motorcycling (n = 54), fishing (n = 23), cycling (road) (n = 21) and Australian Rules football (n = 11). Together the top 10 activities account for 67.3 per cent of all deaths referred to the coroner, while the top 24 accounted for 329 or 84.8 per cent of all deaths. Of importance to note, though, is the cause of death, whether it was as a result of natural or external causes. While Australian Rules football

Table 5.6 Top 24 leisure/sporting activities at time of death of young people < 25 years of age: 1 July 2000 – 31 December 2008

	Death due to natural causes	Death due to external causes	Body not recovered	Unlikely to be known	Total (% of all 388 deaths)
1 Swimming – recreational	5	108	1		114 (29.4%)
2 Motorcycling		54			54 (13.9%)
3 Fishing		23			23 (5.9%)
4 Cycling – road	2	19			21 (5.4%)
5 Australian Rules football	9	2			11 (2.8%)
6 Basketball	5	1		2	8 (2.1%)
7 Surfing/boogie boarding		8			8 (2.1%)
8 Hiking	1	7			8 (2.1%)
9 Jogging/running	1	3		3	7 (1.8%)
10 Trail or general horseback riding		7			7 (1.8%)
11 Water sport, individual (unspecified)	1	5			6 (1.5%)
12 Riding all terrain vehicle	0	6			6 (1.5%)
13 Boating sport (unspecified)	0	6			6 (1.5%)
14 Firearm shooting	1	5			6 (1.5%)
15 Go-carting, motor sport, skateboarding, parachuting/sky diving		5 each			20 (1.3% each)
16 Soccer – outdoor	2	2			4 (1.0%)
17 Jet skiing	0	4			4 (1.0%)
18 Cricket	3	1			4 (1.0%)
19 Snorkelling, water skiing, cliff diving		4 each			12 (1.0% each)
Total (% of all 388 deaths)	30 (7.7%)	293 (75.5%)	1 (0.3%)	5 (1.3%)	329 (84.8%)

had the fifth highest number of deaths over the reporting period, 82 per cent of them were the result of natural causes which may include heart attacks or strokes (Table 5.6).

Further limitations of this data from the perspective of someone who may conduct organised outdoor activities such as hikes, sporting competitions or sea kayak trips include the following: there is no information on what, if any, supervision may have been present, the skills and qualifications of any supervisors and the ratio of supervisors to participants. Further, there is no available information about the skills of the person who died and, finally, there is no information on whether the people who died were wearing relevant personal protective equipment (PPE), such as personal floatation devices (PFDs) in canoeing and kayaking or helmets in equestrian activities.

There are other reports on injuries and deaths in Australian outdoor 'education' (e.g. Brookes 2003a, 2003b; Brookes 2004; Dickson, Chapman & Hurrell 2000). They present some descriptive information, but they draw upon limited and possibly biased samples. The lack of consistency of reporting of incidents (i.e. what is considered a reportable incident?), media focusing upon what may be the sensational rather than the whole picture, whether the sample used is representative of the whole 'population', and the absence of participation data negates any potential to produce death rates. As indicated previously, these issues will be explored further in Chapter 11.

New Zealand data

1 New Zealand National Incident Database Report, 2005

The New Zealand National Incident Database is a voluntary online database designed to collect data on outdoor incidents aimed to provide timely and comparable data on incidents in the outdoors. The one published report (Boyes, Leberman, & McKay, 2005) provides summary charts of 44 non-snow sport incidents (the snow sport incidents are reported separately) of which 62 per cent of injuries were to men. The main activity was tramping, or hiking (27 per cent) followed by ropes courses and initiatives (14 per cent) with 60 per cent of incidents occurring in unsupervised sessions.

2 Accidents and incidents in the adventure and outdoor commercial sectors 1 July 2004 – 30 June 2008

In a report generated as part of the review of the risk management and safety in the adventure and outdoor commercial sectors in New Zealand it is a requirement of the Health and Safety Employment (HSE) Act (1992) that any incident that results in serious harm to any person, employee or visitor to that workplace should be reported (Part 4, Sec 25) (Department of Labour 2010). Schedule 1 of the Act defines serious harm as:

1 Any of the following conditions that amounts to or results in permanent loss of bodily function, or temporary severe loss of bodily function: respiratory disease, noise-induced hearing loss, neurological disease, cancer, dermatalogical disease, communicable disease, musculoskeletal disease, illness caused by exposure to infected material, decompression sickness, poisoning, vision impairment, chemical or hot-metal burn of eye, penetrating wound of eye, bone fracture, laceration, crushing.

2 Amputation of body part.

3 Burns requiring referral to a specialist medical practitioner or specialist outpatient clinic.

4 Loss of consciousness from lack of oxygen.

5 Loss of consciousness or acute illness requiring treatment by a medical practitioner from absorption, inhalation or ingestion of any substance.

6 Any harm that causes the person harmed to be hospitalised for a period of 48 hours or more commencing within seven days of the harm's occurrence (Parliament of New Zealand 1992).

In the five years to 30 June 2009, there were 19 fatalities reported to the Department of Labour (seven canyoning deaths in one accident, four deaths in guided climbing, two each in guided diving and guided heli-skiing), six marine deaths reported to Maritime New Zealand (MNZ) (three in rafting and three in white water boarding) and four deaths reported to the Civil Aviation Authority (CAA) (two each in single accidents in tandem hand gliding/paragliding and commercial microlight flights).

Of the 448 serious harm injuries reported 144 were in guided activities: horse trekking (n = 36), all terrain vehicles (n = 28) and sky diving (n = 18) (32.1 per cent). There were 241 using infrastructural attractions, such as in ski fields (n = 135), luge (n = 32) and go-karts (n = 18), (53.8 per cent). A further seven were in events (1.6 per cent) and 56 in education programs (12.5 per cent) (Table 5.7). The ski field incidents can include members of the public in unsupervised activities.

There were 51 reports of serious harm to MNZ, of which 38 related to rafting, 10 in jet boating and three in kayaking or canoeing. The CAA received 42 reports of serious injury, of which 32 related to tandem hang gliding or paragliding and 10 in tandem parachuting.

To be able to calculate injury rates, the Department of Labour (DOL) noted that it is 'dependent on complete reporting on injuries, the accuracy of injury reports, and precise participation figures' (Department of Labour 2010, p. 28). With these limitations, the DOL were only confident in reporting on limited activities (Table 5.8). The injury rates are per 10 000 participants, not the level of exposure, such as participation hours.

North American data

1 Adventure programs in the US, 1989–90

An early American report on incidents in adventure programs (Liddle & Storck 1995) provides insights into incidents voluntarily reported to the National Safety Network during 1989 and 1990. During that period 832 injuries were reported by 55 programs of which 13 were reported for both

Table 5.7 Serious harm accidents in NZ education settings 1 July 2004 – 30 June 2009

	Frequency	%
Adventure course	36	64.3
Canyoning	1	1.8
Climbing wall	4	7.1
Go-kart	2	3.6
Horse trek	5	8.9
Jet boat	1	1.8
Kayaking	1	1.8
Motorbike	1	1.8
Mountain bike	1	1.8
Rock climbing	1	1.8
Ski field	2	3.6
Tramping/hiking	1	1.8

Source (data): Department of Labour (2010). Stock-take of risk management and safety provisions in the adventure and outdoor commercial sectors in New Zealand. Available from <www.dol.govt.nz/consultation/adventure-tourism/nz-stocktake/index.asp>.

Table 5.8 Rate of NZ adventure and outdoor injuries resulting in serious harm and fatalities by activity 2004–09

	Serious harm per 10 000 passengers or participants	Fatalities per 10 000 passengers or participants
Rafting	0.76	0.06
Jet boating	0.054	0.005
White water boarding	0	0.25
Tandem parachuting	0.5	
Tandem hang gliding and paragliding	1 in 1524	
Hot air balloons	0	0
Microlight passenger flights	0	1 in 250
Para sailing	0	0

years. Of these incidents, 433 were considered serious. The criteria for being included as 'serious' were that:

- the person was removed from the program or activity for at least half a day, or
- treatment was required from a physician beyond a routine examination, or
- long-term treatment or consequences were expected as a result of the injury.

The main known mechanism of injury was a fall (35 per cent), followed by overuse (5 per cent). After combining data from 1988–90, the highest injury rates were reported in sport and recreation games (485.7 per 1 million hours of participation), followed by downhill skiing (273.3), climbing (rock, ice and walls, 97.3), ski touring (76.1) and initiatives (62.9). Looking at injury rates is only the first step, additional investigation needs to be conducted to understand how best to manage risks to physical wellbeing. For example, rock climbing, which may have a high level of perceived risk, also reported higher injury rates than other activities in this study. Yet of the 20 serious injuries that were reported, 11 were on artificial climbing walls, not on natural surfaces. This may be a result of a range of factors, including having a lower perception of risk, insufficient supervision ratios, poorly maintained equipment or even inadequate skills of supervisors.

2 Challenge ropes courses US, 1991

Project Adventure Inc (PA), a leading challenge ropes course designer and trainer in the US conducted surveys of challenge ropes course operators in 1981, 1986 and 1991 (Furlong, Jillings, LaRhette & Ryan 1995). In 1991 a total of 1484 questionnaires were sent out to operators, predominantly in the US, with a return rate of 41 per cent. In these studies 'lost time injuries' was used to indicate a serious incident, which was defined as being where one day or more was lost from work or school the day following the incident. 'Lost time injuries' used here appear to have a higher level of severity than 'serious injuries' used by Liddle and Storck (1995).

The average injury rate per million participant hours over the three studies was 4.33, ranging from 3.67 to 6.22 (Table 5.9). To put these figures into perspective the report drew upon a US Department of Labor survey of job-related injuries which indicated that many other activities had substantially higher injury rates per million hours, for example, backpacking (192 injuries per million hours of participation), downhill skiing (724), basketball (2650) and soccer (4500). The challenge ropes course injury rates compared favourably with other industries such as finance (4.5 injuries per million hours) and educational services (eight).

The challenge course activity with the highest frequency of serious incidents in 1991 was games and initiatives (20), followed by the wall and zip

Table 5.9 Challenge ropes course incidents (1981, 1986, 1991)

Year of study	Surveys sent	Responses (%)	Lost time injuries	Hours on task (million)	Injury rate (per million hours)
1981	246	116 (47%)	78	15.19	5.13
1986	725	392 (54%)	157	42.75	3.67
1991	1484	604 (41%)	93	14.94	6.22
Combined	2209	996 (45%)	250	57.69	4.33

Source: Furlong, Jillings, La Rhette, Ryan (1995).

wire (nine each) and nitro crossing (seven). This does not take into account the number of hours of participation in each of these activities.

3 Adventure programs in the US, 1998–2007

A more recent report from the Wilderness Risk Management Committee and the Association for Experiential Education (Leemon 2008) presents results on incidents that required more than simple first aid. These were voluntarily reported to the incident project. The primary focus was on back-country incidents but did include some front-country incidents, such as at a facility like a summer camp or base camp.

For the reporting period, there were 684 incidents reported by 43 organisations. Of these 70.2 per cent were for more minor injuries such as athletic injuries (sprains, strains, tendinitis) and soft tissue injuries (e.g. blisters, bruises, burns and wounds). Program days were based on the main activity of the day. Thus, it would appear that it would be possible to miscode a program day (i.e. the participation data) to the major activity for the day (e.g. hiking), when the injury may have occurred within a minor activity on that day (e.g. swimming).

For front-country incidents, the injury rates (i.e. injuries per 1000 program days) was 0.31, or 263 incidents over 839 628 program days. The highest injury rate was for snowboarding (16.77), with 30 incidents over 1789 program days. The highest injury rates for activities with more than 2000 program days were for sport and recreational games (1.27), horseback riding (0.87), telemark skiing (0.84), during transportation (0.12) and ropes course elements (high and low) (0.11).

For back-country incidents, the injury rate was 0.52, or 416 incidents over 801 659 program days. While winter camping had the highest injury rate (3.88), this was for five injuries over 1289 program days. The highest injury rates for activities with more than 2000 program days were for mountain biking (2.92), 'other activities' (1.98), flat water canoeing (1.68), swim or dip (1.50), ski touring (1.08), river kayaking (0.92), day hiking or orienteering (0.84) and backpacking (0.77). The most common contributing factor to the incident was a fall or trip (24 per cent), followed by a previous history of a similar injury (nine per cent).

One problem with any voluntary reporting programs, such as with these three North American reports, is that the results may be biased towards organisations that are very interested in injury prevention. Those with less interest, less ability, less time and/or maybe higher or lower injury rates, may choose not to provide data for these projects, thus reported injury rates may be lower than is the case in reality.

4 Paediatric and adolescent sport injuries in wilderness programs

Heggie (2010) reviewed research of sport injuries and deaths in back-country wilderness contexts in Washington state and US National Parks and other expeditions, including results on paediatric and adolescent (12 months – 20 years) wilderness recreation deaths across five counties in Washington state over a 10 year period from 1987–96 (Newman, Diekema, Shubkin, Klein & Quan 1998). This study identified 40 deaths, of which hiking (33 per cent), swimming (20 per cent), and river rafting (10 per cent) were the most common activities. Death was most often by drowning (55 per cent) or closed head injury (26 per cent). The second study Heggie reported on related to recreational injuries sustained by visitors to Mount Rainier National Park and Olympic National Park in Washington State for the period 1997–2001 (Stephens, Diekema & Klein 2005). In the five-year period, there were 535 injuries and 19 deaths. The most common activities at the time of injury were hiking (55 per cent), winter sports (15 per cent), and mountaineering (12 per cent), with the most common type of injuries being sprains, strains and soft tissue injuries (28 per cent), fractures or dislocations (26 per cent), and lacerations (15 per cent). A third study cited related to injuries on National Outdoor Leadership School (NOLS) programs from 1999–2002 (Leemon & Schimelpfenig 2003). There were 1940 incidents involving 1679 students and 233 staff with athletic injuries, e.g. sprains and strains of knees (35 per cent), ankles (30 per cent), and backs (13 per cent) accounted for 50 per cent of all injuries, and soft-tissue injuries for 30 per cent. Falls and slips around camp or while hiking were the leading contributing factors. As a conclusion to this review, Heggie recommended that future research should 'address the challenges of establishing numerator data linked to suitable denominator data, and developing cohort studies that monitor both the injured and non-injured children and adolescents' (Heggie 2010, p. 54). Clarifying numerator data would include having a consistent mechanism for determining what is a reportable incident, while clarification of denominator data requires consistency of whether it is participant numbers or participant 'hours'.

Overview of the available research

The results presented here suggest that participating in outdoor activities is no less 'safe' than many other sport or recreation activities, and at times may be substantially 'safer'. However what these results do suggest is that there is a paucity of consistent and reliable data from which the real physical risk can be assessed across the various dimensions of the outdoor industry such as activity, program type, supervision levels, location and country. While there are snapshots of information, the fact that there is inconsistency in data collection methods, definitions of what may be deemed a reportable or serious injury (e.g. community injury, hospital separations, lost time, serious injury, serious harm), as well as the lack of consistent participation or exposure data (e.g. participant numbers, participant hours, program days) makes comparison next to impossible. What can be concluded from the data presented here is that:

1 For Australia:
- football codes in Australia have the highest number of injuries that result in hospitalisation of all specific sport and recreational activities, with AFL having most injuries
- wheeled motor sports have the highest injury rates per participant numbers
- falls are the major cause of all injury-related deaths
- transport accidents are the major external cause of injury related deaths
- swimming was the main activity for deaths of young people referred to a coroner

2 For New Zealand:
- tramping/hiking accounted for most non-snow sport related injuries
- most injuries occur in non-supervised activities

3 For the US:
- challenge ropes courses have a similar injury rate as the finance injury
- most back-country incidents are of a minor nature
- most supervised adventure, sport and recreational activities have relatively low levels of injuries when compared to other activities.

As noted earlier, another aspect that is omitted from the data presented here is a focus on the contributing factors. For example, Leemon's report (2008) indicates that the major contributing factor for back-country incidents was a fall or a trip. What is not considered is what may have contributed to the fall or trip such as fatigue, hydration, lack of fitness or lack of concentration. Other contributing 'environmental' factors include a tight program design where people feel as if they need to rush to be on time and not take a break, or a group culture that does not support one another physically or emotionally, or the impact of uneven, slippery or steep terrain that is unfamiliar to the participants. This focus on the person ignores the potential impact of the wider 'system' on people's behaviours and choices, including environmental factors (e.g. Reason 2000, 2008). The theme of contributing factors will be explored further in Chapter 11.

Conclusion

A significant part of risk management for organisations or activities in the outdoors is often focused on physical safety. In part, this may be due to the lack of familiarity the wider public has with many of the activities. However, when compared with other sporting and recreation activities, outdoor pursuits have much lower injury reports than other more popular sport and recreational activities. Without additional data it is not clear whether this is a result of the industry's focus on risk management, the importance of supervision levels, skills of supervisors or that each activity is inherently less risky than most sporting activities.

Consistent across most of the data presented here is the lack of consistent, quality injury and mortality data collected over a prolonged period with supporting participation data (i.e. 'exposure') upon which claims may be made about injury incidence severity and the impacts of any interventions. In summary, there is:

- inconsistent or no definition of what might be a reportable injury, i.e. the numerator (what is a 'case')
- inconsistent definitions of participation or exposure, i.e. the denominator
- a mix of voluntary and mandatory reporting which may lead to under or overrepresentation of injuries
- a lack of data on injuries that did not result in hospitalisation which may provide indicators of potential problems.

Most of these issues will be explored further in Chapter 11 on injury surveillance. But as has been stated previously, risk management it is not just about injuries and deaths, but it still remains important to maintain a balanced focus on physical safety, without excluding other factors that lead to uncertainty for an organisation or activity. Taking a broader perspective and exploring the role of the 'system' on an individuals' actions is an important aspect of the overall risk management process.

Points for action for practitioners

- Identify what data has been used to inform your current risk management strategies in relation to physical safety.
- Assess the 'safety culture' in your organisation/situation, how does it support accurate and honest reporting of near misses, accidents and potential safety issues?

- Gather data on incidents and near misses and compare them to activity participation hours.
- Identify the contributing factors to the injuries including previous medical histories, program design, fatigue, dehydration and fitness.
- Use accurate data to inform operating procedures and to develop staff training.
- Use risk communication strategies to clearly convey the real level of risks to clients and the other stakeholders.

Further questions and activities

1 Where you have access to injury data from an organisation or activity:
- What are the activities that have the highest level of risk to physical wellbeing?
- How do injury rates vary with changes in activity type, participation duration and intensity?
- What demographic groups are most at risk, such as age, gender, group type (school, corporate, sporting)?
- What changes have been made to policies, procedures, location choice or staff training as a result of the data?
2 Collect all newspaper articles or online reports on outdoor and sports-related injuries for your state or region, for two 14-day periods, one in winter, one in summer:
- Which activities are most prominent? Consider categories such as team sports vs individual activities, organised vs non-organised activities, 'grass roots' vs elite activity, 'male' sports vs 'female' sports, amateur vs professional.
- Which demographic groups are most at risk (e.g. gender, age, socio-economic status?
- Discuss if and how the media reports on incidents differ depending upon the familiarity of the activity (e.g. an abseiling or a climbing incident vs a football, netball or basketball incident, or whether it is a male or female- dominated sport).
- How would you seek to limit the potential for physical harm in the two activities you identified with most injuries or deaths while still maintaining the fun and adventure of that activity?

References and further resources

References

Australian Sports Commission 2004. 'Participation in exercise, recreation and sport'. Annual Report 2003. Available from <http://www.ausport.gov.au/fulltext/2004/scors/erass2003.asp>

Australian Sports Commission 2010. 'Participation in exercise, recreation and sport'. Annual Report 2009. Retrieved 7 January 2010 from <http://www.ausport. gov.au/information/scors/ERASS/exercise,_recreation_and_sport_survey_past_ reports/erass_2009>.

Boyes, M, Leberman, S & McKay, S 2005. '2005 National Incident Database Report' (non snow sports data). Available from <http://www.outdoorsnz.org.nz/cms_ show_download.php?id=25&st=1>.

Bradley, C & Harrison, J 2008. 'Hospital separations due to injury and poisoning, Australia 2004–05'. Australian Institute of Health and Welfare, cat. no. INJCAT 117. Available from <http://www.nisu.flinders.edu.au/pubs/reports/2008/injcat117. php>.

Brookes, A 2003a. 'Outdoor education fatalities in Australia 1960–2002. Part 1: summary of incidents and introduction to fatality analysis'. *Australian Journal of Outdoor Education*, vol. 7, no. 1, pp. 16–20.

Brookes, A 2003b. 'Outdoor education fatalities in Australia 1960–2002. Part 2: Contributing circumstances: supervision, first aid, and rescue'. *Australian Journal of Outdoor Education*, vol. 7, no. 2, NA.

Brookes, A 2004. 'Outdoor education fatalities in Australia 1960–2002. Part 3: Environmental circumstances'. *Australian Journal of Outdoor Education*, vol. 8, no. 1, pp. 44–56.

Crowther, J (ed) 1995. *Oxford Advanced Learner's Dictionary*. Oxford University Press, Oxford.

Department of Labour 2010. 'Stock-take of risk management and safety provisions in the adventure and outdoor commercial sectors in New Zealand'. Available from <http://www.dol.govt.nz/consultation/adventure-tourism/nz-stocktake/ index.asp>.

Dickson, TJ, Chapman, J & Hurrell, M 2000. 'Risk in outdoor activities: the perception, the appeal, the reality'. *Australian Journal of Outdoor Education*, vol. 4, no. 2, pp. 10–7.

Dickson, TJ & Hurrell, M 2008. 'International visitors to Australia: safety snapshot 2003–05' in C Cooper, TD, Lacey & L Jago (eds). Technical Report. Available from <http://www.crctourism.com.au/>.

Eldridge, D 2008. 'Injury among young Australians'. AIHW bulletin series no. 60 Cat. no. AUS 102. Available from <www.aihw.gov.au>.

Flood, L & Harrison, J 2006. 'Hospitalised sports injury, Australia 2003–03'. AIHW cat. no. INJCAT 79. Available from <http://www.nisu.flinders.edu.au/pubs/ reports/2006/injcat79.php>.

Furlong, L, Jillings, A, LaRhette, M & Ryan, R 1995. '20-year safety study'. Available from <http://projectadventureinc.blogspot.com/2008/09/project-adventures-20-year-safety-study.html>.

Gabbe, BJ, Finch, CF, Cameron, PA & Williamson, OD 2005. 'Incidence of serious injury and death during sport and recreation activities in Victoria, Australia'. *British Journal of Sports Medicine*, vol. 39, no. 8, pp. 573–7.

Greenwald, RM, Gwin, JT, Chua, JJ & Crisco, JJ 2008. 'Head impact severity measures for evaluating mild traumatic brain injury risk exposure'. *Neurosurgery*, vol. 62, no. 4, pp. 789–98.

Heggie, TW 2010. 'Paediatric and adolescent sport injury in the wilderness'. *British Journal of Sports Medicine*, vol. 44, no. 1, pp. 50–5.

Henley, G, Kreisfled, R & Harrison, JE 2007. 'Injury deaths, Australia 2003–04'. AIHW cat. no. INJCAT 89. Available from <http://www.nisu.flinders.edu.au/pubs/reports/2007/injcat89.pdf>.

International Organization for Standardization 2009. 'ISO 31000: Risk management – Principles and guidelines' (under development). Available from <http://www.iso.org/iso/catalogue_detail.htm?csnumber=43170>.

Leemon, D 2008. 'Adventure program risk management report: incident data from 1998–2007'. Paper presented at the 15th Annual Wilderness Risk Management Conference.

Leemon, D & Schimelpfenig, T 2003. 'Wilderness injury, illness, and evacuation: National Outdoor Leadership School's Incident Profiles, 1999–2002'. *Wilderness & Environmental Medicine*, vol. 14, no. 3, pp. 174–82.

Liddle, J & Storck, S (eds) 1995. *Adventure Program Risk Management Report: 1995 Edition. Narratives and Data from 1989–1990*. Association for Experiential Education, Boulder, CO.

Louv, R 2006. *Last Child in the Woods*. Algonquin Books of Chapel Hill, Chapel Hill, NC.

McMahon, B 2007. 'Australia's fatal charms claim thousands of tourists'. *The Guardian*, 6 February 2007. Retrieved 28 July 2007 from <www.guardian.co.uk>.

National Coroners Information Service (2009). 'Unpublished report: deaths of young people (under 25 years) whilst engaging in sporting/leisure activities in Australia: 01/07/2000–31/12/2008'. Melbourne, Vic: Victorian Institute of Forensic Medicine, Melbourne.

Newman, LM, Diekema, DS, Shubkin, CD, Klein, EJ & Quan, L 1998. 'Pediatric wilderness recreational deaths in western Washington State'. *Annals of Emergency Medicine*, vol. 32, no. 6, pp. 687–92.

Parliament of New Zealand 1992. *Health and Safety in Employment Act*. Retrieved from <http://www.legislation.govt.nz/act/public/1992/0096/latest/DLM278829.html>.

Pless, IB & Hagel, BE 2005. 'Injury prevention: a glossary of terms'. *Journal of Epidemiology and Community Health*, vol. 59, no. 3, pp. 182–5.

Reason, J 2000. 'Human error: models and management'. *BMJ*, vol. 320, 768–70.

Reason, J 2008. *The Human Contribution*. Ashgate Publishing, Aldershot, UK.

Stephens, BD, Diekema, DS & Klein, EJ 2005. 'Recreational injuries in Washington State National Parks'. *Wilderness and Environmental Medicine*, vol. 16, no. 4, 192–7.

van Mechelen, W & Verhagen, E 2005. 'Injury prevention in young people – time to accept responsibility'. *Lancet*, vol. 366, S46.

Williamson, J 2007. *Accidents in North American Mountaineering* (vol. 60). American Alpine Club, Golden, Co.

Further resources

Abbreviated Injury Scale (AIS) <http://www.aaam1.org/ais/>.

Accidents in North American Mountaineering <http://www.americanalpineclub.org/pt/accidentsinnorthamericanmountaineering>.

Dickson, TJ & Hurrell, M 2008. *International Visitors to Australia: Safety Snapshot 2003–05*. Cooperative Research Centre for Sustainable Tourism, Gold Coast.

Home and Leisure Accident Surveillance System, UK (HASS and LASS), includes annual reports from 1999 <http://www.hassandlass.org.uk/query/index.htm>.

International Classification of Diseases (ICD) <http://www.who.int/classifications/icd/en/>.

Roberts, WO 2004. *Bulls Handbook of Sports Injuries*, 2nd edn. McGraw Hill, New York.

Wilderness Risk Management Committee (WRMC) and the Association for Experiential Education (AEE) Incident Data Reporting Project <www.aee.org/accreditation/wildernessCommittee>.

Program design and activity selection

Eric Brymer and Tonia L. Gray

To accomplish great things, we must not only act, but also dream; not only plan, but also believe.

Anatole France (1844–1924), member of the French Academy, winner of the Nobel Prize for Literature

FOCUS QUESTIONS

1   Explain the philosophy and goals of your program and/or activity.
2   How do the activities you have selected support your goals?
3   Does the sequencing of your activities optimise the program's impact?
4   How does your equipment choice reflect your philosophy and/or goals?
5   How does the choice of location/environment support your goals?
6   Have you assessed the impact of risk-taking aspects in your program in terms of social, physical, emotional and psychological growth?

CASE STUDY

Edited version from *Bush and Adventure Therapy: Letting Nature In*, Val Nicholls and Tonia L. Gray (2008).

The use of the natural environment as an agent of change is a key characteristic which differentiates bush and adventure therapy (BAT) from more traditional forms of therapy or counselling. Simply put, BAT aims to promote personal growth and positive attitudinal and behavioural change through the experience of challenge and adventure within a remote and natural environment.

The natural environment does not just provide a setting for action and 'doing'. BAT acknowledges the restorative effects of simply 'being' in nature. By contrast, while many participants welcome the opportunity to tap into the calming and rejuvenating powers of nature, some do not.

The behaviour of 14-year-old Scottie is a common reality with the early stages of BAT programs. Throughout the first two days of his six-day BAT journey Scottie crushed insects, terrorised possums, cursed and defaced rocks and yelled abuse at the rain and the 'f***ing trees'.

So how might the setting of BAT assist a participant like Scottie whose vision of himself is blurred by anger, fear and negative self-talk and whose relationship with nature is alienated? Psychologist and facilitator of BAT, Norah Trace, explains the process: 'Adventure therapy can allow us to slow down the entire nervous system, access calm emotions, and form new neural networks and patterns which in turn, influence our perceptions, emotions, and cognitions . . . the mind slows down and looks more deeply into what is present in self and the world, and is more able to consider how to create well being.' (Trace 2004)

BAT research has identified that participants are most tuned in to nature when they are alone. However, a recent study into the role of stillness and quiet time in BAT programs revealed that, in the past, most participants avoided any opportunity to be alone. All the same, the study found that as participants relaxed into the program, gained in their sense of trust and security and appreciated that there were no performance benchmarks, 'no rush', they were increasingly inclined to take time alone to simply enjoy being in nature (Nicholls & Gray, 2007).

Scottie soon recognised that he was in the company of older men who cared for him and young girls who begged him to sing them to sleep. Throughout the BAT program he struggled with physical and emotional challenges but did his best to adapt and express his thoughts and feelings. One night he sat on a cliff top staring in silence at a silver sea, one morning he took a minute or two to listen to the birdsong. By day six his growth in self-esteem was palpable. As the group struggled its way up a steep and slippery slope, Scottie grabbed hold of a sapling, turned to me with a huge grin and said, 'You know what? I'm starting to like these f***ing trees!'

Introduction

Risk and risk-taking are complex, culturally determined constructs with positive and negative connotations (Brymer 2010a). What one culture or individual considers risk another will consider normal. For this chapter we define risk as subjective perceptions of challenging events that include uncertainty, dangers and hazards. Most often, risk is portrayed as physically oriented dangers but they might also relate to psychological, emotional, social and spiritual hazards. From this perspective, risk-taking is the active search for experiences that might be perceived as dangerous or hazardous (Madge & Barker 2007), but still has the potential for gain. Risk-taking is a universal dimension of human experience, arising throughout all stages of life (Madge & Barker 2007). It is a pervasive quality of all human activity, whether it is the first baby steps taken and losing your balance, or riding a two-wheeled bike after detaching the training wheels. Risk is unavoidable as we negotiate the day-to-day activities within our learning landscape, especially if we seek to transcend our accustomed limits or stretch our abilities. The experience of risk-taking is contradictory. On the one hand, it is saturated with potential danger, misfortune, ambiguity, adversity and even despair, but on the other hand it is also filled with opportunity for growth, jubilation, rapture, exhilaration and increased mastery.

Contextualising risk

Elements of risk are integral components of the human experience and thus an innate part of program design and activity selection. Within the domain of adventurous sports and outdoor recreation, the profession has been subjected to intense and rigorous scrutiny because of potential for harm. In today's legal and financial climate it would be understandable if organisations involved in outdoor program design focused on the prevention of physical harm (see Chapter 3 for more discussion on the legal context).

The reader could be forgiven for thinking that outdoor or adventure programs are just about the search for dangerous situations, yet the statistics do not support that perception (see Chapter 5 for more detail). Indeed there does seem to be an assumed link between many outdoor programs and the unnecessary need for risk, at a level where death might potentially be the eventual outcome. Lyng (2004, 2005), for example, proffered that outdoor activities were in a similar category to many delinquent behaviours:

> What do skydiving, rock climbing, and downhill skiing have in common with stock-trading, unprotected sex, and sadomasochism? All are high risk pursuits. Edgework explores the world of voluntary risk-taking, investigating the seductive nature of pursuing peril and teasing out the boundaries between legal and criminal behavior; conscious and unconscious acts; sanity and insanity; acceptable risk and stupidity. (Lyng 2004, cited in Madge and Barker 2007, p. 12)

However, outdoor activities have also been presented as a worthwhile medium for those, mainly young men, who might be inclined to take risks in more socially undesirable areas (Farley 1991; Wilson & Lipsey 2000). There are many organisations that deliver targeted and very successful programs on a premise similar to this (Wilson & Lipsey 2000). This risk emphasis might be too simplistic an association (Brymer 2010a). In reality, outdoor programs are often considered fun and associated with positive social, psychological and ecological activities (American Institutes for Research 2005; Brymer, Downey, & Gray 2009; Brymer & Oades 2009; Dillon, Rickinson, Teamey, Morris, Young Choi, Sanders & Benefield 2006; Maller, Townsend, St.Ledger, Henderson-Wilson, Pryor, Prosser & Moore 2008; Pryor, Townsend, Maller & Field 2006). It is these positive components that are the main foci for the development of many outdoor programs. However, this does not mean that we should ignore or make light of the potential uncertainty, indeed such events as those introduced in Further resources in Chapter 5 should be analysed and learnt from. In the end, effective programming is underpinned by the acceptance and management of risks and not just those that might result in serious harm.

This chapter explores client-centred approaches to program and activity design in the context of risk-taking. The central tenant is that program design and activity choice are part of the 'coordinated activities' that form risk management, as indicated in ISO 31000. The program design and activity choice, by considering the impact of uncertainty on objectives, will take into account the aims and desires of the participants as well as the capabilities of the organisation. In this way a provider of outdoor activities (education, sport or recreation) will be better placed to deliver a safe experience that aligns with participant desires, needs and interests.

Know thyself and thy client

What are the aims and objectives of your organisation? What is it that your organisation hopes to achieve? What are you hoping to accomplish through your program design and activity selection? These basic questions need to transcend your program design. The traditional perception of outdoor programs, including experiential education, has focused on the development of recreational skills and/or educational aims. From this stance outdoor programs are seen as a means to develop 'hard skills' such as the ability to navigate a particular wild river or 'soft skills' such as the development of effective team communication. This simple classification developed into a categorisation that was based on whether a program was aimed at changing the way people think, behave or feel. Generally speaking, the classification of programs covered four broad domains: recreational, educational, developmental or therapeutic. At the same time program delivery evolved from a pure activity focus to emphasise the facilitation process and the holistic and rhythmical experience encouraged through facilitation styles such as those advanced by the 'dramaturgy' approach (Martin, Leberman & Neill 2002).

Over the last two decades, growth in the diversity of outdoor activities available to society and the change in focus of many traditional activities have prompted an expanded perception of outdoor programming. For example, interest in so-called extreme sports (e.g. skydiving, whitewater rafting, paragliding, parkour, bungee and surfing) has grown exponentially outstripping the growth rates of any other sporting activity (American Sports Data 2002; Pain & Pain 2005). Additionally, many of the traditional outdoor activities have been transformed into competitive disciplines with internationally recognised competitions (e.g. freestyle kayaking and adventure racing). Outdoor activities have also been promoted as a means to develop a more meaningful relationship with the natural world (Brymer & Gray 2010; Martin 2009).

Paradoxically, at the same time, modern society has arguably become more risk averse and safety focused (refer to Chapter 1 for more discussion). As a result, many activities are considered by mainstream society to be unacceptably dangerous, despite evidence to the contrary (Brymer 2010a; Gill 2007), see also Chapter 5. From a risk management viewpoint, outdoor organisations are being asked to demonstrate greater levels of credibility and accountability (see Chapter 7 for more information on program evaluation). However, many types of outdoor programs use the one-size-fits-all approach where clients are moulded into predetermined activity sets packaged as effective outdoor programs (Loynes 1998; Stremba 2009). This approach mirrors the general McDonaldisation of society (Ritzer 2010) and allows organisations to rely on a leader base with a very specific and narrow skill set. The efficient delivery of the program is the primary emphasis and the client is relegated to a secondary concern.

Whilst this process may appear to be predictable and controlled it also tends to de-humanise and de-skill. Risk of physical harm could easily be managed providing the activity ran as planned, but there may also be an associated risk of the loss of learning about one's self or nature. This is not to suggest that the one-size-fits-all approach is unwarranted for today's consumer as indeed there may be legitimate scope for such programs that produce a consistent almost guaranteed service. The important issue is that an organisation should carefully determine what they are able to deliver, accept the constraints and ensure that the program meets the client needs. An organisation might also need to carefully consider the distinction between the client, who may be a teacher, an organisation, a parent or a staff member, versus the participant who is the individual on the program or doing the activity. Who are you designing the program for and how can you balance the mix? The organisation might be paying the bill, the teacher or human resource manager might be evaluating the experience, but it is the participant who ultimately takes part.

From a risk management perspective, it is imperative to understand your organisational philosophy and objectives, what is your raison d'être? What is it that distinguishes you from any other organisation or program? This then guides what it is that you will do or offer in your programs and activities. For example, a commercial tourism operator running trips to Mt Everest with a commercial focus will offer different program designs and choose different activities and have different staff and equipment needs than a teacher running outdoor photography courses for at-risk young people at their local high school as part of a program aimed to reconnect them with themselves and their community.

In practice, risk management begins before the program is designed. An organisation will need to determine what they are capable of delivering and work to understand the client needs. Undertaking a thorough needs analysis to determine client and participant requirements is a useful exercise. At the same time, program designers would need to review resource requirements such as staff expertise and equipment requirements with regards to client needs and determine whether the activity and environment is suitable. This course of action will provide valuable information about participant prior skills and the desirability of a pre-program course. The assessment of potential risks should be undertaken as the program is being designed. This process will help inform the choice of activities and challenges and provide guidance for a client-centred program.

Interestingly, the one-size-fits-all or cookie-cutter outdoor program might become redundant (Stremba 2009), particularly as the internet and social media provide people with a wealth of real-time information of the diversity of opportunities available to them. Today's consumer anticipates a more holistic, memorable and personal experience that engages them emotionally, physically and psychologically (Pine & Gilmore 1998). To this end Pine and Gilmore provided many examples of organisations encountering difficulties because they relied on delivering the same old service. Outdoor organisations wishing to thrive in the current economic environment must continually refresh the experience to ensure participants do not feel that they are being subjected to old stale programs. As a result, many facets traditionally considered supplementary to the outdoor program or activity, such as transport, meal time, quiet time, relaxation time and free time, might now be best considered an integral part of the total experience. For instance, when considering the program design it might also be prudent to reflect on the food you are thinking of preparing, does it meet your philosophical aims? Should your food selection reflect the program values? For example, if sustainability is important to your program should this factor also be reflected in your choice of foods and methods of meal preparation? Could meal time be a core activity for your program? What is it that your client wants? What is it that you can deliver? What then is the most appropriate program design?

Holistic program design

An organisation should also have a clear model of the participant. For example, if you are focusing on the development of recreational or sporting skills do you have a clear view on how your participants acquire and develop skills? Have you considered the relationship between the individual, the task and the environmental? Is your selection of equipment appropriate for the participant and your program aims? (Brymer & Renshaw 2010) Equally, if you are designing outdoor education programs or organisational development programs do you have a model of the learner (e.g. child, young person or adult) and how they learn? Or are you just following the processes you were taught without considering if they truly reflect the learning process or are appropriate for your organisation or client. The reason it is important for a leader to possess a clear understanding of the learner and the learning process is that s/he will be able to make effective decisions which emphasise the learner rather than the leader. A leader without this comprehension will usually fall back on methods used in another context that might not be appropriate. The challenge is to ensure that your particular model reflects your participant. Are you purely focused on the traditional physical or cognitive structure or does your model truly respond to the varied constraints manifest by the individual, the environment and the task in hand? (Chow, Davids, Button, Shuttleworth, Renshaw & Araújo 2007).

Historically, outdoor and experiential programs have been primarily physical activities, which were conducted, briefed and debriefed as part of 'the adventure wave' (Schoel, Prouty, & Radcliffe 1988). Early in the last decade, Martin (2001a, 2001b) questioned the need for a more holistic approach that took into consideration the physical, intellectual, emotional and spiritual aspects of personal development. Figure 6.1 outlines the interplay of social (group work, relationships, interdependence), physical (outdoor activities such as hiking, canoeing and skiing), creative (art, photography and craft) and reflection (solo, journal writing and quiet time). Martin (2001a) proposed that all four should be interspersed sequentially throughout a program in order to obtain maximum gain. In other words, programs should not solely be physical, but they need to be counterbalanced with a holistic approach which includes 'quiet time' (Nicholls & Gray 2007).

The dramaturgy wave (Figure 6.1) highlights the different facets of the person who is engaged in the program and how there may need to be 'space' within programs to support the development of these facets. For example,

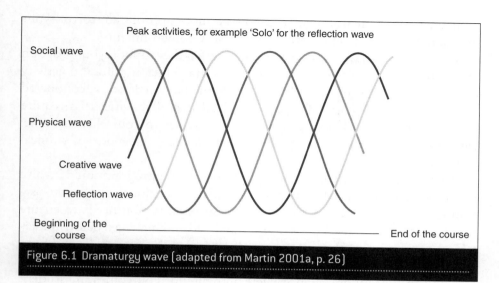

Figure 6.1 Dramaturgy wave (adapted from Martin 2001a, p. 26)

'busyness' may need to be replaced with solitude and stillness to promote reflection, while creativity and innovation may be supported through non-physical activities requiring more right-brain thinking. Conversely, those who are more creative and reflective may be challenged in their thinking about their physical bodies through engagement in a range of sequenced physical activities that build their confidence and competence.

Programs and activity design

The scope and sequence of outdoor programs can be designed to meet a variety of client and participant needs and interests. You will need to determine what your organisation is intending to deliver, whether this meets your philosophy and capacity and whether your aims meet those of the client and participant. When designing your program is it appropriate to focus on fun? Do you need to fill every minute of the program or will the program best meet client needs if it is slower or if there is time in the program to be alone? If you have high-energy participants will you need to keep them busy to stop them injuring themselves?

Ensure you offer and design programs that reflect your organisation's purpose as well as the needs and objectives of the clients and participants. As part of the design process you might also need to make sure that you choose environments that reflect participant needs and experiences. Is your choice of environment based on your own interests or those of your participants? Undertaking a program in wilderness environments might be ideal for many participants but if the group you are considering have little experience outside their own urban environment it might be more appropriate to run your program in less challenging, and often sensitive, environments.

Activity selection should also consider whether they support your program aims. For example, if you are trying to encourage lifelong physical activity it may not be appropriate to run a program that needs to be conducted in remote areas with lots of experienced leaders and activities that require expensive gear. Could your program be run closer to your client's home, with less equipment and thus modelling a more accessible model of physical activity?

Depending on the intended aims, the scope of your program could involve numerous and diverse risks. Such risks could be educational, emotional, psychological, spiritual, social and physical. An organisation needs to ensure that potential risks have been assessed, analysed and managed before undertaking any program. However, there also needs to be enough flexibility to manage risks that might arise during a program. The challenge for operators is to find an appropriate balance where both intended outcomes and student safety needs are met. If the balance is correct, outdoor programs can be a profound medium for personal growth. However, if safety has not been adequately considered then there is a real possibility of disaster (Martin, Cashel, Wagstaff & Breunig 2006).

The processes put in place for the management of risk needs to be specific to each program. Program design needs to be client-focused and therefore take into account the needs of particular clients and ensure that the organisation and staff have the skills and expertise that match the specialist needs of each client group (Stremba & Bisson 2009). Effective programs should consider the individual (e.g. physical, emotional, historical, cultural, spiritual, prior experience), environmental (e.g. social, peer group, wilderness) and task (e.g. purpose, activity) related constraints of each specific group (Brymer 2010b; Brymer & Renshaw 2010).

As part of the risk management process the program designer should also consider safety and emergency procedures (e.g. chain of command, communication, vehicle users, emergency response and incident reporting), activity specific requirements such as equipment, group management, program delivery, student/staff ratios and instructor competencies) (Dickson & Tugwell 2000). These policies, plans and processes should be documented and checked against industry norms.

Activity standards and industry norms

One example of published industry norms are the Adventure Activity Standards (<http://www.orc.org.au/activity_standards.php>) in Australia. These Standards have been developed to provide guidance for program designers intending to use a variety of outdoor activities. At the time of writing there are 15 published Standards and three draft Standards. The Adventure Activity Standards have been produced as a set of minimum requirements and expected guidelines for undertaking specific adventure activities. They were developed under consultation with the industry and cover issues such as leader–participant ratios, leader competencies, a section on 'defences against claims by participants', and other sections on planning, leader responsibilities, equipment and minimal impact (details can be found on the ORC website).

The advantage of such a system is that program managers have a set of general guidelines to follow even if these may not be context specific. A potential disadvantage might be that, as the name suggests, society might perceive them to be 'formal' standards. This might lead to an expectation that organisations should blindly follow the documented procedures. It might also lead to organisations actually blindly following the 'Standards' without contextualising the guidelines to their own situation. Program managers will need to avoid treating the published standards as step-by-step rules and ensure that they instigate and document, policies, procedures and processes that ideally suit their specific needs. Failure to contextualise the Standards (e.g. for local conditions and organisational capacity) could lead to disastrous psychological, emotional, social, education or physical outcomes. As an example, Hogan (2002) pointed out generic activity guidelines are also limited by decisions made in the field. He used the example of a mass drowning that resulted from a scout kayak trip in Lake Alexandrina in South Australia. Essentially, the findings of the coroner indicated that the leaders of the trip breached scout generic rules for kayaking in that area. However, Hogan noted that the coroner report found that the generic standards were inadequate particularly with regards to taking heed of client prior experiences. Brookes (2003) established that the trip leaders did not have the required skills to manage the event:

> it is clear that the capacity of supervisors to effect rescues was overwhelmed by the conditions and by multiple capsizes; most of those who survived did so by making their own way to shore, helping others where they could but not attempting futile rescues. (p. 35)

Of course, another potential limitation is that strict adherence to published standards might limit appropriate creativity and the inclusion of new activities. It is often the case that guidelines appear after an activity has been in place for some time. Organisations wishing to be appropriately innovative might find that the idea comes before the guidelines.

The equipment choices that a program designer makes are also a vital part of the risk management process. From an educational perspective, equipment choices might detract from the intended aims and the learner's ability to develop. For instance, if you are designing a program to teach recreational skills in canoeing it is important to choose equipment that fits the individual. Selecting equipment such as boats and paddles that are all the same size does not reflect the fact that people are all different sizes with different leg lengths, arm lengths and body lengths. The one-size-fits all approach to equipment choice ignores the fact that people have different physical backgrounds or that your clients might be at different stages in psychological or emotion readiness. For example, will wearing strange gear like harnesses and helmets be a big enough challenge or will it make your participant feel vulnerable (i.e. social rejection by peers, laughed at by colleagues or a source of ridicule by co-workers) without having to go over 50 metre cliffs? Depending on the context, a well-designed program might even consider belay methods, choosing activities that can be done in everyday trainers or the advantages of bivvies over tents. In some instances it might be prudent to have certain less readily available gear for rent or use as an integral part of the program. Essentially, even equipment choice should be carefully considered. You will need to choose equipment that supports the program aims and client profiles.

Staff skills and qualifications

To support your organisational and program objectives, what skills and expertise will your staff need? Will you rely on staff with specific qualifications and/or competencies, or do you prefer hiring staff with years of experience? Alternatively, do you train your own leaders? There has been an ongoing debate about the need to formalise staff skills, qualifications or competencies for at least three decades (Attarian 2001). In many countries professional organisations with expertise in a particular activity have developed pathways for skill development and leadership proficiency. Recognised associations with specialist knowledge in canoeing (e.g. British Canoe Association), mountaineering (e.g. Union of International Mountain Leader Associations) or skiing (e.g. Canadian Ski Instructors Alliance) have well established curriculum to support the professional development of outdoor leaders. Some leadership development schemes, such as those delivered by the National Outdoor Leadership School (NOLS), are broader in their delivery aims, accepted in many parts of the world and enable prospective leaders to gain holistic outdoor skills and leadership qualifications.

In Australia, recognised qualifications or competencies have been absorbed by the vocational education industry and delivered as qualifications or competency sets. The Outdoor Council of Australia (OCA) also administers a program that registers outdoor leaders who have achieved industry standards in activity leadership but not necessarily qualifications. The benefit of these processes is that a potential leader can gain knowledge in a structured and methodical manner that might take a lifetime (or more) to develop through experience alone. For example, in Australia a potential leader with little or no outdoor experience can gain a qualification that indicates they are ready to lead multi-activities in less than a year.

Despite the plethora of programs and schemes, there is still a view that certification has not met industry needs or resolved issues around participant safety. To this end, Attarian (2001) argued that leader certification was inadequate due to the diverse range of geographical, program and environmental contexts. Hogan (2002) acknowledges the potential danger in relying on qualifications as the sole means of determining proficiency to lead groups in the outdoors. He argued that effective risk management in outdoor activities is absolutely dependent on the judgment capabilities of those undertaking the risk assessment. Judgment is further dependent not just on an individual's level of knowledge but also on experience and reflection. From this stance, appropriate experience might be more suitable than qualifications. As a result many organisations train their own staff based on program and activity specific criteria and industry standards. However, while helpful to that organisation, it might mean that the training will not be recognised by any other organisation or country.

Depending on the context, leaders could need a high level of technical expertise, pedagogical skill, therapeutic or psychological training and even interpretative know-how (Brymer & Gray 2006). The challenge confronting an organisation is to determine what mix or blend of skills and capabilities are required to ensure a successful program. In many instances there might be external restrictions from insurance institutions or industry bodies to guide this process; however, this is not always the case.

A further concern for program planners in school-based programs is the role of the visiting teacher. Within many organisations, it is appropriate for a teacher with little experience of the activity set or environment to be considered as a responsible part of the broader leadership team. This is particularly so as they often retain a duty of care to the students, even though they may be outside their normal area of operations (refer also to Chapter 2). However, the responsibilities of the teacher should be carefully considered. For instance, if the teacher had to initiate a rescue or look after a group in hazardous situations would they have the skills to do so? For example, in the Lyme Bay situation (see Chapter 3) above it might actually be that the accompanying teacher is the first to require aid.

Conclusion

Risk and uncertainty are an integral part of being human. From birth until death we are confronted with a vast array of risks, whether they are emotional, social, physical, spiritual or psychological. However, developing a formal program that is structured around risk presents an array of potential pitfalls. This chapter has outlined the basis of program design and activity selection that are embedded in the production of client-centred and safe outdoor activities. From a risk management perspective, we have argued for sound prior planning and a realistic understanding of your own capacities and the needs of your client and participants. Program design is becoming more complex as outdoor activities are now situated in a changing legislative, insurance and land and water management environment. Activities that were once peripherals are arguably becoming central to the program design. Equipment and activity selection should ideally fit the participant needs and program intentions. Those delivering and designing programs need to understand their participants and have appropriate knowledge of how they learn and develop: knowledge that includes an understanding of the relationship between the individual, the task and the environment.

This ever-growing complexity places the onus on the organisation to ensure that the program reflects their capacity and that resources meet the needs of the program. The organisation and program planners need to be vigilant as they strive to meet the needs and interests of an ever-evolving participant.

Points for action for practitioners

- Ensure your organisational philosophy, goals and objectives align.
- Consider how your program design and marketing materials reflect your organisational philosophy.
- Evaluate your programs (see Chapter 7) to determine whether you are delivering what you say you will deliver.
- Redesign any programs that do not reflect your philosophy and clients' desires to reflect the attributes of your clients, the community (including staff) and the environment.

Further questions

1 What is the raison d'être of your program?
2 It can be rewarding and fulfilling for young people to live on the edge. How much 'edgework' is embedded into your programs?
3 Can you justify the cost benefit to your potential clients/participants?
4 Does your program design and activity selection mirror your anticipated outcomes?
5 What mix of skills and capabilities are required of your staff to ensure the delivery of a successful program?

6 How 'holistic' is your program in terms of social, creative, physical and reflective components?

7 How much 'quiet time' is purposely sequenced into your program?

References and further resources

References

ABC 2001. 'Six found guilty over Interlaken canyoning deaths'.

American Institutes for Research 2005. *Effects of Outdoor Education Programs for Children in California*. California, Palo Alto.

American Sports Data 2002. 'Generation Y' drives increasingly popular 'extreme' sports. Retrieved from <http://www.americansportsdata.com/pr-extremeactionsports.asp>.

Attarian, A 2001. 'Trends in outdoor adventure education'. *Journal of Experiential Education*, vol. 24, no. 3, pp. 141–9.

BBC 2004. 'Schools "shying away from trips"'.

Brookes, A 2003. 'Outdoor education fatalities in Australia 1960–2002. Part 2: contributing circumstances: supervision, first aid, and rescue'. *Australian Journal of Outdoor Education*, vol. 7, no. 2, pp. 34–42.

Brymer, E 2010a. 'Risk and extreme sports: a phenomenological perspective'. *Annals of Leisure Research*, vol. 13, no. 1&2, pp. 218–39.

Brymer, E 2010b. 'Skill development in canoeing and kayaking: an individualised approach' in I Renshaw, K, Davids & G Savelsbergh (eds), *Motor Learning in Practice: A Constraints-led Approach*. (pp. 152–160). Routledge, London, pp. 152–60.

Brymer, E, Downey, G & Gray, T 2009. 'Extreme sports as a precursor to environmental sustainability'. *Journal of Sport and Tourism*, vol. 14, no. 2–3, pp. 1–12.

Brymer, E & Gray, T 2006. 'Effective leadership: transformational or transactional?'. *Australian Journal of Outdoor Education*, vol. 10, no. 2, pp. 13–9.

Brymer, E & Gray, T 2010. 'Dancing with nature: rhythm and harmony in extreme sport participation'. *Adventure Education & Outdoor Learning*, vol. 9, no. 2, 135–49.

Brymer, E & Oades, L 2009. 'Extreme sports: a positive transformation in courage and humility'. *Journal of Humanistic Psychology*, vol. 49, no.1, pp. 114–26.

Brymer, E & Renshaw, I 2010. 'An introduction to the constraints-led approach to learning in outdoor education'. *Australian Journal of Outdoor Education*, vol. 14, no. 2, pp. 33–41.

Chow, J-Y, Davids, K, Button, C, Shuttleworth, R, Renshaw, I & Araújo, D 2007. 'The role of nonlinear pedagogy in physical education'. *Review of Educational Research*, vol. 71, pp. 251–278.

Dickson, TJ & Tugwell, M 2000. *The Risk Management Document: Strategies for Risk Management in Outdoor and Experiential Learning*, 2nd edn. The Outdoor Recreation Industry Council of NSW, Sydney.

Dillon, J, Rickinson, M, Teamey, K, Morris, M, Young Choi, M, Sanders, D, et al 2006. 'The value of outdoor learning: evidence from research in the UK and elsewhere'. *School Science Review*, vol. 87, no. 302, pp. 87–111.

Farley, F 1991. 'The type-T personality' in L Lipsitt & L Mitnick (eds), *Self-regulatory Behavior and Rrisk Taking: Causes and Consequences*. Ablex Publishers, Norwood, NJ.

Gill, T 2007. *No Fear: Growing up in a Risk Averse Society*. Calouste Gulbenkian Foundation, London.

Haddock, C 1993. *Managing Risks in Outdoor Activities*. New Zealand Mountain Safety Council, Wellington, NZ.

Hogan, R 2002. 'The crux of risk managment in outdoor programs – minimising the possibility of death and disabling injury'. *Australian Journal of Outdoor Education*, vol. 6, no. 2, 71–9.

Loynes, C 1998. 'Adventure in a bun'. *Journal of Experiential Education*, vol. 21, no. 2, pp. 35–9.

Lyng, S 2004. *Edgework: The Sociology of Risk-taking*. Routledge.

Lyng, S 2005. 'Sociology at the edge: social theory and voluntary risk taking' in S Lyng (ed) *Edgework: The Sociology of Risk-taking*. Routledge, Abingdon, pp. 17–49.

Madge, N & Barker, J 2007. *Risk and Childhood*. RSA Risk Commission, London.

Maller, C, Townsend, M, St. Ledger, L, Henderson-Wilson, C, Pryor, A, Prosser, L et al 2008. 'Healthy parks healthy people: the health benefits of contact with nature in a park context: a review of current literature' in *Social and Mental Health Priority Area, Occasional Paper Series*. Faculty of Health and Behavioural Sciences, Melbourne, Australia.

Martin, A, Leberman, S & Neill, JT 2002. 'Dramaturgy as a method for experiential program design'. *Journal of Experiential Education*, vol. 25, no. 1, pp. 196–206.

Martin, AJ 2001a. 'Dramaturgy: an holistic approach to outdoor education'. *Australian Journal of Outdoor Education*, vol. 5, no. 2, pp. 34–41.

Martin, AJ 2001b. 'Towards the next generation of experiential education programmes: a case study of Outward Bound'. Unpublished doctoral thesis, Massey University, Palmerston North, New Zealand.

Martin, B, Cashel, C, Wagstaff, M & Breunig, M 2006. *Outdoor Leadership: Theory and Practice*. Human Kinetics, Champaign, IL.

Martin, P 2009. 'Loving nature through adventure: examining the human-nature interaction'. In B Stremba & CA Bisson (eds), *Teaching adventure Education Theory: Best Practices* (pp. 359–368). Champaign, Ill: Human Kinetics, Champaign, IL, pp. 359–68.

Nicholls, V & Gray, T 2007. 'Sense and sensibility: looking at the reality and romance of human/nature relationships'. *Australian Journal of Outdoor Education*, vol. 11, no. 1, pp. 19–25.

Nicholls, V & Gray, T 2008. 'Bush and adventure therapy: letting nature in'. *Park Watch*, no. 232, pp. 22–33.

Pain, MTG & Pain, MA 2005. 'Essay: risk taking in sport'. *The Lancet*, vol. 366, no. 1, S33–4.

Pine, BJ & Gilmore, JH 1998. 'Welcome to the experience economy'. *Harvard Business Review*, July–August, pp. 97–105.

Pryor, A, Townsend, M, Maller, C & Field, K 2006. 'Health and well-being naturally: "contact with nature" in health promotion for targeted individuals, communities and populations'. *Health Promotion Journal of Australia*, vol. 17, no. 2.

Ritzer, G 2010. *The McDonaldization of Society*, 3rd edn. Pine Forge Press, Thousand Oaks.

Schoel, J, Prouty, D & Radcliffe, P 1988. *Island of Healing: A Guide to Adventure Based Counselling*. Project Adventure, Hamilton, MA.

Stremba, B 2009. 'The four uses of outdoor adventure programming' in B Stremba & CA Bisson (eds), *Teaching Adventure Education Theory: Best Practices*. Human Kinetics Champaign IL, pp. 99–109.

Stremba, B & Bisson, CA (eds) 2009. *Teaching Adventure Education Theory: Best Practices*. Human Kinetics, Champaign, IL.

Tempest, SKS & Ennew, C 2007. 'In the death zone: a study of limits in the 1996 Mount Everest disaster'. *Human Relations*, vol. 60, no. 7, pp. 1039–64.

Trace, N 2004. 'Adventure therapy as opportunity for self-reorganisation' in S Bandoroff & S Newes (eds) *Coming of Age: The Evolving Field of Adventure Therapy*. Association for Experiential Education, Boulder, CO, pp. 107–19.

Wilson, SJ & Lipsey, MW 2000. 'Wilderness challenge programs for delinquent youth: a meta-analysis of outcome evaluations'. *Evaluation and Program Planning*, vol. 23, no. 1, pp. 1–12.

Further resources

Shields LBE, Hunsaker JC, Stewart DM 2008. 'Russian roulette and risk-taking behaviour: a medical examiner's study'. *The American Journal of Forensic Medicine and Pathology*, vol. 29, no. 1, pp. 32–9. Retrieved from <http://www.scribd.com/doc/15829912/Russian-Roulette-and-RiskTaking-Behavior-A-Medical-Examiner-Study>.

Program evaluation

Tonia L. Gray and James T. Neill

What gets measured gets done.
If you don't measure results, you can't tell success from failure.
If you can't see success, you can't reward it.
If you can't reward success, you're probably rewarding failure.
If you can't see success, you can't learn from it.
If you can't recognize failure, you can't correct it.
If you can demonstrate results, you can win public support.

Osborne & Gaebler (1993)

FOCUS QUESTIONS

1 What is program evaluation?
2 Why evaluate programs?
3 What are the main types of program evaluation?
4 What are the main approaches to program evaluation?
5 What steps are involved in program evaluation?

CASE STUDY

On 16 November 2010 the Victorian State Labor Premier, John Brumby, was on the election campaign trail travelling to Bendigo unveiling his election policy – opening more kindergartens, more resources for primary schools and the 'radical' idea of helping youth transition to adulthood – a life skills program which would include an opportunity for all year nine students to experience a two-week out-of-classroom program (for city students to go to the country and country students to go to the city). The goal was to develop life skills, such as how to save, lead and help their community (Government of Victoria 2010).

'Education for Life: the Year 9 Experience' would run for a school term, focusing on life skills such as leadership training, saving and budgeting, volunteering, community service and bushfire awareness – to build resilience and independence among young people. The centrepiece would be a two-week camp which would include outdoor, environmental, cultural and sport activities in order to build on their new life skills and develop strong bonds with their classmates. The camp could include a city experience for rural students, a regional setting for suburban students, outdoor challenges and leadership programs (Brumby 2010).

Had Labor won the Victorian election (it did not) the programs would have been closely scrutinised by educational experts, the media and political critics. The public would expect a well-designed and well-evaluated program and potentially a world-class, evidence-based program could be developed with such significant political, social and financial support. Program effectiveness could be compared with other types of life skill training programs around the world. Cost-effectiveness would also be closely examined – which programs deliver the best outcome per unit of cost? If evaluation indicated that the programs were relatively ineffective or cost-inefficient, then the program would be criticised as a waste of money and potentially as a reckless, dangerous exercise.

What is clear from this scenario is that program evaluation is a critical component of outdoor programs and will be critical for all stakeholders – students now and into the future, teachers, schools, politics and society. All will be to some extent reliant on the design, conduct, analysis, results and reporting about valued program processes and outcomes.

Introduction

Most practitioners seek to promote program goals such as improved self-confidence, inter- and intra-personal skills, environmental sensitivity and physical fitness, to name just a few. But how can we objectively assess the extent to which such goals are achieved? What is the risk if desired outcomes are not being achieved? Could the same outcomes be achieved more effectively through other methods? Are the outcomes achieved cost effective? What evaluation methods could be used to examine the extent to which a program is achieving its mission and program objectives? Is it enough to rely on anecdotal stories and everyday perceptions? Or is that too risky? From a risk

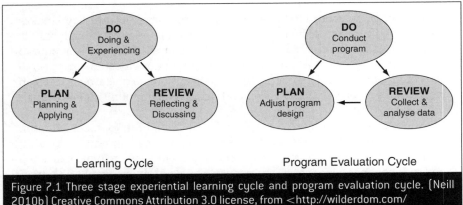

Figure 7.1 Three stage experiential learning cycle and program evaluation cycle. (Neill 2010b) Creative Commons Attribution 3.0 license, from <http://wilderdom.com/images/3StageELC.png>).

management perspective, knowing what you achieve, how you achieve and ways you can improve your processes and outcomes will be of benefit in risk communication, program design, staff training, organisational development and sustainability.

Quality control is vital for organisations, both internally and externally. Internally, program evaluation can be used to monitor quality and drive program development. Externally, the political and social climate is increasingly expecting transparent performance data from service providers. In this day and age, it would be unwise for an organisation to invest significant time, effort and money into running programs without measuring the degree of success in achieving the stated outcomes.

In a thriving organisation, program evaluation stimulates a learning culture. Program evaluation provides the review step of the do–review–plan experiential learning cycle (Figure 7.1) that is often championed in outdoor and experiential education. Reflective analysis of program processes and outcomes can fuel action research plans for improvement and help to develop better models and programs.

The possibility that a program may be using flawed processes or not achieving its stated outcomes should motivate an organisation to take evaluation seriously. Ideally, program evaluation is used not just to assess program performance, but also to guide program and staff development. In a learning organisation, program evaluation is part of a systematic action learning or quality improvement cycle, much like an experiential learning cycle (Figure 7.1).

This chapter introduces program evaluation methods and practices with advice tailored to evaluating outdoor and experiential learning programs.

Historical dimensions of program evaluation

Proponents of outdoor and experiential education often argue that there is enduring personal and social transformation through adventure education (Gray 1997a, 1997b; Neill 2010b). For the most part, however, anecdotal evidence and 'warm fuzzies' have not been grounded in rigorous, systematic research. The vast majority of outdoor and experiential programs run because we have a gut feeling that what they do is valuable (Neill 2010b), however there is a lack of empirical data to support the typical claims about outdoor-based programs. Neill (1997b) exemplifies this point:

> To date, the vast majority of outdoor education programs have been sustained by an act of faith. We can choose to continue walking along the path of faith, however, this will require praying harder than ever that schools, teachers, parents, and funding bodies don't dare question the evidence for that faith. (p. 198)

In essence, outdoor and experiential education suffers from a credibility crisis. Research is needed to inform practice and, in turn, to enhance the credibility of the profession (Gass 1992; Neill 1997a; Richards 1994). Many practitioners purport that quality research and evaluation is needed to deepen our understanding of the educational processes and impacts of such programs (Dickson, Gray & Mann 2008; Gray 1997b; Hanna 1992: Neill 2010a). There may be a mix of qualitative and quantitative research (these will be considered in greater detail later). In order to facilitate the value of the research to the wider audience what may help is to develop an integrated research agenda. This would help build upon the existing strengths and gaps in the research and provide a means for new and existing researchers as well as practitioners to learn from one another.

Aspects of evaluation

What is evaluation?

Evaluation is literally *e-value-ation* – or determining the value of something. It refers to a systematic process of asking questions, gathering data, analysing, reporting and then implementing arising recommendations. Program evaluation applies this process to the operations and outcomes of intentionally designed intervention programs.

Research and evaluation are related but are not synonymous. Evaluation is more basic and less time-consuming (Priest 2001) and focuses on specific programs. Research attempts to generalise from a sample to a larger population of programs and participants. Evaluation seeks to monitor and improve

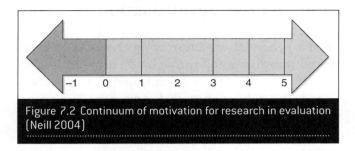

Figure 7.2 Continuum of motivation for research in evaluation (Neill 2004)

practice and outcomes, whereas research generally seeks to address theory underlying the effectiveness of practice.

Why evaluate programs?

Why might an organisation decide to evaluate its programs? Priest (2001) discussed three key reasons for conducting program evaluation:

1 Accountability is about meeting stakeholder demands. External stakeholders may include sponsors, funders and the community. Internal stakeholders may include participants, staff and the board. Stakeholders would generally like to know about the extent to which stated objectives are being achieved.

2 Improvement involves identifying program strengths and weaknesses and strategically improving on these, for example, to improve safety practices, increase educational value or maintain cost-effectiveness.

3 Marketing involves acquiring program evaluation effectiveness in order to enhance program image, kudos and saleability. Before undertaking evaluation, it is important to clearly specify the reasons for conducting the research.

An alternative model by Neill (2004) suggests a continuum of motivations or demotivations for conducting research and evaluation (see Figure 7.2).

Organisations can start from any point and need not progress linearly (e.g. a change in leadership can cause a big leap up or down). A negative score (such as −1) refers to active resistance, 0 to a neutral stance and a positive number refers to depth of motivation to engage in research or evaluation.

What are the main types of evaluation?

Priest (2001) describes five purposes or models of program evaluation:

1 Needs assessment: what are some gaps that the program will fill?

2 Feasibility study: given the constraints, can the program succeed?

3 Process evaluation: how is the implementation program progressing?

4 Outcome evaluation: were program goals objectives achieved?

5 Cost analysis: was the program financially worthwhile or valuable?

Table 7.1 Characteristics of qualitative and quantitative research designs in educational research

	Qualitative	Quantitative
Purpose	To study relationships, cause/effect	To understand social phenomena
Design	Developed prior to the study	Evolves during study
Approach	Deductive; tests theory	Inductive; generates theory
Tools	Uses standardised instrument	Uses face-to-face interaction
Sample	Uses large samples	Uses small samples
Analysis	Statistical analysis of numeric data	Narrative description/interpretation

Adapted from Lankshear & Knobel (2005).

What are the main approaches to program evaluation?

A systematic approach to program evaluation assumes a scientific orientation, however an excellent program evaluation cannot just be designed on paper – it will generally require good people skills, effective management and someone prepared to learn program evaluation skills. Ideally, program evaluation is not a separate activity but rather business-as-usual, with evaluation playing a continuous and integral role in a quality improvement process. There are many ways to approach program evaluation – each with merits and limitations. The approach described in this chapter draws on qualitative, quantitative and action research methods. We emphasise that each evaluation should be customised according to particular needs.

Qualitative versus quantitative methods

According to Thorndike (1918, p. 16) 'whatever exists at all, exists in some amount. To know it thoroughly involves knowing its quantity as well as its quality'. This encapsulates the basis of research and evaluation – it is a search to measure the quality and quantity of phenomena of interest. Distinguishing between quantitative and qualitative is relatively straightforward. Qualitative methods seek to find 'meaning' via interpretation of, for example, words contained in stories, artefacts and pictures. For example, information about a participant's connections with nature and how this might have changed over time could be gleaned from interviews or focus groups in which participants share their respective stories and interpretations. For further distinctions between qualitative and quantitative approaches see Table 7.1.

Quantitative methods

Quantitative methods involve numerical data and statistical data analysis. Quantitative data is often referred to as 'empirical data', as it is evidence-based and numerical in structure. As Lankshear and Knobel (2005, p. 63) state it 'will use objectivity-seeking methods for data collection and analysis, that are replicable so that findings can be confirmed or disconfirmed, and that are systematic and cumulative'.

Examples of quantitative measures are height (measured with a ruler), weight (measured with scales), IQ scores (measured through standardised IQ tests), exam results and so on. Strengths of quantitative data include objectivity, generalisability and time and cost efficiency of gathering and processing data. However, a word of caution – whilst quantitative numbers can be useful, they may 'miss' contextual or fine detail that can be gathered in one-on-one interviews or focus group meetings.

Measurement tools suitable for outdoor and experiential education

There are readily available measurement tools which can be used in program evaluations (see summary in Table 7.2, with details in Neill 2011a).

Table 7.2 Types of measurement instruments that may be used for outdoor and experiential education research and evaluation

Types of instruments	Example measures and constructs
Community, group, school and workplace	Community engagement, group cohesion, school climate, workplace effectiveness
Environmental attitudes and knowledge	Local environmental knowledge, environmental awareness, Connectedness to Nature (Mayer & Frantz 2004).
Personal and social development	Coping, life effectiveness, communication skills
Personality and psychological profiling	Myers–Briggs Type Indicator, 360 degree feedback, Personality profiles
Physical health and development	Physical self-concept, physical activity, health and wellbeing
Program quality surveys	Satisfaction with quality of program
Psychological and behavioural health	Mental health, resilience, psychological wellbeing and distress
Self-constructs	Self-esteem, self-confidence, self-efficacy, self-concept
Youth-at-risk outcomes	Personal, social, behaviour

Adapted from Neill (2011a).

Consider carefully whether such measures are likely to measure what you are targeting. It is also important to investigate the reliability and validity of the measures (Howitt & Cramer 2005) as well as any cost and conditions associated with use of the instrument. It can be helpful to get started with program evaluation using a pre-existing tool before considering custom-developed evaluation tools over time. Further information about designing survey questions is available in survey design resources such as Fowler (2002) and Nardi (2006).

Example evaluation instrument: Life Effectiveness Questionnaire

The Life Effectiveness Questionnaire (LEQ) is a commonly used instrument for measuring the effects of personal growth (adapted from Neill 2011a intervention programs). The LEQ measures generic life skills which are theoretical amenable to change (Neill 2007a, 2008a) and may be used with adolescents and adults. The LEQ is free to use and adapt. Participants can complete the LEQ at the beginning and end of a program and potentially also prior to the program and at follow-up. Observer data can also be collected. The 24-item, 8-factor LEQ-H (Table 7.3) is the most popular version, but there are also versions for use with youth-at-risk and corporate groups. Users

Table 7.3 The eight LEQ-H factors and descriptions

Factor	Description
Achievement motivation	Motivated to achieve excellence and put the required effort into action to attain it
Active initiative	Initiates action in new situations. Likes to be busy, energetic and actively involved in things
Emotional control	Capacity to stay calm in new, changing or stressful situations
Intellectual flexibility	Adapts thinking and accommodates different perspectives when presented with better ideas
Self-confidence	Confidence in personal abilities and success of one's actions
Social competence	Effectiveness, confidence and competence in social interactions
Task leadership	Leads and motivates other people effectively when a task needs to be done
Time management	Makes optimal use of time, efficient time management, with minimal time wastage

are also encouraged to consider adapted versions which may better suit their particular program goals (e.g. Neill 2007b).

Qualitative methods

All research ultimately has a qualitative grounding (Campbell 1974). In other words, the nature of what we usually wish to evaluate is fundamentally subjective, such as how one thinks or feels about one's self or perceived safety of an outdoor activity. We may choose to apply a quantitative measure to extract numerical data – or we may ask participants and the evaluator to convert their perceptions into language. Such *non-empirical data* uses the evaluator(s) as the data recording device. Qualitative data can provide 'rich' data and can facilitate deep understanding. Qualitative data collection methods include focus groups (small group discussions), one-on-one interviews, narratives, photos, videos and stories. The main disadvantages of qualitative data is that it can be subjective and influenced by the personal bias of the evaluator (Carlson 2010) and that it can be time consuming to collect and analyse. The main advantage is that 'rich' descriptions about individual's experiences may tell more about the meaning of an experience than the numbers ever can.

Examples of qualitative questions for participants:

1 What has been the most meaningful aspect of the camp for you?
2 Based on your time so far at camp, what do you think will be the main benefits of these experiences for you?
3 What effect do you think this experience will have on your life in later years? How? What makes you think that?
4 What do you think are likely to be the most difficult things for you to deal with here on camp? What makes these so difficult?
5 What are the main differences between this camp and life back home? Are these differences important? Why? Why not?

Mixed methods research design

Mixed method research blends quantitative and qualitative approaches and is becoming increasingly commonplace (Creswell 2009; Henderson 1993; Rudd & Johnson 2010). Mixed methods may lead to a more robust study design by gathering data from more than one source. This will build on the strengths of one approach (for instance, questionnaires capture large sample sizes) and offset the weaknesses of the other (such as interviews and focus groups can be time consuming and only capture a small number of participants). See Table 7.4 for other reasons to use mixed methods. Examples of mixed methods designs in outdoor and experiential education include

Table 7.4 Why use mixed research methods?

Benefit	Feature/s
Confirmation	Seeks convergence, corroboration of results from the different methods
Development	Seeks to use the results from one method to help develop or inform the other method
Expansion	Seeks to extend the breadth and range of inquiry by using different methods for different inquiry (different methods used to address different questions)
Complementary	Seeks elaboration, illustration of the results from one method with the results from the other method (different methods used to address different aspects of the same questions)

Adapted from Greene, Caracelli & Graham (1989).

Gray (1997a), Martin and Legg (2002) and Bobilya, Kalisch, McAvoy, and Jacobs (2005).

Action research

The key purpose of program evaluation is to improve programs which is also a key focus of action research. Lewin (1948) coined the term 'action research' to describe a reflective process of progressive problem solving to address specific issues and arrive at appropriate solutions. Action research may use a combination of quantitative or qualitative methods for data collection. Action research should be an integral component of outdoor and experiential education programs which aim to improve strategies, methods, practices, and knowledge of the environments within which they take place. The following eight basic components may be used to augment an action research process.

What steps are involved in program evaluation?

Expanding on the three-step do–review–plan model suggested earlier in Figure 7.1, the following eight steps are suggested and described:

1 Identify a problem
2 Review the current research
3 Formulate a research question or hypothesis to be answered
4 Devise a plan and research methodology to test the problem
5 Execute the plan
6 Collect and interpret data

7 Act on data (revise, modify, improve materials or equipment)

8 Share with others (in-house dissemination, publications, conference presentations etc.).

Step one: identify a problem

An evaluation study should focus on a specific problem (or set of problems, e.g. prevalence of particular injury type, achievement of program objectives etc.). The problems that are identified will guide the framework and method for the study. Thus, it is vital that meaningful, tangible problems of importance to the program and its stakeholders are identified. There is no point in conducting an evaluation if a clear problem to be solved is not identified.

Three important aspects of a well-focused evaluation project include, firstly, whether it is significant to the profession or the organisation and whether the outcomes of the evaluation will make a difference? Secondly, do you anticipate that the program evaluation findings will be a cue to action, such as modifying an instructional strategy or redesigning an equipment error? Lastly, is the research project doable and feasible in terms of human resources, time, cost and effort?

Step two: review the literature

A literature review should be conducted. This should be organised around the identified problem and be directly related to it. A good literature review will almost always save valuable time by helping to find out what is already known (and what is not), such as identifying others working in the same area, the key theories and studies to date as well as typical research methods, tools and resources (Bourner 1996, as cited in Kervin, Vialle, Herrington & Okely 2006, p. 43).

Step three: formulate/conceptualise a research question or hypothesis

Based on Steps one and two, brainstorm possible research questions and consider each of them carefully. The more specific these questions are the better. Vague questions can lead to problems down the track. It should be possible for each question to have an answer. Questions provide clear goals for an evaluation project. Make sure they express exactly what you want to know and that they address all aspects of the problem that are of interest. By framing the evaluation problem as questions, the goal becomes to provide the best possible answer(s) to the stated question(s). Here are some examples of research questions that might be asked in an evaluation study:

1 How do participants improve their environmental knowledge through an environmental education program?
2 At what times of day are injuries most frequent on outdoor programs?
3 What is the relationship between participant fatigue and injury severity?
4 To what extent are participants satisfied with the program? Are women and men equally satisfied with the program?
5 How does program length influence participant experiences and outcomes?
6 Do new activities have better educational outcomes than old activities?
7 Is the program worth the cost in dollars, staff time and disruption to school and family?

Step four: choosing the most appropriate research methodology or strategy

The nature of your research questions should influence the data collection methods (qualitative, quantitative, mixed methods or action research). You may choose to do a descriptive analysis (e.g. to identify the first aid skills of new career instructors) or you may investigate relationships (e.g. between participant age and knee injuries or the impact of new reflective facilitation techniques on learning outcomes).

Depending on your research question you may choose to collect data once (e.g. at the end of an experience) or you may choose to collect data on more than occasion (e.g. at the beginning and end of a program). You may also choose to collect data from a control or comparison group to determine whether your program is the cause of any change. Detailed examples of various research designs are described in Rossi, Freeman and Lipsey (1999) and Shadish, Cook and Campbell (2002).

Step five: collect data

As mentioned earlier in this chapter, data is either quantitative (e.g. tally scores, presentation at emergency departments, survey results) or qualitative (e.g. narratives or dialogue with those in the field or in focus groups). To begin with, you could use data that a program already possesses, such as medical authority forms, customer feedback, age of equipment and history of accidents in the field.

Ideally, data should be gleaned from several different sources to ascertain whether your results are consistent. This is called triangulation. Triangulation is where 'multiple sources of data are compared and contrasted with each other to build a coherent analysis of gathered data' (Kervin et al 2006, p. 203). Triangulation helps to improve validity.

Step six: analyse data

The goal of data analysis is to identify patterns or trends in relation to each of the research questions. Data analysis can be conducted using a spreadsheet, statistical software package or online survey software. Efficient processing of results of ongoing program evaluation is critical in closing the feedback loop. If you replicate a previous design, then it may also be possible to replicate the statistical techniques. Descriptive statistics and visualisation of the data (e.g. using graphs) should be provided. In addition, Neill (2002, 2008b) recommends using effect sizes to allow ready comparison to other studies and meta-analyses.

Step seven: take action based on results

Your evaluation results should inform your practice. Incorporate the results into program debriefs, course reviews and performance reviews. Do not overly rely on a single evaluation or over-react, but, on the other hand, do not ignore clear trends. Perhaps a new program design, sequencing or facilitation strategy is needed to improve student learning? Perhaps there are problems with a particular site location, activity, piece of equipment or instructor? Or perhaps the program evaluation methodology itself could be improved to better address the problem?

Step eight: disseminate your findings

Working in outdoor and experiential learning can be a lonely and solitary activity with successes and failures all too rarely transferred to others. Consider how best to disseminate the findings to stakeholders such as participants, parents, instructors, managers, directors, board members, industry members, academia and the media. Dissemination could be through journals, conference presentations and websites such as on-line discussions that can provide dynamic platforms for information exchange. We encourage all programs and practitioners to do some form of evaluation, whether qualitative, quantitative, mixed or action research and to circulate the findings.

Program evaluation needs assessments and checklists

There is no need to reinvent the wheel – handy program evaluation guides are available to help assess program evaluation goals and methods. Checklists help to make sure each aspect of the evaluation plan has been considered and that key steps are undertaken. Using needs assessments and checklists will quickly help to shape and inform your thoughts about evaluating your program. Recommended program evaluation checklists include Gass and Neill (2001), Courtworker.com (2007) and Stufflebeam (2010).

Common practices in program evaluation

In wondering about the design of your program evaluation it might be helpful to know more about common practices. Richards, Neill and Butters (1997) surveyed attendees at the 10th National Outdoor Education Conference in Australia about the nature of their outdoor education work and program evaluation practices. More than half of the recipients reported working with programs which evaluated participants' and teachers' overall satisfaction with the program and satisfaction with operational aspects of the program (such as food, accommodation etc.). The key sources of data were participants, instructors and accompanying teachers or client representatives. The main types of evaluation were group discussions with participants, written survey questions, observations of the program and individual discussions with participants.

Program evaluation tips

1 What data do you already have? Has the program evaluation potential of this data been realised? If not, learn from previous evaluation efforts to help develop a better program and an improvement method of program evaluation.
2 It is better to do some program evaluation than no evaluation.
3 Start small and develop a program evaluation approach over time, with trial and error, rather than trying to design an overly grandiose single program project.
4 Engagement with stakeholders is key – what do they want to know?
5 Develop a written program evaluation plan so you are clear about what questions the evaluation is trying to answer and how you are going to gather and analyse evidence.
6 Make connections with evaluation experts in your field such as in universities, ask for their advice or offer to provide them with access to your program as a research site for them.
7 If you find a good program evaluation study that matches your needs, consider replicating it.

Conclusion

A program without good quality program evaluation risks losing an important internal quality monitoring mechanism as well as external public support and funding. Programs well supported by evaluation are likely to be stronger, more mature programs with greater longevity. This chapter has demonstrated a clear need for program evaluation and some ways to approach program evaluation. It is not difficult or onerous, but it does require an open and objective mind and a commitment to improvement. Practitioners need to embrace this mindset and engage in evaluation themselves in order to have the best possible data for program improvement and to communicate with external stakeholders.

Points for action for practitioners

- How do you justify the existence of your program to politicians and policy-makers?
- What program evaluation has already been conducted about your program? Do your peers and colleagues know about the aspects of your program that have merit in terms of physical, emotional, social, spiritual and environmental benefits? (Collate and make accessible.)
- Why do you want to evaluate? Who in the organisation wants program evaluation and why? Who in the organisation might be most resistant to program evaluation and why?
- Develop a written plan, including the evaluation objectives, proposed methods for data collection, type of analysis, dissemination, budget and timeline with milestones. Get the plan peer-reviewed and revise accordingly. Consider options then commit to implementation.
- Consider whether the evaluation is to be done in-house, or would it be better to involve an external evaluator?

References and further resources

References

Bobilya, A, Kalisch, K, McAvoy, L & Jacobs, J 2005. 'A mixed-method investigation of the solo in a wilderness experience program' in K Paisley, A Young, C Bunting & Bloom, K (eds) *Coalition for Education in the Outdoors Seventh Biennial Research Symposium Proceedings*. Coalition for Education in the Outdoors, Cortland, NY, pp. 1–18.

Brumby, J 2010. 'Labor to invest in new school camps and accommodation for Year 9 experience'. Retrieved from <http://www.alpvictoria.com.au/news-events-media/news/labor-to-invest-in-new-school-caps-and-accommodation/>.

Campbell, D 1974. 'Quantitative knowing in action research'. Kurt Lewin Award Address, Society for the Psychological Study of Social Issues, presented at the annual meeting of the American Psychological Association, New Orleans.

Carlson, J 2010. 'Avoiding traps in member checking'. *The Qualitative Report*, vol. 15, no. 5, pp. 1102–13.

Courtworker.com 2007. 'Program evaluations metaevaluation checklist' based on *The Program Evaluation Standards* Daniel L Stufflebeam 1999. Retrieved from <http://www.courtworker.com/user/docs/program_metaeval.pdf>.

Creswell, JW 2009. *Research Design: Qualitative, Quantitative, and Mixed Methods Approaches* 3rd edn. Sage, Thousand Oaks, CA.

Dickson, TJ, Gray, T & Mann, K 2008. *Australian Outdoor Adventure Activity Benefits Catalogue*. University of Canberra, ACT. Retrieved from <http://www.oric.org.au/IndustryNews/OutdoorActivityBenefitsCatalogueFinal270808.pdf>.

Fowler, FJ Jr. 2002. 'Designing questions to be good measures' in FJ Fowler, *Survey Research Methods* 3rd edn. Sage, Thousand Oaks, CA, pp. 76–103.

Gass, M 1992. 'Theory and practice'. *The Journal of Experiential Education*, vol. 15, no. 2, pp. 6–7.

Gass, M & Neill, JT 2001. 'Introduction to program evaluation'. Presentation to the 29th Annual International Conference of the Association for Experiential Education, 2 November 2001. Retrieved from <http://wilderdom.com/html/NeillGass2001EvaluationNeedsAssessmentforAEE6pageversion.doc>.

Government of Victoria (2010). 'Victoria's premier John Brumby speaks in Bendigo'. <http://www.thegovmonitor.com/economy/victorias-premier-john-brumby-speaks-in-bendigo-42757.html>.

Gray, T 1997a. 'The impact of an extended stay outdoor education program on adolescent participants'. Unpublished doctoral thesis, University of Wollongong.

Gray, T 1997b. 'Examining the fruits of the outdoor education tree from a gender perspective'. *Proceedings of the 25th International Conference*, Association for Experiential Education Conference, 23–26 November, Asheville, NC, pp. 113–10.

Hanna, G 1992. 'Ripples in the water: Reflections on experiential education research designs'. *Proceedings of the 20th International Conference of the Association for Experiential Education*, Banff, Canada, 8–11 October, pp. 231–5.

Henderson, K 1993. 'The yin-yang of experiential education research'. *The Journal of Experiential Education*, vol. 16, no. 3, pp. 49–54.

Howitt, D & Cramer, D 2005. 'Reliability and validity: evaluating the value of tests and measures' in *Introduction to Research Methods in Psychology*. Pearson, Harlow, Essex, pp. 218–31.

Kervin, L, Vialle, W, Herrington, J & Okely, T 2006. *Research for Educators*. Thomson Social Science Press, Melbourne.

Lankshear, C & Knobel, M 2005. *A Handbook for Teacher Research*. Open University Press, England.

Lewin, K 1948. *Resolving Social Conflicts: Selected Papers on Group Dynamics*. Gertrude W Lewin (ed). Harper & Row, New York.

Martin, A & Legg, S 2002. 'Investigating the inward sounds of Outward Bound' (Outward Bound New Zealand). *Australian Journal of Outdoor Education*, vol. 6, no. 2, pp. 27–36.

Mayer, FS & Frantz, CM 2004. 'The Connectedness to Nature Scale: A measure of individuals' feeling in community with nature'. *Journal of Environmental Psychology*, vol. 24, pp. 503–15.

Nardi, P 2006. 'Developing a questionnaire' in *Doing Survey Research: A guide to Quantitative Methods* 2nd ed. Pearson, Boston, MA.

Neill, JT 1997a. 'Gender: how does it effect the outdoor education experience?'. *Proceedings of the 10th National Outdoor Education Conference*, Collaroy Beach, Sydney, Australia. Jan 20–24, pp. 183–92.

Neill, JT 1997b. 'Outdoor education in schools: what can it achieve?'. *Proceedings of the 10th National Outdoor Education Conference*, Collaroy Beach, Sydney, Australia. Jan 20–24, pp. 193–201.

Neill, JT 2002. 'Meta-analytic research on the outcomes of outdoor education'. Paper presented to the 6th Biennial Coalition for Education in the Outdoors Research Symposium, Bradford Woods, IN. Retrieved from <http://wilderdom. com/research/researchoutcomesmeta-analytic.htm>.

Neill, JT 2004. 'Hierarchy of research & evaluation motivations'. Retrieved from <http://wilderdom.com/research/HierarchyResearchMotivations.html>.

Neill, JT 2007a. 'Life effectiveness questionnaire: a research tool for measuring personal change'. Retrieved from <http://wilderdom.com/leq.html>.

Neill, JT 2007b. 'A measurement tool for assessing the effects of adventure-based programs on outcomes for youth-at-risk participants'. Retrieved from <http://wilderdom.com/tools/leq/YouthDevelopmentLEQScalesPaper.htm>.

Neill, JT 2008a. 'Enhancing life effectiveness: the impacts of outdoor education programs'. Unpublished doctoral dissertation, Faculty of Education, University of Western Sydney, NSW, Australia. Retrieved from <http://wilderdom.com/phd>.

Neill, JT 2008b. 'Why use effect sizes instead of significance testing in program evaluation?' Retrieved from <http://wilderdom.com/research/effectsizes.html>.

Neill, JT 2010a. 'Experiential learning cycles: overview of 9 experiential learning cycle models'. Retrieved from <http://wilderdom.com/experiential/elc/ExperientialLearningCycle.htm>.

Neill, JT 2010b. 'Program evaluation and outdoor education: an overview'. Presentation at the 16th National Outdoor Education Conference, Notre Dame University, Fremantle, Western Australia, 10–13 January 2010. Retrieved from <http://wilderdom.com/wiki/Neill_2010_Program_evaluation_and_outdoor_education:_An_overview>.

Neill, JT 2011a. 'Index to tools, instruments & questionnaires for research & evaluation of intervention programs'. Retrieved from <http://wilderdom.com/tools/ToolsIndex.html>.

Osborne, D & Gaebler, T 1993. *Reinventing Government: The Five Strategies for Reinventing Government*. Plume, New York.

Priest, S 2001. 'A program evaluation primer'. *Journal of Experiential Education*, vol. 24, no. 1, pp. 34–40.

Richards, A 1994. 'From exposure to engagement or awareness to action'. *Journal of Adventure Education and Outdoor Leadership*, vol. 11, no. 2, pp. 6–8.

Richards, GE, Neill, JT & Butters, C 1997. *Statistical Summary Report of Attendees at the 10th National Outdoor Education Conference, Collaroy, NSW, 1997*. National Outdoor Education & Leadership Services, Canberra, Australia. Retrieved from <http://wilderdom.com/abstracts/RichardsNeillButters1997NOECSurvey.htm>.

Rossi, PH, Freeman, HE & Lipsey, MW 1999. *Evaluation: A Systematic Approach* 6th edn. Sage, Thousand Oaks, CA.

Rudd, A & Johnson, RB 2010. 'A call for more mixed methods in sport management research'. *Sport Management Review*, vol. 13, no. 1, pp. 14–24.

Shadish, WR, Cook, TD & Campbell, DT 2002. *Experimental and Quasi-experimental Designs for Generalized Causal Inference*. Houghton-Mifflin, Boston.

Stufflebeam, D 2010. 'Metaevaluation checklists'. Retrieved from <http://www.wmich.edu/evalctr/checklists/metaevaluation/>.

Thorndike, EL 1918. 'The nature, purposes and general methods of measurements of educational products' in GM Whipple (ed) *National Society for the Study of Educational Products: Seventeenth Yearbook*. Public School Publishing, Bloomington, IL, pp. 16–24.

Further resources

Neill, JT 2011b. 'Program evaluation in outdoor education, adventure education, & other experiential intervention programs'. Retrieved from <http://wilderdom.com/evaluation.html>.

Trochim, WMK 2006. 'Introduction to evaluation'. Retrieved from <http://www.socialresearchmethods.net/kb/intreval.htm>.

Wikipedia 2010. 'Action research'. Retrieved from <http://en.wikipedia.org/wiki/Action_research>.

Risk communication

Clare Dallat

> The single biggest problem in communication is the illusion that it has taken place.
>
> George Bernard Shaw (1856–1950)

FOCUS QUESTIONS

1   What is 'informed consent' and how can we ensure we provide it?
2   Why do people perceive what may seem to be the same risk so differently and how can we use this to inform our risk communication?
3   What practical steps can we employ in our risk communications to ensure that parents and other stakeholders feel appropriately informed to make a decision regarding their child's participation in an outdoor program?
4   How can we ensure we are communicating *both* the risks and benefits of participation?

CASE STUDY

On 20 April 2010 an explosion on BP's Deepwater Horizon drilling rig in the Gulf of Mexico resulted in 11 people dead. The worst marine oil spill in the US history caused an environmental and economic disaster for the Gulf of Mexico, and a financial and public relations nightmare for BP. Before this catastrophe the oil industry had been lobbying for more offshore drilling suggesting that a major oil spill was unlikely, and, if it did occur, the industry had the ability to minimise the damage. The April disaster was evidence that the industry was wrong on both accounts. Additionally, they overestimated the benefits and underestimated the potential costs of offshore drilling. BP's 'management' after the event also magnified the public outrage when the CEO made comments such as 'the Gulf of Mexico is a very big ocean. The amount of volume of oil and dispersant we are putting into it is tiny in relation to the total water volume' (14 May 2010) and on 30 May 2010 'the environmental impact of this disaster is likely to be very, very modest'. By February 2011 the costs were estimated at over 40 billion US dollars, not to mention the environmental or social costs to the Gulf Coast communities who were still recovering from Hurricane Katrina in 2005.

Introduction

The following chapter draws upon recent cases, literature and research into risk communication in a small group of schools in Victoria, Australia, as an example of risk communication with stakeholders. In conducting the research, the author sought to understand how communicators were defining risk and then argues for a more balanced view where the benefits of participation is highlighted, communicated and understood as well as the potential for harm, so that parents can then weigh up these factors and make a decision. This approach complements ISO 31000 as presented in this book. ISO 31000 suggests that 'communication and consultation with external and internal stakeholders should take place during all stages of the risk management process' (SASNZ 2009, p. 14). The communication should include information about the risks, causes, consequences and management strategies. Communication and consultation is important as each stakeholder will make a decision about their participation based upon their own perception of the risk which may vary according the their 'values, needs, assumptions, concepts and concerns' (SASNZ 2009, p. 15). To support the decision making of the stakeholder, ISO 31000 suggests that 'communication and consultation should facilitate truthful, relevant, accurate and understandable exchanges of information' (SASNZ 2009, p. 15).

The stakeholders who may need to be communicated with will vary by organisation, activity, program and location. Internal stakeholders include staff and boards or councils while external stakeholders may include participants, parents/guardians, teachers, land managers, insurers, other suppliers or activity providers and shareholders.

Lessons learned

It is apparent in coronial reports, recommendations and litigation following several outdoor education incidents both in Australia and around the globe, that communication between schools and parents could be improved. Several of these incident investigations suggest that parents were inadequately informed of the risks involved, or were given insufficient information on which to base their consent (Ajango 2005; Holden 2002). Holden (2002) reviewed coroners' cases related to school excursions, and highlighted the importance of consent, stating that it must be truly 'informed' whereby 'evidence of consent is evidence of reasonable care, it is only relevant if the consent is informed consent, based on a full appreciation of the risks involved in the activity' (Pullar cited in Holden 2002 p. 25).

Informed consent was also highlighted in the Cathedral Ranges incident in 1983, a landmark for outdoor education in Victoria: a student badly sprained her ankle and while the staff were attending to her, another student from the group fell nearby and sustained fatal injuries. The student who suffered the ankle injury successfully sued for emotional trauma at having to witness her classmate die. Among other findings, Judge Lazarus found that 'the information provided to parents did not advise them of the rugged and hazardous conditions' (cited in Stewart 2000, p. 346).

Currently, all Victorian government school outdoor education programs are required to have a designated 'teacher in charge' of the program (DEECD 2006). School principals generally employ an outdoor education teacher or coordinator for this role. This person is expected to assemble the program, which includes the risk communication information, to enable parents to make an informed decision. It may be the case that, in the absence of clear guidelines and support material, the risk communication strategies may vary widely from school to school, and specifically from coordinator to coordinator. Thus, the research summarised here (Dallat 2009) focused on the school outdoor education coordinator and the risk communication with the parents by seeking to understand the current risk communication strategies employed by Victorian government school outdoor education coordinators to satisfy the Department's requirements that 'Parents/guardians asked to sign consent forms must be given sufficient information about the nature of the proposed activity and the risks involved, and the degree of supervision, to enable them to make an informed decision' (DEECD 2006, Parental Guardian Approval and Information, para. 4.4.2.4).

Prior to sharing the findings of the study, an examination of the relevant theoretical perspectives of risk communication is warranted.

Review of relevant literature

Since its emergence approximately thirty years ago risk communication has now firmly established itself as a discipline in its own right across a wide range of situations (World Health Organization 2002). From the time when it became apparent that the messages being delivered by the risk experts were not being received by the public as initially intended, risk communication has grown to become an important aspect in the overall management of risk within both public and private institutions (Fischhoff 1995).

The Society for Risk Analysis defines risk communication as a process that involves the exchange of views and information between people, larger groups and organisations. It involves numerous messages related to the levels of risk, the concerns, reactions, opinions or to the legal or institutional arrangements for risk management (US Public Health Service 1995). Adler and Kranowitz (2005) defined risk communication in a way that clearly places importance on both the risks *and* benefits of hazards. In their view risk communication is 'the method by which the public can be informed as to the potential risks and benefits of specific projects and programs' (p. 18).

Why communicate about risks?

Risk is about uncertainty. For all activities in the outdoors, as in life, there will be a level of uncertainty. Calman (2002) considered that the primary motivation for communicating risk is to arm the individual or community with adequate information in order to make choices about the consequences of the risk. Previously, Otway and Wynne (1989) cautioned the need for adequate balance, in that risk communication should create the appropriate amount of concern regarding the hazard, yet not so much as to create unnecessary panic. They refer to this as the reassurance-arousal paradox.

The expectations of more demanding and increasingly 'outraged' public are also changing (Calman 2002; Sandman 1987). Previously Beck (1992) contended that we are now living in a 'risk society' characterised by increased pessimism, epitomising a move away from the previous aspects of industrial and materialistic 'positives' to the 'negatives' or 'harm' of such activities, an opinion that one would argue is as relevant today. The discussion has focused on what might go wrong and consequently on the provision of the necessary systems, procedures and tasks to mitigate such risk. These demands come from a public insisting on a more significant role in decision-making about hazards likely to affect them. Scholars and policy makers have also called for more public participation in complex risk decisions (Irwin 1995; Sandman 1987; Wynne 1992).

Over time, risk communication has evolved into a multi-faceted phenomenon. Covello & Sandman (2001) suggested that there have been four

Table 8.1 The nature of risks

Risks are considered more acceptable if they are perceived to be:	Risks are considered less acceptable if they are perceived to be:
Voluntary	Imposed
Under an individual's control	Controlled by others
Having clear benefits	Having little or no benefit
Distributed fairly	Unfairly distributed
Natural	Man-made
Statistical	Catastrophic
Generated by a trusted source	Generated by an untrusted source
Familiar	Exotic
Affecting adults	Affecting children
Affecting you personally	Affecting others

Source: Adler & Kranowitz (2005).

'generations' of risk communication as to how risk communicators, primarily in an environmental context, view the role of the public. These can be described as following, with the emphasis often being upon the first generation:

- ignore the public
- learn how to explain risk data better
- risk seen as consisting of two almost independent, basic elements, hazard and outrage, therefore the essence of risk communication is not just explaining risk numbers – it is also reducing (or increasing) outrage
- treat the public as a full partner.

Although there has been growth and development in risk communication, it should be noted that successful risk communication does not necessarily result in better decisions. For example, people may be aware of the risks of smoking, drink driving or prolonged exposure to the sun, but they still choose to behave in ways that increase their risk of injury or illness. An alternate view of successful risk communication is that 'it raises the level of understanding of relevant issues or actions for those involved and satisfied them that they are adequately informed within the limits of available knowledge' (National Research Council 1989, p. 2).

Table 8.1 highlights the benefits of a collaborative approach where the public, such as parents and children on outdoor programs, are fully informed and 'welcomed' into the decision-making process, as in Covello and Sandman's fourth generation. Helping students and parents understand the expected benefits that may be achieved through the program (as well as the risks involved) and ensuring parents have the genuine final say in whether or not their child attends are vitally important as to how risks will be perceived.

However, the aim of treating the public as a full partner may be hindered by the dominant model of risk communication, the so-called 'deficit' model.

The 'deficit' model of risk communication

The deficit model of risk communication assumes that the public is a *tabula rasa*, meaning that each member of the public is a blank slate patiently waiting to be filled with 'knowledge' (University of Leicester Department of Criminology 2005). With this approach, parents may be treated as if they have no knowledge at all about outdoor education. The deficit model also employs language that favours expertise and specialism (Otway 1992). For example, outdoor education co-ordinators who have specific technical skills, knowledge and language (e.g. personal flotation devices, harness, belay ropes, Nordic skis), may communicate risk in a way that favours such a discourse, albeit without being aware or cognizant of it. Thus parents may be prevented from engaging in active dialogue about their child's participation in an outdoor education program simply because they lack the knowledge and/or the technical language to converse confidently with the coordinator.

A further characteristic of the deficit model is that the public are approached as an 'undifferentiated, homogeneous mass' (University of Leicester Department of Criminology 2005). All recipients are therefore treated the same. The deficit model employs a single, one-way communication flow that is always initiated by the experts and is aimed towards a passive recipient who is waiting to receive the information. Finally, the majority of risk communication strategies adopting this model are 'single use' only and no opportunities for feedback are provided (University of Leicester Department of Criminology 2005). This dominant model, with its focus on single one-way communication, contradicts the intent of ISO 31000 which recommends that communication be two-way and continuous with the stakeholders.

Trust and relationships

In seeking to communicate with the public, two aspects are of importance: trust and relationships. It has been previously suggested that the public is generally willing to permit professionals, who they trust, to make decisions on their behalf as long as the decision-makers maintain the public's trust (Royal Academy of Engineering 2002). For example, internationally renowned risk communication expert, Peter Sandman, (Personal communication, 8 January 2007) considers that while there may be low trust in the organisation that is proposing that a hazardous waste site be located near their homes, parents in general have much higher trust in the school systems educating their children. When high levels of trust exist, parents may then be more likely to unquestioningly believe what they are being told regarding the risks and/or benefits involved with their child's participation in an outdoor education program. This then increases the need to ensure that the communication is effective, that the information is conveyed in such a way that people can receive and understand the message and that they feel free to ask questions for clarification.

The second aspect relates to relationship building through effective communication. The Royal Academy of Engineering (2002) suggested that, where possible, the people making the risk decisions and those likely to be impacted by them should know each other personally, with risk communication messages being delivered in as many mediums as possible. The content of the message must be sensitive to the receiver's frame of reference (Covello, Sandman & Slovic 1988; Royal Society 1992). For example, terms used routinely by outdoor educators (e.g. remote) may mean something quite different to parents given their different frames of reference. Through having a relationship the messages between the parties may be varied to meet identified needs as well as encouraging debate and dialogue. These varied frames of reference and viewpoints are central to an important area of risk communication research called risk perception.

Risk perception

Risk perception is the body of research investigating peoples' identification of risk and their concerns about it. It is very much to do with the feeling that if we perceive that something is dangerous (even if the professionals do not), there will be an impact on how we feel and respond to that risk. Slovic (1992) suggested that this area of research is considered critical to risk communication in that:

> Perceptions of risk play a prominent role in the decisions people make in the sense that differences in risk perception lie at the heart of disagreements about the best course of action between technical experts and members of the general public. (p. 2)

In order to better understand how and why people perceive risk differently, we must first investigate what is understood about the term *risk*. Slovic (1992) examined the multiple meanings of the term risk and noted it is used to describe a hazard, probability, a consequence or a potential threat. The fact that there are multiple and vastly different meanings to the word is a major challenge in communication. As mentioned previously, within a technical framework the likelihood and severity of hazards and therefore the 'risks' are viewed as being quantifiable in an objective manner by risk assessment processes. A social scientific approach, however, holds the view that risk is intrinsically subjective; in this regard 'risk' is not something that can be separated from the cultural and social background or the thinking mind of human beings. Rather, risk is a construct that humans have created to cope with the uncertainty and dangers of life. This social science view therefore negates the concept of risk being 'real' or 'objective.' The only things that may be real are the dangers themselves (Slovic 1992).

Zink and Leberman (2001) suggested that the outdoor education literature is somewhat at odds with this subjectivist view of risk and the desire to quantify risk is prevalent within outdoor education. This is evidenced through equations of risk-measuring probabilities and likelihood as well as the development of incident databases to track incidents. The DEECD defines risk as 'the chance of something happening that has the potential to cause loss, damage or injury and thus impact upon the achievement of the school's goals, targets and priorities. Risk is measured in terms of consequence and likelihood' (DEECD 2006, para. 6.14). This technical view of risk is predominantly negative, in that risk is seen as something to be avoided as well as something that can be objectively measured. There is no mention in this definition of the benefits that may come from taking risks. Risk, in this context, is viewed as something to be 'managed' and 'overcome'. By contrast, the ISO 31000 definition of risk as the 'effect of uncertainty on outcomes' seems to offer a much more balanced definition where the rationale for venturing out in the first place as well as the benefits to be achieved are equally considered.

Building upon the literature, the following section provides an overview of some insights gained during the research of a sample of Victorian schools and is followed by suggestions for practical applications.

Research insights

The research conducted by Dallat (2009) was undertaken in 2006 with a group of seven Victorian schools that conduct some form of overnight outdoor education program. The respondents were aged 26–52 years, three of whom where women and four men. Five of the interviewees had tertiary qualifications in outdoor education and their outdoor education experience ranged from four to twenty-four years. Data was collected via interviews and analysis of documents to determine the methods of communicating risk employed by outdoor education coordinators in Victoria, as well as the motivations behind such an approach.

What became apparent throughout this research is that communicating risk to parents was viewed as more of a 'task' than a 'process'. Parents were treated more as external stakeholders and not as integral components of the decision-making. Risk was expressed primarily in terms of loss or harm in the communication to parents, yet the coordinators personally spoke passionately of the benefits they believed students could gain from participation in an outdoor education program. Overall, the results of this study demonstrate that the method and the process of risk communication principally correlated with the 'deficit' model of risk communication with one-way communication by the experts to the unknowledgeable recipients.

Key findings were:

1 The most common method to communicate risk was via some form of written documentation (ranging from two–fifteen pages). In some cases this was supported by a website and/or DVD with visual images of activities.

2 For three of the schools, student participation was compulsory for completion of a unit, which may influence whether a parent reads all the material provided; further, the fact that a risk is involuntary may make it less acceptable.

3 For five of the schools, the benefits of participation were articulated in the material, but in one instance, it was simply suggested that it was to fulfil the course aims, objectives and work requirements for their high school subject.

4 Four of the outdoor education co-ordinators used a standardised risk communication approach across their school, regardless of program, venue or year level; this may have the benefit of consistent messages, or alternatively, the risk of people skipping over key information when they are very familiar with the content and/or layout.

5 Most programs documented specific risks that may be encountered, with some providing broad statements such as 'programmed activities involve an element of risk'.

6 All co-ordinators provided their risk communication in English only, even though one school had 60 per cent of its population originating from a Chinese background. This may be problematic for parents who either do not read English well, or at a sufficient level to make an informed decision.

7 The dominant discourse about risk seemed to imply that risk is 'real' and therefore can be managed in an objective and rational way.

8 By contrast, three coordinators used the term safe in their risk communication strategies. However given that *safe* may be defined as 'free from hurt, injury, danger or risk' (Macquarie Essential Dictionary 1999, p. 700) it may be contradictory to suggest that a program is safe, when risk is an often accepted aspect of an outdoor education program.

Practical applications for risk communicators

To develop practical strategies for risk communication a few others points need to be considered. There are numerous approaches available to risk communicators to help them assess and evaluate risk perception.

One practice is to compare risks to assist the public put these risks in 'perspective' (Slovic, Kraus, & Covello 1990). This has also been employed in the outdoor education literature when attempting to show the relative safety of outdoor education activities compared to other activities, such as driving and school yard activities (Bailie 2007). However, several scholars have urged caution in the use of risk comparisons (Slovic et al 1990) because while two hazard sources may have similar probabilities, they may indeed have very different qualitative characteristics, for example, comparing the risk of driving with that of a child's compulsory participation in a white-water rafting program in a remote setting. The qualitative characteristics of the hazards are quite different for these two activities, while driving is familiar, generally controllable and voluntary; white-water rafting may be unfamiliar, compulsory and the environment can be quite uncontrollable.

Message maps have also been used to help organise and communicate complex information. This method involves distilling information into easily understood messages conveyed in a maximum of three sentences per 'message'. To facilitate maximum understanding the messages are written at a primary school level (US Department of Health and Human Services 2006). Currently in Victoria, there is no formally adopted process/template for communicating risk to parents.

The review of relevant literature has highlighted the complexity of designing effective risk communication where the end result is someone who, with the new information they now have, can make a truly informed decision about the relevant risks. However, the difficulty of achieving this can be seen with the popularity of the 'deficit' model of risk communication, where among other characteristics, communication is essentially one-way and the communicator is positioned as the 'expert' imparting knowledge on the passive receiver. Factors to consider include understanding how different people perceive risk, the importance of trust, language use specifically surrounding the word 'risk' and the importance of understanding the benefits that may come with accepting the risk.

Based upon these points, the literature review and the research summarised here, the following are suggestions for implementing effective risk communication strategies as part of the overall risk management process. As noted in ISO 31000, 'communication and consultation with internal and external stakeholders should take place during all stages of the risk management process' (p. 14) and thus should not only occur as a pre-event or pre-program strategy, but must be part of the overall trust and relationship building process.

Communication methods

Use as many channels of communication as possible – these could include websites, photographs, personal contact, Google Earth, videos. Having multiple means of communication which can be accessed at different times and in different places will more accurately represent the actual program and the most anticipated and likely prevalent conditions. This will make it possible for the parents to interact with multiple types of images, as opposed to only having text on a page.

Listen well

Invite and provide multiple means for parents to ask questions. Is it clear that the coordinator is accessible and welcomes questions? How can you develop a relationship where dialogue is encouraged? Do not assume that parents are not interested if they do not contact you.

Competence

Avoid the use of jargon and other expert language. Communicate risk in a way that is clear, fosters understanding for people who may have no knowledge of outdoor education and which does not undermine the knowledge that some parents may have. For example, if you have students who have been on three of your programs before, design your risk communications in a way that respects and draws upon the increased knowledge level of your parents, but does not omit core messages.

Inclusiveness

Ensure that you are able to communicate with all of your parents. Are there non-English speakers or parents who may not be able to read? All parents, regardless of their speaking or reading ability will be required to provide informed consent. Look at your parent population and consider if your school needs to alter its current delivery method for communicating information. The multiple channels of communication will also support this.

Know what the benefits are

Being able to demonstrate the benefits of a program or activity will help balance the overall risk communication process. This is achievable through regular evaluation of program outcomes against the objectives, as well as through being engaged in broader industry research on the benefits of your program. (Refer also to Chapter 7 on program evaluation in this book).

Acknowledge uncertainty

Be wary of stating your programs are 'safe' (refer also to Chapter 3 on the legal context in this book) or of falling into the 'telling them what they want to hear' trap. Honesty is vital. Do you have an adequate response to a parent who asks you 'Will my child be safe?' As is evident from the research on risk perception, people are generally willing to accept the risks if they are clear and agree with what benefits are likely to be gained in return. Have you or your school/organisation clearly thought about what your outdoor program achieves, can you demonstrate what it achieves through evaluations and can you communicate this in a consistent, confident manner?

Conclusion

In order to continue to provide outdoor education opportunities for young people in an increasingly 'blamist' society, risk communication must be treated as a high priority amongst all involved in the planning and approval of such programs. Although this may be complex and time consuming, the end result will hopefully be a parent who, based on the information they have, can make a conscious decision weighing the costs and benefits of their child's participation against the costs and benefits of them not participating.

Points for action for practitioners

- Sit down with key stakeholders within your school/organisation and discuss why your program exists, what it is trying to achieve in terms of benefits and what the foreseeable risks are, considering the perception of risk.
- Invite some parents who are both advocates and critics of your programs to engage in a discussion about how they feel they could be better informed about the risks and benefits of your program.
- Swap your risk communication with another similar program/school and do a peer analysis; it is cheaper than an external consultant and a great way of finding out what you do well and how you can improve.

Further questions

- Conduct a short analysis of the risk communication your school/ organisation has in place by using some of the main themes of this chapter as your benchmark.

- Do an internet search of similar organisations/schools and review their risk communication for ideas and suggestions as to how to improve yours.

References and further resources

References

Adler, PS & Kranowitz, JL 2005. *A Primer on Perceptions of Risk, Risk Communication and Building Trust*. The Keystone Centre, CO.

Ajango, D 2005. *Lessons Learned II – Using Case Studies and History to Improve Safety Education*. Watchmaker, Palm Springs, CA.

Bailie, M 2007. 'And by comparison'. Retrieved 30 March 2007 from http://www.aals.org.uk/guidance_details.php/pArticleHeadingID=144.

Beck, U 1992. *Risk Society*. Sage, London.

Calman, KC 2002. 'Communication of risk: choice, consent and trust'. *The Lancet*, vol. 360, no. 9237, pp. 160-8.

Covello, V & Sandman, PM 2001. 'Risk communication: evolution and revolution' in A Wolbarst (ed), *Solutions to an Environment in Peril*. John Hopkins University Press, Baltimore, pp. 164-78.

Covello, VT, Sandman, P & Slovic, P 1988. *Risk Communication, Risk Statistics and Risk Comparisons: A Manual for Plant Managers*. Chemical Manufacturers Association, Washington, DC.

Dallat, CE 2009. 'Communicating risks with parents; exploring the methods and beliefs of outdoor education coordinators in Victoria'. *Australian Journal of Outdoor Education*, vol. 13, no. 3, pp. 3-15.

DEECD 2006. 'Schools reference guide: student safety and risk management'. Department of Education and Early Childhood Development. Retrieved 12 December 2006, from <http://www.education.vic.gov.au/management/governance/referenceguide/default.htm>.

Delbridge, A, Bernard, J, Blair, D, Butler, S, Peters, P & Yallop, C (eds) 2003. *Macquarie: Australia's National Dictionary* 3rd edn. The Macquarie Library, Sydney.

Fischhoff, B 1995. 'Risk perception and communication unplugged: twenty years of progress'. *Risk Analysis*. vol. 15, no. 2, pp. 137-45.

Holden, S 2002. 'Coroners, excursions and duty of care'. *Educare News*, vol. 130, pp. 24-5.

Irwin, A. (1995). *Citizen Science*. Routledge, London.

Macquarie Essential Dictionary 1999. The Macquarie Library, Sydney

National Research Council 1989. *Improving Risk Communication*. National Academy Press, Washington, DC.

Otway, H 1992. 'Public wisdom, expert fallibility: toward a contextual theory of risk' in S Krimsky & D Golding *Social Theories of Risk*. Praeger, Westport, CT, pp. 215-22.

Otway, H & Wynne, B 1989. 'Risk communication: paradigm and paradox'. *Risk Analysis*. vol. 9, no. 2, pp. 141-5.

Royal Academy of Engineering 2002. *The Societal Aspects of Risk*. Westminster, London.

Royal Society 1992. *Risk: Analysis, Perception and Management*. Report of the Royal Society Study Group, London.

Sandman, P 1987. 'Risk communication: facing public outrage'. *EPA Journal*, vol. 13, no. 9, pp. 21–2.

SASNZ 2009. *AS/NZS ISO 31000 Risk Management – Principles and Guidelines*. Standards Australia and Standards New Zealand, Sydney, NSW.

Slovic, P 1987. 'Perception of risk'. *Science*. vol. 2, no. 36, pp. 280–5.

Slovic, P 1992. 'Perception of risk: reflections on the psychometric paradigm' in S Krimsky & D Golding (eds) *Social Theories of Risk*. Praeger, New York, pp. 117–52.

Slovic, P, Kraus, N & Covello, VT 1990. 'What should we know about making risk comparisons?'. *Risk Analysis*. vol. 10, no. 3, pp. 389–92.

Stewart, D 2000. 'A preventive risk management perspective'. *International Journal of Educational Reform*, vol. 9, no. 4, pp. 342–8.

University of Leicester Department of Criminology 2005. *Module 2 – Managing Risk and Crisis*. University of Leicester, Leicester, UK.

US Department of Health and Human Services 2006. 'Pandemic influenza pre-event message maps'. Retrieved 7 January 2007 from http://www.pandemicflu.gov/news/pre_event_maps.pdf.

US Public Health Service 1995. 'Risk communication: working with individuals and communities to weigh the odds'. Retrieved 12 December 2006 from http://odphp.osophs.dhhs.gov/pubs/prevrpt/archives/95m1:htm/

Wynne, B 1992. 'Risk and social learning: reification to engagement' in S Krimsky & D Golding. *Social Theories of Risk* (pp. 275–301). Praeger, Westport, CT, pp. 275–301.

Zink, R & Leberman, S 2001. 'Risking a debate – redefining risk and risk management: a New Zealand case study'. *The Journal of Experiential Education*, vol. 24, no. 1, pp. 50–7.

Further resources

O'Neill, P 2004. 'Developing a risk communication model to encourage community safety from natural hazards'. *4th NSW Safe Communities Symposium*. Retrieved from http://www.ses.nsw.gov.au/multiversions/2304/FileName/Developing_a_risk_communication_model.pdf.

Peter M. Sandman Risk Communication Website <http://www.psandman.com/>.

World Health Organization, Risk Communication and Food Safety http://www.who.int/foodsafety/micro/riskcommunication/en/.

Technology, risk and outdoor programming

James T. Neill and Tonia L. Gray

If there is technological advance without social advance, there is, almost automatically, an increase in human misery.

Michael Harrington

We are stuck with technology when what we really want is just stuff that works.

Douglas Adams, *The Salmon of Doubt* (2002)

The first rule of any technology used in a business is that automation applied to an efficient operation will magnify the efficiency. The second is that automation applied to an inefficient operation will magnify the inefficiency.

Bill Gates

FOCUS QUESTIONS

1   What goes into your backpack for an outdoor trip? What stays out? How do you decide? Why?
2   In the pursuit of safety and risk management through technological aid are we losing our independence and connection with the outdoors?
3   Are modern day 'adventurers' over-reliant on 'gadgets' and 'gizmos' to buffer their inadequacies or for legal requirements?
4   Are modern electronic devices innocuous or intrusive?
5   What technologies can be used to help administer, operate and market outdoor programs?

CASE STUDY ONE & TWO

Modern communication technologies provide a major boost to rescue efforts. However, over-reliance on such technologies and under-reliance on prior planning, preparation and contingency planning is creating a new set of problems. When would you use a personal rescue beacon? Consider the following two scenarios.

1 'Tourists found thanks to beacons'

The hiring of a Personal Locator Beacon (PLB) from the Snowy Region Visitor Centre in Jindabyne was crucial in the quick rescue of a group of Victorian Scouts over the weekend.

The group, aged from 11 to 14 years and their leader and one parent, hired the beacon on Friday before taking off for a mountain bike trek on the Saturday.

Poorly prepared for the trek, they had not packed suitable cold weather clothing, a map, a compass or emergency camping equipment.

They set out from Dead Horse Gap on mountain bikes with the aim of making it to the Pinch in one day. A wrong turn saw the group lost near the Tin Mines Trail and the Jacob's river.

Inspector Peter Rooney from Cooma Police Station said police received notification from Australian Marine Search and Rescue (AMSR) that the beacon had been activated.

'They (AMSR) dispatched a fixed wing aircraft with infra red capabilities and they quickly located the group. The aircraft flew over the group until the emergency personnel could reach them at around 5.30 am.

No one was injured but the temperature was down to 6 degrees.'

Manager for Business and Tourism at the Snowy Region Visitor Centre Steve Redden reminded people using the Kosciuszko National Park these summer holidays to always be prepared for changes in conditions.

The beacons are available for hire at a cost of $20 for a two-week period and can be collected from NPWS offices in Jindabyne, Khancoban, Tumut or Perisher.

The devices are not a GPS though and all users should carry a readable and current topographic map as well. This was the second activation of a PLB since they were introduced into the area before winter.

In a third incident, yesterday morning a group of schoolgirls hiking near Mount Twynam activated their PLB.

NSW Police said at 6.00 am the group became disoriented due to fog while walking towards Guthega.

The SouthCare Helicopter responded but there were no injuries and although worried, the group had not become lost (*Summit Sun*, 10 December 2009).

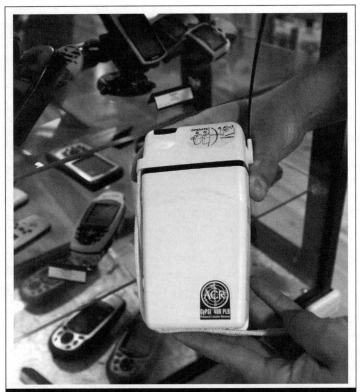

Figure 9.1 A Personal Locator Beacon
(*Source:* AP Image/Ted S. Warren)

2 'Free EPIRBS save lives'

The free Person Locator Beacons commonly known as EPIRBs (Emergency Position Indicating Radio Beacon) service, in the Blue Mountains, instituted by Benbro Electronics, in cooperation with the Police Rescue Service and the NSW National Parks and Wildlife Service, is proving a great success and may have saved a life, while assisting the speedy rescue of two other bushwalkers, who also felt that they were in imminent danger.

Since the launch of the free-loan EPIRBs, in October last year, more than 150 bushwalkers have taken advantage of the pocket-sized emergency beacons, which can alert authorities to their position to within fifty metres when activated, even in remote areas. During the peak bushwalking season, up to 15 beacons were lent out every weekend. The EPIRBs were purchased and donated by Benbro Electronics, whose Technical Director John Bennett OAM is himself an avid bushwalker and canyoner. He had become concerned after a number of deaths in the Blue Mountains, when people had either become lost or were injured in falls. Two of the recent rescues facilitated by the loaned EPIRBs involved serious injuries and, in one case, the walker could have died if he had not been lifted out quickly. In another, 33 school students from a Blue Mountains college had to be led out of the wilderness when one of their number suffered an injured leg and was evacuated via police helicopter.

The EPIRBs are available to bushwalkers who register their trip intentions at either the National Parks and Wildlife centre at Blackheath during office hours or the 24-hour police stations at Springwood and Katoomba after hours.

John Bennett, the originator of the scheme, stressed that the EPIRBs were not intended to replace good preparations. He said that they are merely a backup, in case trouble is encountered. He added: 'No bushwalker, whether experienced or not, should ever venture into the Australian bush without an Emergency Beacon, a map, a compass and the ability to use them'. (BENBRO)

CASE STUDY THREE

Outdoor activity and safety equipment helps to enable us to participate in a wide variety of activities. However, every activity and piece of equipment carries negative risk (e.g. of harm) as well as positive risk (e.g. of enjoyment). Even safety equipment itself can be dangerous, as the following example shows.

3 'Boy's death sparks trampoline warning', ABC News, Friday 6 August 2010

A Hobart coroner has warned parents to position trampolines free from obstructions after a five-year-old boy accidentally hanged himself.

Blair Anthony Hepburn died of asphyxia in his New Norfolk backyard in July 2010. He had been playing on a trampoline positioned under a clothesline.

Coroner Chris Webster says the child was wearing a bicycle helmet and the helmet's chin strap got caught on one of the struts of the clothesline.

The child's father immediately ran outside and lifted his son down but it was too late.

Coroner Webster says it seems the trampoline had been moved underneath the clothesline to utilise space in the Hepburns' backyard.

He says the death is the result of a tragic accident and he has recommended trampolines not be put under clotheslines, trees or similar obstructions (ABC News, 2010).

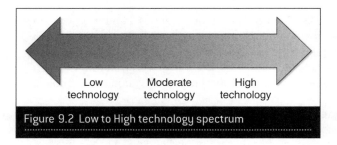

Figure 9.2 Low to High technology spectrum

Introduction

> [We] travel to access points in cars or buses, we have planned our route using topographic maps and guide books, we carry a lightweight pack with a mixture of freeze-dried and fresh foods to be cooked on our stove followed by a sleep on a self-inflating mattress within a waterproof and breathable tent or bivvy. But when does more technology become too much technology? Is it possible that for some people the only purpose for outdoors is a place to use their latest technological toy? Dickson (2004 p. 50)

This chapter discusses benefits and pitfalls of technological and communication devices in outdoor activities and programs. Technological advancement is moving rapidly and includes gear such as clothing, footwear or outdoor activity equipment and mobile devices such as Emergency Position Indicating Radio Beacons (EPIRB), satellite phones, mobile phones, Global Positioning Systems (GPS), laptops, notebooks, tablets and smart phones. Look down a trip gear list or a pre-departure checklist and you will see a myriad of technology. (For example, see this Stanford University Wilderness Backpacking Gear List: <http://www.stanford.edu/class/ges7/cgi-bin/drupal/students/gear_list>.)

What goes into your backpack for an outdoor trip? What stays out? How do you decide? Why? Some people revel in taking as little gear as possible – whilst others love taking lots of high-tech gear, clothes and devices – and many of us find ourselves somewhere in between. Take a moment to consider where your personal preference lies on the spectrum in Figure 9.2. Do you prefer minimal and basic gear or do you prefer having specialised high technology equipment and sophisticated mobile devices? What about your friends or colleagues, what do they think? You could ask a group this question and invite them to line up to indicate their personal preference, and ask them to explain why, particularly those people at the extremes.

Technology has a complex relationship with outdoor experience programs. On the one hand, coping with the relative absence of technology is one of the hallmarks of outdoor and experiential programs. Yet, because of the relative absence or deprivation of typical twenty-first century daily life technologies (such as houses, hot water, refrigerators, televisions, air-conditioners, cars, desktop computers), the technology that is used in outdoor and experiential programs is minimal but critical (e.g. in abseiling and climbing activities one relies on a rope as a life line, in emergency situations a mobile telecommunication device could also be a lifeline). Outdoor programs frequently rely on quite sophisticated technology, although this is often 'behind the scenes' and in many cases is intentionally hidden beyond participant awareness (e.g. instructors might keep two-way radios hidden, roads might be removed from maps and participants probably do not realise that the area has been well-reconnoitred).

Consider the implications for participants' experiences and likely program impacts when we approach, for example, cross-country navigation with either: a) a hand-held GPS, b) a map and compass or c) no artificial navigation aids (e.g. relying on memory, Sun/Moon/starts and topography)? How might the choice of technology influence the experience? On what basis should we be choosing which technologies to take and not to take? Should everyone carry a personal locating beacon? Should mobile phones be encouraged or discouraged on an expedition? Should students be engaged in electronic social networking activities while on an outdoor program? Should camping and wilderness areas provide wifi access? Should climbing routes be bolted (Kennedy, 1989, 1990 as cited in Priest & Gass 2005)? Or should we be focusing on providing minimal technology experiences in order to help people learn to live independently, without modern housing, consumer goods and electronic gadgetry?

Such questions and many more arise from examining the uneasy relationship between the outdoors and technology. The reader is warned that there are few straightforward answers – an open mind is recommended. The best answers are likely to vary widely depending on the specific circumstances. Technology is slippery and ever evolving, continuing to offer fascinating opportunities, challenges, possibilities and dilemmas and critically, for this chapter, technology presents a range of risks for positive and negative outcomes of outdoor-experience programs.

What is technology?

Technology is artificial aids or tools which augment or facilitate human functioning – or more simply 'technology is how people modify the natural world to suit their own purposes' (The International Technology Education Association, ITEA 2007, p. 2). It is derived from the Greek word *techne*, meaning art or artifice or craft. Technology means the act of making or crafting, but more generally it refers to 'the diverse collection of processes and knowledge that people use to extend human abilities and to satisfy human needs and wants' (ITEA, p. 2).

Evolution of technology

> Technology has been going on since humans first formed a blade from a piece of flint, harnessed fire, or dragged a sharp stick across the ground to create a furrow for planting seeds, but today exists to a degree unprecedented in history. (ITEA 2007, p. 2)

> Every advance in civilization has been denounced as unnatural while it was recent. (Bertrand Russell)

Technology, arguably, distinguishes humans. Or does it? Beavers build dams. Birds build nests. Wombats burrow holes. Our ancestors sharpened sticks, developed fire-lighting techniques, made crafts from earth, bones and skins and created language. Modern humans make post-industrial cities and mobile digital aids. All of these are survival-enhancing actions via 'artificial' modification of the natural environment.

Human technology is rapidly changing and is increasingly ubiquitous, affording many obvious survival advantages – we generally live in better buildings, drive better cars and use better computers than our predecessors. But at what cost have we achieved such gains? Have our cultural technologies outpaced our genetic adaptation? Have we thrown out the baby (heart and soul) with the bathwater (discomforts of subsistence living)? Should outdoor programs concentrate on connecting people with nature rather than technology? Or is this a false dichotomy? Can there be a symbiosis between low and high technology, risk and meaningful outdoor programming (Neill 2010)?

Evolution of indoors

Life evolved outdoors. Humans subsequently developed technologies for creating dwellings with walls and doors, leading to a distinction between indoors and outdoors. In 2010 more than 50 per cent of the human population lived in urban areas. In 1800 three per cent lived in urban areas, in 1900 14 per cent, in 1950 30 per cent and in 2050 it is estimated to be 70 per cent (Population Reference Bureau 2010). We are now witnessing generations of people being brought up almost entirely indoors and in artificially constructed outdoor urban environments, surrounded by and immersed in modern technology. Has this happened too rapidly for our genetic evolution? At least a significant part of us is wild animal and benefits physically and psychological from engaging in natural environments with a relative absence of technology. Nevertheless, unless we go fully naked, there is always some technology involved in mediating human experiences of the outdoors.

Table 9.1 Reasons for using technology in the outdoors

Reasons for using technology in the outdoors
Comfort (e.g. sunglasses, clothing)
Safety (e.g. altimeter, rope, first aid kit, mobile communication)
Protection (e.g. clothing, helmets)
Food preparation (e.g. utensils, stove)
Water storage (e.g. bottles, backpack systems)
Transport and area access (e.g. plane, vehicle, helicopter)
Outdoor activity equipment (e.g. canoe, skis)
Navigation (e.g. map, compass, GPS)
Interest, education and entertainment (e.g. books, activities, games)
Recording, reflecting and sharing (e.g. journal, photos, audio, video)

Reasons for using technology in the outdoors

Technology and outdoor and experiential education 'are not unusual bed-fellows' (Dickson, 2004, p. 50). Ask yourself this question: Why do we use technology in the outdoors? Write down the reasons you can think of. Compare them to the reasons suggested in Table 9.1. This is a good exercise to do with a group of people so you can share your answers and look for underlying themes. For each piece of technology consider its risk implications – how could it decrease or increase the likelihood of negative and positive outcomes? What alternative technologies could be used and how would this impact on the risk profile? Also consider the reliability of each of the technologies? How likely is it for each of the technologies to be misused or to fail in such a way as to affect outcomes of value?

Reasons for *not* using technology in the outdoors

> Technology . . . the knack of so arranging the world that we don't have to experience it. (Max Frisch)

The poignant question 'should outdoor programs concentrate on connecting people with nature rather than technology?' was raised earlier in this chapter. 'Purists' in outdoor and experiential education vehemently argue that technology usage in the outdoors is an impost on the rawness, simplicity and naturalness of experience. Given this stance, a paradox exists between the 'primitive' nature of being in the wild places and the use of advanced technology to explore and interpret such places. From this point of view, embracing innovations in communication equipment and devices

---

'Tired from a hike? Rescuers fear Yuppie 911'

FRESNO, Calif. — Last month two men and their teenage sons tackled one of the world's most unforgiving summertime hikes, the Grand Canyon's parched and searing Royal Arch Loop. Along with bedrolls and freeze-dried food, the inexperienced backpackers carried a personal locator beacon — just in case.

In the span of three days, the group pushed the panic button three times, mobilising helicopters for dangerous, lifesaving rescues inside the steep canyon walls.

What was the emergency? The water they had found to quench their thirst 'tasted salty'.

If they had not been toting the device that works like Onstar for hikers, 'we would have never attempted this hike', one of them said after the third rescue crew forced them to board their chopper. It's a growing problem facing the men and women who risk their lives when they believe others are in danger of losing theirs.

Technology has made calling for help instantaneous even in the most remote places. Because would-be adventurers can send GPS coordinates to rescuers with the touch of a button, some are exploring terrain they do not have the experience, knowledge or endurance to tackle. (Associated Press 2010)

Figure 9.3 Overdependency on technology

---

barricades 'from the very place, the outdoors, that we have chosen to be in' (Dickson 2004, p. 48).

According to the purist perspective, permitting the adoption of mobile and satellite phones, Global Positioning Systems (GPS) and other similar devices into our fieldwork, gives permission for another artificial layer of 'perceived' comfort creeps into the experience. Participants can become overly reliant on these external technologies rather than developing and refining their own innate judgment and skills. The goals of outdoor programs are generally to develop life-long skills, not to become wedded to technology as a quick-fix answer. How many rescue helicopters have responded to an Emergency Position Indicating Radio Beacon (EPIRB) being prematurely activated? People tend to call for help as a knee-jerk reaction to being unsure of their location or when facing inclement weather. In most instances, these calls are proven futile and costly to the taxpayer (see Figure 9.3).

Incorporating technology into wild and remote places creates an additional 'layer' of alienation or disconnect, from nature. Dickson (2004) cautions 'in the name of safety and risk management, we are losing interaction and connection with the outdoors as well as the "venture" that makes for an outdoor adventure' (p. 48). The word 'adventure' is derived from *ad venio* meaning 'whatever comes' (Zweig 1974) and this includes uncertainty in outcomes (Cline 2003). If leaders in outdoor and experiential learning 'depend upon environments to be controlled, with high-tech clothing and equipment as well as communication devices to direct and save us, then we are in jeopardy of totally losing any sense of adventure and of losing the potential for interaction and connection with the natural world' (Dickson 2004, p. 53). Our affinity with nature and concomitant sense of place may be adversely affected by high tech gizmos and gadgets (Henderson & Frelke 2000).

Some wilderness philosophers go as far as advocating for the maintenance of wild places with minimal technological intrusion. Leo McAvoy's 'rescue-free wilderness' proposal advanced the somewhat radical perspective that there be areas of wilderness deemed rescue-free – where people go in at their own peril because no external rescue assistance will be provided (McAvoy 1990; McAvoy & Dustin 1981, 1983).

Given that at least some presence of technology in outdoor experiences is inevitable, it begs the question, 'What is the impact of technology on our outdoor experience?' Or as, as Dickson (2004, p. 51) muses 'does technology add to, subtract from, or is it neutral with respect to our experience of the outdoors?' Neill (2007, 2010), on the other hand, argues that technology versus outdoors is a false dichotomy (humans have always used technology in the outdoors) and that the uneasy philosophical tension between the outdoors and technology provides opportunities to provide programs which explore a spectrum of low, medium and high technology-based outdoor experiences.

For many participants who are technophiliacs or techno-addicts, disassociating or disengaging from technology can be as 'foreign' as going on the expedition itself. The disequilibrium and dissonance bought about by not being connected 24/7 to social networks such as Facebook, texting, emails, Twitter, blogs and so on can be challenging in and of itself, let alone dealing with the program, and is thus likely to contribute to issues such as homesickness (Rofe 2010). Technology advocates, on the other hand, argue for risk, safety, recreational and educational benefits which can be gained by using various technologies.

Types of technology in outdoor programming

Brainstorm a list of technologies that are used in the planning or delivery of outdoor programs. When you are done, compare your responses with the list in Table 9.2. Consider which of these technologies are you familiar and unfamiliar with.

Level of technology in outdoor programming

For any given need or function in outdoor experiences, there is a spectrum of applicable technologies, ranging from low to moderate to high. Low

Table 9.2 Technologies used in planning and conducting outdoor programs

Technology
Building & construction (e.g. admin, storage, preparation, training and accommodation facilities)
Powered travel (e.g. aeroplanes, trains, buses, motorised vehicles)
Trip reconnoitring (e.g. area information, maps, 3D virtual fly-through)
Hazard, risk and accident trends and statistics
Weather forecasting and live weather tracking
Global positioning system (GPS), route tracking, geotagging
Digital media (e.g., audio, photo and video recording and sharing)
Documentation (e.g., area, procedures, proformas, curriculum, web resources)
Internet-based development, storage and sharing of program information
Communications (e.g. phones, radios, location-tracking)
Research and evaluation (e.g. surveys, data, spreadsheets/databases, reports)
Outdoor gear, equipment and clothing (e.g. clothing, shelter, food, cooking and specialist gear for outdoor activities such as hiking, climbing, and paddling)
Medical and first-aid (e.g. pharmaceuticals, first aid kits, splints, stretchers)
Web 2.0 technologies (e.g. office tools, social media, social networking, blogging, micro-blogging, wikis, VoIP, tagging, rss, podcasting, vodcasting and other interactive technologies for collaborative content creation, sharing and re-mixing)
Emerging technologies (e.g. smart phones/clothing/gear, mobile power charging, wifi mesh, biofeedback, augmented realities, virtual technologies, robot teachers)

Partially based on Boyle (2008a, 2008b) and Dingle (2004).

technologies use relatively simple, primitive tools (e.g. pre 1900s). Moderate technologies use commonly available, everyday tools (e.g. pre 1990s). High technologies involve specialised gear, artificial environments and digital technologies (e.g. post 1990s). Table 9.3 provides relevant examples of low, moderate and high outdoor activities.

Technology, risk and safety

The use of technology in the outdoors, ideally, would be judicious in order to promote positive risk and decrease negative risk (Neill 2003). But when introducing any technology we should also consider potential decreases in positive risk and increases in negative risk. Consider the case, for example, in Figure 9.4. It seems the man and his friends falsely assumed that

Table 9.3 Examples of low, moderate and high outdoor activities

Activity	Low	Moderate	High
Navigation	Mud map, sextant	Map and compass	GPS
Hiking footwear	Hand-made sandals	Sneakers	Boots with crampons
Fire-lighting and cooking	Flint, rocks, sticks, earth	Safety matches and metal pots	Auto-igniting pressurised liquid fuel stove
Lighting	Fire	Hand-held, battery powered torches/ flashlights	Rechargeable LEQ and halogen head-torches
Water expedition	Self-made raft	Wooden or fibreglass Canadian canoe	Plastic, kevlar or carbon fibre kayak
Rock-climbing	Free climbing on outdoor wall	Manual belay and harness using self-placed anchors and protection	Auto-belay via bolts on indoor wall
Camping	Wrap in a blanket	Sleeping bag and bivouac	Tent

'Man dies in abseiling fall from bridge'

A 24-year-old man has died while abseiling from a bridge north of Alice Springs. Police said they were called to the Geoff Moss Bridge about five kilometres from Alice Springs at 8.45pm (CST) on Saturday.

It was believed the victim was abseiling from the bridge with friends when his harness flipped upside down.

The man fell out of the harness onto rocks below, resulting in severe head injuries.

"Bystanders attempted to perform first aid on the man, however were unsuccessful and the man died at the scene," NT Police said in a statement on Sunday.

Police were not treating the incident as suspicious, but said it highlighted the dangers associated with this type of activity.

"Abseiling from height is a dangerous activity at any time and must be conducted with a great deal of care, preferably with professional guidance," NT duty superintendent Robert Burgoyne said in the statement.

"Correct safety precautions are essential, especially at night." (AAP 2010, 14 November 2010, 2.19 pm)

Figure 9.4 Example of outdoor fatality involving equipment

Table 9.4 Positive and negative effects of technology on positive and negative risk in outdoor programs

Type of technology effect	Type of risk	
	Negative	Positive
Negative	Negative risk increases e.g. taking more gear on a hiking trip leads to an increased pack-weight leading to greater risk of injury	Positive risk decreases e.g. taking a smart phone on a hiking trip creates distraction from getting to know self, other people in the group and the environment
Positive	Negative risk decreases e.g. access to weather forecasts helps to plan activities and to avoid high risk activities in poor weather conditions	Positive risk increases e.g. asking a group member to read each morning from a book of inspiring quotes could help to facilitate personal development

the harness would be sufficient to prevent him from the negative risk of falling.

The potential positive and negative consequences of using and not using various low, medium and high technologies in the outdoors should be considered in light of the program's aims and objectives. One solution is unlikely to fit all. Practical examples of technology positive and negative impacts of technologies on positive and negative risk in the outdoors are provided in Table 9.4.

Other case studies

Case study: 'Sydney to Hobart 1998'. The media enthusiastically reports on incidents in sport and recreational activities that occur due to technology failures, equipment mishaps or a combination of both. In the Sydney to Hobart Yacht race in 1998 six people died due to miscommunication with weather tracking devices. From a technology standpoint, the Bureau of Meteorology was criticised for not doing more to alert the club of an upgraded forecast on the severe storm south of Eden the day before the fleet was due there.

Case study: 'Friend or Foe?' As a leader, have you ever had the serenity of the wilderness experience interrupted by a participant's mobile phone coming into service range and beeping madly and incessantly? This generally occurs while climbing a ridge line and getting closer to satellite reception. Some leaders would argue that the pristine, uncluttered and therapeutic

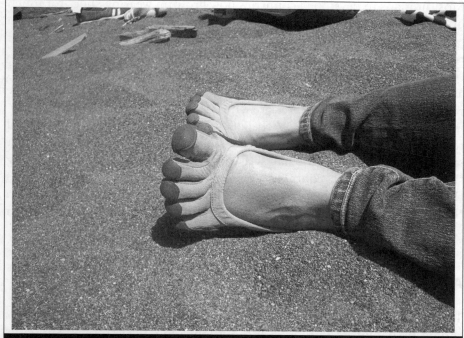

Figure 9.5 Technology and footwear. Vibram five fingers shoes are a minimalist footwear which offer a compromise between barefoot and shoes.
Source: Brett L 2006. <http://commons.wikimedia.org/wiki/File:Five_Fingers_shoes.jpg>. Copyright: Creative Commons Share-alike 2.0, <http://creativecommons.org/licenses/by-sa/2.0/deed.en>.

dimension of an expedition is ruined, stymied and adversely affected by the intrusion of technology into wild places. What are your thoughts?

Technology becoming passé

Almost any technology is at significant risk of becoming quickly outdated and obsolete. Some specific examples are chosen for exploration, with this caveat in mind.

Minimal footwear

An interesting debate is taking place among podiatrists, sport scientists, athletes, physiotherapists as well as people in the street about the relative merits and risks of barefoot versus shod walking and running (Figure 9.5).

Most humans in developed countries now grow up wearing shoes for much of the time and many adults rarely go without shoes. Shoes are a common piece of technology that we often take for granted. They provide a form of risk management to help prevent damage to the feet from abrasion and cutting and to provide cushioning impact for feet, ankles and knees. However, as anyone who has caught a shoe and twisted their ankle or had over-use running injuries might appreciate, shoes also carry negative risks (Lieberman, Venkadesan, Daoud & Werbel 2010; Wharburton 2001). In a maximal technology approach, a participant in the outdoors is often advised to get specialised boots for particular activities (e.g. hiking boots, rock-climbing shoes, river shoes). In contrast, a minimalist technology approach argues that humans are healthier barefoot, when their toes are free to move, when they are able to use a more natural gait and when they are in closer touch with their environment (Downey 2009).

Audio and video availability on mobile devices

There is considerable debate about the extent to which mobile devices should be permitted in indoor and outdoor school classrooms. Similarly, outdoor programs are continually morphing, rethinking and adapting to find an appropriate balance. Arguably, much of the decision-making regarding students' allowed use of mobile devices is based around fear and prevention of potentially adverse consequences of technology use (e.g. cyber bullying). However, many progressive technology users and educational technology experts advocate for allowing greater use of mobile devices within educational environments (e.g. a Sydney girls' school is trialling allowing students to call a friend during an exam). Mobile devices can increasingly perform a dazzling array of functions, for example accessing, storing, playing, recording and sharing audio and video files (see Table 9.5).

Location tracking

Personal satellite messenger and tracker

Low-cost devices (such as the SPOT Satellite Messenger and Personal Tracker) are now readily available with affordable subscription plans which allow emergency contact, help signalling, position tracking and messaging via the satellite network from almost anywhere in the world. The position tracking function can be used to automatically update one's geo location on Google Maps (e.g. <http://www.nzkayaker.com/map>). Some outdoor

Table 9.5 Possible approaches to one technology: podcasting in outdoor education

Recordings of student reflections: solo
Capturing a learning moment on the edge
Data collection – audio of birdsong, frog
Noises, waves, wind, storms etc.
Field lectures interpretive walk
Audio stimulus material for reflection and inspiration
Informational use of travel time

Source: <http://www.slideshare.net/digger_boyle/ technology-and-outdoor-ed-presentation/44>.

programs are using such satellite tracking technology to keep track not only of groups but also individuals (<http://au.findmespot.com/en/>, <http:// www.gpstrackersandmore.com/>, <http://www.globalcomsatphone.com/ spot/>, <http://www.findmespot.com/en/index.php?cid=101>, <http:// www.vehicle-tracking-gps.com/gps-monitoring-plans-goji.htm>).

Conclusion

Technology has entered our life at an unparalleled or unprecedented speed. Today, our experiences in outdoor and experiential education are 'fashioned' by layers of high-tech commodities and equipment. The pioneers in adventure education did not have the luxuries that we have at our fingertips. The old Dunlop volley shoes, pure wool knitted jumpers and rudimentary navigation devices have been replaced with the creature comforts of thermal underwear, Gortex jackets, state-of-the-art hiking boots and GPS navigation equipment. The rhetorical question remains – who gained the most out of the adventure?

References and further resources

References

AAP 2010. 'Man dies in abseiling fall from bridge'. *Sydney Morning Herald*. Retrieved 14 November 2010 from <http://news.smh.com.au/breaking-news-national/ man-dies-in-abseiling-fall-from-bridge-20101114–17shq.html>.
ABC News 2010, 'Boy's death sparks trampoline warning'. 6 August 2010. <http://www.abc.net.au/news/stories/2010/08/06/2975505.htm>.
Associated Press 2009. 'Tired from a hike? Rescuers fear Yuppie 911'. <http://www. msnbc.msn.com/id/33470581/ns/us_news-life>.

BENBRO (2010) <http://www.benbro.com.au/index.php?option=com_content& task=view&id=29&Itemid=37>. Accessed 25 Nov 2010.

Boyle, I 2008a. 'Technology in outdoor education'. Presentation to the Outdoor Recreation Industry Conference, Sydney, Australia. Retrieved from <http://www. slideshare.net/digger_boyle/technology-and-outdoor-ed-presentation>.

Boyle, I 2008b. 'Using information technology in the administration and delivery of outdoor education programs'. Presentation to the Outdoor Education Association of Queensland Conference, July. Retrieved from <http://www. slideshare.net/digger_boyle/utilising-information-technology-in-outoor-education-administration>.

Cline, PB 2003. 'Re-examining the risk paradox' in *Wilderness Risk Management Conference Proceedings, State College, PA*. Wilderness Risk Management Committee, Lander, WY, pp. 23–7.

Dickson, TJ 2004. 'If the outcome is predictable, is it an adventure? Being in, not barricaded from, the outdoors'. *World Leisure*, vol. 4, pp. 48–54.

Dingle, M 2004. 'The impact of technology on outdoor education'. Presentation at ACHPER Conference. Retrieved from <http://www.voea.vic.edu.au/events/pd/ presentations/The_Impact_of_Technology_on_Outdoor_Experience.ppt>.

Downey, G 2009. 'Lose your shoes: is barefoot better?'. *Neuroanthropology: For a Greater Understanding of the Encultured Brain and Body*. Retrieved from <http:// neuroanthropology.net/2009/07/26/lose-your-shoes-is-barefoot-better/>.

Henderson, KA & Frelke, CE 2000. 'Space as a vital dimension of leisure: the creation of place'. *World Leisure Journal*, vol. 42, no. 3, pp. 18–24.

International Technology Education Association 2007. *Standards for Technological Literacy*. Retrieved from <http://www.iteea.org/TAA/PDFs/xstnd.pdf>.

Lieberman, DE, Venkadesan, M, Daoud, AI & Werbel, WA 2010. Biomechanics of foot strikes and applications to running barefoot or in minimal footwear'. Retrieved from <http://barefootrunning.fas.harvard.edu/>.

McAvoy, L 1990. 'Rescue-free wilderness areas' in JC Miles & S Priest (eds) *Adventure Education*. Venture, State College, PA, pp. 335–43.

McAvoy, L & Dustin, D 1981. 'The right to risk in wilderness.' *Journal of Forestry*, vol. 79, no. 3, 150–2.

McAvoy, L & Dustin, D 1983. 'In search of balance: a no-rescue wilderness proposal'. *Western Wildlands*, vol. 9, no. 2, pp. 3–5.

Neill, JT 2003. 'Where has the adventure gone? Bringing risk back into the outdoors'. Keynote presentation at the Annual Outdoor Recreation Industry Council (ORIC) Conference, Olympic Park, Sydney, October, 2003. Retrieved from <http://wilderdom.com/abstracts/Neill2003WhereHasTheAdventureGone. htm>.

Neill, JT 2007. 'Technology and the outdoors: some experiential possibilities'. Presentation to the Outdoor Recreation Industry Conference, Sydney, Australia. Retrieved from <http://wilderdom.com/wiki/Technology_and_the_outdoors: Some_experiential_possibilities>.

Neill, JT 2010. 'Technology and outdoor education: some experiential possibilities'. Presentation to the 16th National Outdoor Education Conference, Fremantle, Western Australia, 10–13 January. Retrieved from <http://wilderdom.com/wiki/Neill_2010_Technology_and_outdoor_education: _Some_experiential_possibilities#Materials>.

Population Reference Bureau 2010. *Human Population: Urbanization*. Retrieved from <http://www.prb.org/Educators/TeachersGuides/HumanPopulation/Urbanization.aspx>.

Priest, S & Gass, M 2005. *Effective leadership in adventure programming* 2nd ed. Human Kinetics, Champaign, IL.

Rofe, S 2010. 'An investigation of a short-term outdoor education expedition's role in fostering resilience in young adolescence through a field-based case study'. unpublished honours thesis, University of South Australia.

Stonehouse, P 2007. 'Recording in the wilds: a reflection on research-technology needs on an expedition'. *Australian Journal of Outdoor Education*, vol. 11, no. 1, pp. 47–9.

Summit Sun 2009. 'Tourists found thanks to beacons'. *Summit Sun*, 10 Dec 2009.

Wharburton, M 2001. 'Barefoot running'. *Sportscience*, vol. 5, no. 3. Retrieved from <http://sportsci.org/jour/0103/mw.htm>.

Zweig, P 1974. *The Adventurer: The Fate of Adventure in the Western world*. Dent and Sons, London.

Further resources

Technology in outdoor education:
<http://www.slideshare.net/digger_boyle/utilising-information-technology-in-outoor-education-administration>
This presentation is narrated, it encompasses all uses of technology not just risk.
<http://www.slideshare.net/digger_boyle/technology-and-outdoor-ed-presentation>
000 preparedness what do you do when it goes wrong.
<http://www.slideshare.net/digger_boyle/emergency-preparation-in-outdoor-education>
YouTube videos can be directly embedded in a PowerPoint Presentation using an add-on.
River crossing: use of video to highlight river crossing hazards or protocols.
<http://www.youtube.com/watch?v=JlEll8chHZk>
<http://www.youtube.com/watch?v=l1yNaCFJZQk>
Highlighting rough terrain and talking about spotting during a bush walk
<http://www.youtube.com/watch?v=QNiY_UeucIc>
Using Memory Map 3D fly through to get a feel of terrain prior to a trip
<http://www.youtube.com/watch?v=8WF1SBXY4vw>
Cliff side management
<http://www.youtube.com/watch?v=3HQUIJdBPw0>
Video to show how to belay with a GriGri
<http://www.teachertube.com/members/viewVideo.php?video_id=120095&title=Belaying_with_a_GRI_GRI>
Prepare participants before they arrive with a video briefing. Some of the short clips above come from this larger video.
<http://www.teachertube.com/members/viewVideo.php?video_id=25010&title=Bushwalking_Preparation_Video_Apple_Tree_Flat>

Using VoiceThread to create a discussion around risk management. This VoiceThread is an example of how VoiceThread can be used. Students can type a response or add a voice to the slide.
http://voicethread.com/#u132978.b178277.i947728
Using VoiceThread to prepare students for an upcoming trip. How to pack a pack.
http://voicethread.com/#u132978.b537227.i2875717
How to poo in the woods: how to videos can be developed.
http://www.youtube.com/watch?v=z9xlK5yl5Po

Severe weather

Paul Colagiuri

Twenty years from now you will be more disappointed by the things that you didn't do than by the ones you did do.

So throw off the bowlines. Sail away from the safe harbour. Catch the trade winds in your sails. Explore. Dream. Discover.

Mark Twain

FOCUS QUESTIONS

1   How does weather impact on the benefits and dangers involved in conducting programs and activities outdoors?
2   How do outdoor organisations develop an understanding of the current and forecast weather conditions in the areas in which they are operating?
3   How do organisations communicate weather information with groups who may be spread across a wide and often remote area?
4   How do outdoor organisations use weather information, at all levels, to make decisions about the programs which they are designing and conducting?
5   How do individual leaders and practitioners in the outdoors respond to severe weather when they encounter it in the field?

CASE STUDY

From the *Pitt News*, the daily newspaper of Pittsburgh University

As editor of Accidents in North American Mountaineering since 1974, Williamson warned that bad preparation, not the mountain or the weather, causes deaths and accidents. "There's no such thing as bad weather," Williamson said. "It's weather. It's what you get." "The leading cause of accidents is trying to stick to a schedule and trying to please other people," he added. "You don't climb up something you can't climb down."

Introduction

Outdoor activities and programs, by their very nature, are outdoors and by being outdoors the weather will always be an integral part of the experience. They are at the mercy of nature. Sometimes the situation is immensely favourable and provides an amazing sunny day, with a perfect tide for a canoeing trip, or a cool clear day for hiking which ensures majestic views and panoramas. It is easy to reflect on these or similar days as being perfect, framing the outdoor experiences of our participants in the very best light. On other days, the weather can of course be most uncooperative. Managers of outdoor activities and programs can spend many late nights reorganising programs when the weather forecast, quite simply and rather unfortunately, is just not going to support the planned activities. Those same managers would no doubt also remember the immense feeling of achievement they see in the faces of participants who have 'survived' a few days hiking and camping in the rain. It becomes clear that weather, good or bad, should not be considered an inconvenience, but seen as an integral part of the very fabric that makes the outdoors such a powerful place for education, recreation and development.

We must of course recognise that different weather brings different risks. For example, the same bushwalk completed by the same group on two different days six months apart, often present two different cases for risk management. Certainly, there are common risks but as we apply dynamic risk assessment to each situation, different risks appear. A simple descent down a small rocky creek carries significantly more physical risk on a wet day than on a dry day. A long flat walk along a ridge top fire trail requires the management of some additional risks on a steaming hot summer's day as opposed to a cool clear day in winter.

It is hard to categorise what might be 'good' weather or 'bad' weather. We have learnt that weather means different things to different people.

Heavy rain in the lead up to a planned program might be problematic for a hiking trip with creeks flooding and restricting access or tracks becoming too slippery to safely traverse. The same rain might be a blessing to a kayaking program that may have been cancelled due to low water levels without the rain. Additionally, as explored further in Chapter 11, in societies where people live in built environments where the temperature and humidity is tightly controlled, an individual's ability to adapt to differences in weather may be limited, especially when compared to the professional who is regularly working in the outdoors in different environmental conditions. Further, differences in weather may add to the experience through challenging participants in areas such as equipment selection, waterproofing and packing of their equipment, route planning and group management. For this chapter, the focus is upon severe weather, a term that has become much more common in recent times.

When does weather become *severe weather* and for whom is the weather severe? There are many people who live and work in extreme environments, people around the world willingly ski in –25 degrees Celsius, while people on cattle properties in north and central Australia would think nothing of working outdoors in 35 degrees Celsius or more and with high humidity, yet this may not be appropriate for participants in optional recreational or educational outdoor activities.

Geoscience Australia considers severe weather as one of eight natural hazards, the others being bushfire, cyclone, earthquake, flood, landslide, tsunami and volcano, and further describes severe weather specifically as including intense low pressure systems, thunderstorms, lightning, hail, storm wind gusts and tornadoes (Geoscience Australia 2010). At a more practical level, the Australian Bureau of Meteorology (BOM) sets out criteria used in the issuing of severe weather warnings. Table 10.1 lists the various phenomena and the criteria used in the decision to issue a severe weather warning.

It becomes apparent that whilst the categorisation of severe weather and the criteria for the issuing of severe weather warnings are quite detailed and specific, the impact of that weather on people in the outdoors can vary greatly. Weather means different things to different people conducting different programs, with different objectives, in different locations, therefore the risks must be managed differently. Perhaps it is best to consider severe weather as weather with the potential to have a severe impact on the participants of specific outdoor programs and activities.

This chapter aims to outline ways in which organisations conducting outdoor programs and activities may use the risk management process to manage the unique risks that are created by the weather. In particular, the chapter will focus on severe weather events and explore ideas and methodologies for organisations to consider in the development of their own protocols.

Table 10.1 Criteria for issuing severe weather warnings

Phenomenon	Severe Thunderstorm Warning	Severe Weather Warning
Wind (gusts)	Gusts 90 km/h or more	Gusts 90 km/h or more
Wind (average)		Widespread winds over land of 63 km/h or more (gale force)
Tornado	All tornados	
Blizzard		Widespread blizzards in alpine areas
Flash floods	Heavy rainfall that is conducive to flash flooding or a reported flash flood	Heavy rainfall that is conducive to flash flooding or a reported flash flood
Large hail	Hail with diameter of at least 2 cm (size of $2 coin)	
Storm tide		Abnormally high tides caused by winds (expected to exceed highest astronomical tide)
Large waves		Unusually large surf waves expected to cause dangerous conditions on the coast (dependent on location – but generally surf exceeding 5 m, less in the tropics). Large surf is commonplace in South Australia, Victoria and Tasmania, so warnings are only issued there for extreme events.

Source: Bureau of Meteorology (2010b) Bureau of Meteorology: Severe Weather Warning Education.

Severe weather events and the outdoor industry

Severe weather events have now become an uneasy companion to accidents and incidents in the outdoors. Regrettably, almost every incident involving the outdoor industry reported in the Australian media has some connection to severe weather events such as high winds or flooding. This unfortunate association not only highlights the significance of severe weather as a risk in the outdoors but also the potential for public opinion to focus on the negative implications of weather on activities in the outdoors.

As a simple example, at the time of writing this piece, a Severe Weather Warning was in effect for 10 of the 15 forecast districts of the state of New South Wales, warning of locally damaging winds associated with a fast-moving cold front. It is perhaps hard to argue with the concerns of a parent for their child who might be on an outdoor program anywhere in that area. Particularly when the warning specifically states the following, which appears on every Severe Weather Warning issued: 'Emergency services advise you to keep clear of fallen power lines, stay indoors away from windows and keep children indoors.' (Severe Weather Warning issued by the BOM on 9 June 2010).

The challenge, of course, is to unpack the two situations: those weather conditions, severe or otherwise, that may require mitigation or even avoidance, and those situations that simply highlight the need for better preparation, communication and understanding.

Two recent situations help to highlight this point:

1 1 On 15 April 2008 a tragic incident occurred in New Zealand when a flooding canyon took the lives of six students and one teacher participating in an Outdoor Education program with their school. The Coronial enquiry highlights, amongst other things, issues relating to the collection of weather forecasts: the communication of this information with leaders in the field, and the use of this information in decisions about program changes. Every organisation in the industry should use this tragedy to review their own procedures for processing weather information and communicating it to the field (Devenport 2010).

2 In February 2009, in the days following the tragic Black Saturday bushfires in the state of Victoria in Australia, there were several days of high fire danger. On these days, a directive was issued by the Education Department in Victoria that no student from any school in the state should attend any camp or excursion on that day. Obviously a sound decision for those camps in bushfire-affected areas and bush locations, but hard to accept for those camps in urban areas or locations where the risks associated with bushfire were very low. This directive, along with many other cancelations of school camps in the ensuing period, had a significant negative impact on the industry.

Those working in the outdoors must recognise the unique challenge of both managing very real and significant physical risks associated with severe weather as well as managing the risk of loss of business and confidence that may occur with poor public perception of weather and its effects on the safe conduct of outdoor programs.

Managing risks associated with severe weather

A common military adage is that no battle plan ever survives actual contact with the enemy, highlighting the fact that no matter how much one plans any

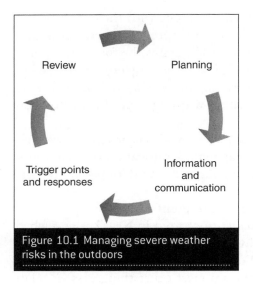

Figure 10.1 Managing severe weather risks in the outdoors

activity conducting it in a dynamic environment means that the environment, not your plans, will define much of the way in which that activity pans out. In order to effectively manage weather-related uncertainty in the outdoors, there are many areas that need to be addressed in the planning of activities, taking into account the dynamic nature of the outdoors.

As such, managing weather risks in the outdoors really should be a two-step process.

1 The potential impact of weather should be considered in the original development and risk management of any outdoor activity or program

2 The dynamic nature of weather should be factored in as an ongoing risk management process within the daily operation of the program.

The flowchart in Figure 10.1 and the following notes suggest some critical ways in which weather, severe or otherwise, should be integrated into the conduct of outdoor activities.

1 Planning

When considering what outdoor activities to engage in, at what time and in what place, it is critical to ask 'Why?'. If, for example, a family on a summer holiday chooses to hire sea kayaks for a leisurely paddle around the bay, then their experience and their aims and objectives for that activity would probably mean that they would cancel or postpone their trip in the event of rough seas and stormy weather. For the same outdoor activity, sea kayaking, in a different context, such as two young adventurous Australians seeking to cross the Tasman Sea, rough seas and stormy weather would be considered a given and in this context the uncertainties would need to be managed not simply avoided.

Having established the context as a guiding beacon – the planning of any outdoor activity obviously has to carefully consider the weather. The aims and objectives of the activity, the skill and experience level of the participants, the equipment to be used, the time of year, time of day and the local environment should all be considered in making a decision of what to do where to do it. Planning has to specifically consider the potential for severe weather events and has to make the distinction between what may just be inconvenient or uncomfortable as opposed to that which carries unacceptable physical risk that requires mitigation.

2 Information and communication

Gathering information should be considered an ongoing process, from collecting typical weather for that time of year as part of the planning process, to accessing the most current weather forecast before embarking, through to having access to current information, such as severe weather warnings, during the activity.

The internet has given us unprecedented access to weather information, it is now possible to view live radar images and river height gauges where once all we could do was wait for the hourly news and weather report. However, while the range and quality of information is vast, its effectiveness is only as good as our ability to access it or have it communicated to us while we are in a remote location. Other methods of information gathering should also be considered as an important way of seeing the whole picture. Local knowledge and experience is critical, particularly with conditions such as floods where historical situation-specific knowledge is often far more valuable than what may discovered on the internet. We must also integrate forecast information with what we are actually seeing on the ground. Weather observations are made at designated stations within forecast districts – these are usually located within towns in that area where most outdoor activities are conducted in the more remote parts of that area – and as such there can be subtle or even significant differences in the weather being encountered in the field away from the weather observation points.

As a coordinator of outdoor programs for many years I often find myself being asked over the radio 'What is the weather doing?' I stare into a computer screen and talk into a radio many kilometres away. Obviously, there is much that I can contribute with the vast amount of information I can access. However, the leader on the other end of that radio has much to contribute too, as they are looking at the sky, their campsite and their participants, and in the end they need to be making decisions based on their knowledge, skills,

Table 10.2 Examples of environmental trigger points and potential responses

Trigger point	Response
Temperature reaches 32 degrees	All bushwalks are scheduled for morning periods only
River height at gauge reaches 1.6 m	No river crossings to be conducted
Fire Danger Rating is listed as Severe (FDI 50–74)	All remote bushwalks are replaced with on site activities
Severe thunderstorm warning is issued for area being used	All groups move to pre-designated severe weather sites

experience and observations at that time, as well as the forecast information provided to them.

The next challenge, of course, is establishing a system to effectively communicate the available weather information with the people 'in the field' making decisions about where people go and what they do there. However, at the same time the leader in the field needs to feel confident and competent to make decisions when this information is not available, such as when the power is out, the communication system is down or they are out of radio or phone contact. This highlights the importance of training and development for outdoor leaders and to highlight the uncertainties involved with severe weather as an important part of their training.

As a further consideration, communications systems used in outdoor activities are often 'one way' – a satellite telephone or radio, for example, may often be kept switched off and stored in a dry bag and only activated to make contact with someone at 'base' for a scheduled call in or if assistance is required. This 'one way' system does limit the ability of that person at 'base' to pass on dynamic information, such as the issuing of a severe weather warning.

3 Trigger points and responses

In order to be able to effectively respond to the range of detailed and relevant weather information it is essential to have a clear plan in place that will determine the next steps. Trigger points are measurable aspects of weather that can be used to initiate certain actions and can be used to respond to any weather situation that has the potential to impact on the safety or outcomes of an outdoor program or activity, not just severe weather warnings. Table 10.2 lists a few examples of trigger points and responses.

Trigger points can be an effective way for organisations to pre-plan their responses to various weather events. These are also useful, as part of your risk communication, to inform the client about how you will aim to respond to the uncertainty of working in the outdoors (see also Chapter 8). Established relevant trigger points will be dependent on knowledge of the local conditions under different circumstances. Various considerations for trigger points are listed in the sections following on some specific weather situations.

Alternate plans should be established to provide a course of action to be enacted if trigger points are reached. For example, if a river height reached a certain level, and that was the trigger point to avoid a particular bushwalk route, then having another walk available that does not involve a river crossing is an effective alternative.

It is also important to plan ahead so that if a trigger point is reached and an alternate plan is needed, then it is possible to make that adjustment. For example, a group of canoeists half-way through a journey across a lake will have little opportunity to get off the water, if that is the response triggered by a severe thunderstorm warning. In this case the skills of the leaders and participants and equipment choice will be essential components for managing this situation.

4 Review

Obviously review is a critical part of all risk management, and especially important in the case of severe weather. The realisations of weather as compared to that which was forecast, the effect of river levels on various creek crossings and the way in which operations were able to be adapted to respond to a severe thunderstorm warning are all great things to be reviewed and added to the local knowledge bank for future programs or activities.

Severe weather events

There are many severe weather types that are identified as being particularly relevant to the conduct of activities in the outdoors including such things as severe wind, floods, extreme temperature, lightning strike, blizzards and bushfire. The following section seeks to guide the development of risk management strategies by organisations and individuals for outdoor activities in response to each of these severe weather events.

The problem with any severe weather event is that it may occur without warning. All people working in the outdoors need to be able respond to those events most likely to occur in their area of operations, with or without the availability of weather warnings, radar and communications with outside parties from their remote location.

1 Severe wind, severe thunderstorms and lightning

Severe wind can be associated with weather warnings issued in a number of situations including severe thunderstorm warnings, coastal and closed water wind warnings, gale warnings and severe weather warnings. Lightning as well as hail are often other factors associated in particular with severe thunderstorm warnings.

Wind is typically forecast and recorded based on average speed and the speed at which it gusts to. Wind speed and direction can vary greatly across any given area and be significantly affected by local topography. Where wind is forecast to average over 63km/h or to gust at over 90km/h, a severe weather warning noting dangerous winds is issued by the Australian Bureau of Meteorology (BOM). These warnings are issued and updated on the BOM website and are broadcast via local media outlets.

Planning

Wind and the severe weather warnings associated with it have the potential to impact significantly on outdoor programs and activities. Strong wind for water-based activities can separate participants, capsize craft and hamper recovery efforts and on land the risk of trees and branches falling is significantly increased.

Naturally, there are times of the year and times of the day when severe thunderstorms are more common and usually the chance of thunderstorms is forecast in advance of actual warnings being issued. However, we should always prepare for the possibility. As an example, in February 1999 a severe hailstorm struck the eastern suburbs of Sydney causing damage in the order of one billion Australian dollars. In a report on the Bureau of Meteorology's forecasting and warning performance, the following observations were made:

> The storm was highly unusual in meteorological terms. Not only did it produce some of the largest hail ever recorded in Sydney, but it occurred at a time of year when severe thunderstorms are normally rare and at a time of day when the probability of storms developing, or existing storms maintaining their intensity, is low . . . The meteorological indicators (observations, synoptic conditions, climatological record) did not exhibit the combination of background conditions which would normally be expected to lead to development of severe thunderstorms. (Director of Meteorology 2000)

As such, we must at all times have plans in place to act, should a warning come into place, or severe weather simply arrive without warning. Establishing designated severe weather sites within the area of an outdoor program is an excellent first step in responding to warnings of severe wind, for example, a clearing free of trees for a group to camp overnight, or a building where groups can move to take shelter during a storm. These sites should be pre-determined and outdoor activities planned in such a way that these sites can be accessed should they be needed.

Information and communication

Information on forecast winds and storms as well as the development of severe weather warnings is readily and clearly accessed via the BOM website. Observations in the field are critical also as often smaller storm cells affect areas outside the warning area and regularly winds are affected by local topography and conditions.

Communication is obviously a big consideration in this regard also, many severe weather warnings, particularly severe thunderstorm warnings, are issued in the afternoon and so a two-way system of communications is needed to be able to pass the information on to groups in the field. This two-way communication also enables local information to be passed back from the field so that it can also be disseminated to others in the local area.

Trigger points and responses

Often the issuing of severe weather warnings is an unfolding process, usually beginning with some reference in the daily forecast, followed by a general warning that becomes more and more specific as time unfolds. A sample severe thunderstorm warning graphic is given in Figure 10.2, outlining the warning area, the area under immediate threat and the location of the storm.

In establishing trigger points it must be considered how long the response will take to enact, in order to consider how early in the process the trigger should be set. If, for example, a number of groups were engaged in outdoor activities on the grounds of a base camp where the designated response to severe weather was to move indoors, then this can be enacted in a matter of minutes so the trigger could be the final detailed warning. For a group heading off on a multi-day hike into a remote area then the forecast of possible thunderstorms may be the trigger to alter the plan and make use of severe weather campsites regardless.

Review

The review of planned outdoor activities that are affected by severe weather warnings is critical in an ongoing approach to risk management. Many severe weather warnings never eventuate, but rather than simply being relieved, organisations should consider what would transpire if the weather reached its full potential. Review can also help to build local knowledge of how forecast weather translates in that particular environment, helping in the planning of future activities and the development of future trigger points and responses.

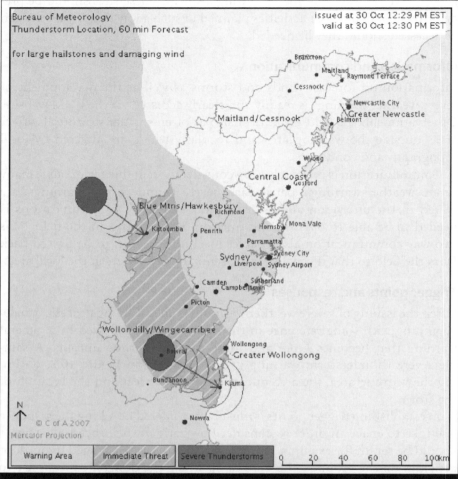

Figure 10.2 Sample detailed severe thunderstorm warning
Source: The Bureau of Meteorology (2010a) About graphical severe thunderstorm warnings in New South Wales.

2 Floods

Unquestionably, flooding impacts on outdoor activities and without sound risk management has the potential to cause significant harm. Flooded local creeks can isolate groups on bushwalks, flooded rivers can increase risks for canoeists, low lying campgrounds can flood and become inaccessible. These examples, along with many others, highlight the significant risks associated with flooding, some physical risks and some concerning the need to cancel trips if suitable alternatives are not considered. It should also be considered that in many cases, local flooding may bear little resemblance to the weather at a specific location, but may reflect the rainfall encountered higher upstream in a particular catchment area.

Flood warnings are usually issued for major river systems and often contain anticipated peak river heights and times based on recent rainfall and river activity. These warnings are directed towards townships and outlying settlements in flood-prone areas, not necessarily to people in the outdoors in more remote locations.

Planning

When planning outdoor activities and considering the impact of flooding, it is critical to consider the aims of that activity and the skill level of the participants. For example, many experienced kayakers will only paddle a particular river when it is in flood, while many school-based outdoor organisations will cancel water activities when river levels rise beyond their normal level.

It is essential to develop plans that allow alternatives should rivers or creeks begin to rise.

In June 2007, 12 students with two teachers completing a bushwalk in the Blue Mountains west of Sydney became isolated due to a swollen creek and activated a Personal Locater Beacon in order to be rescued. The following extract from local media provides an interesting perspective on the situation:

> weather forecasts and details of the group's walk had been sent in advance to police at Katoomba and to the NSW National Parks and Wildlife Service.
>
> "Neither of those groups advised us not to go, so we feel that we had all the preparations made," he told ABC radio.
>
> "We sent the information through on Thursday afternoon, just advising them of the walk to begin Friday, and maybe that timeline will prove to have been too short.
>
> "But neither group advised us not to go," he said.
>
> Police want to meet this week with the teachers who led the bushwalk in wet weather, saying they may have unnecessarily put lives at risk.
>
> The group . . . were rescued on Sunday after spending the night stranded by a rising creek . . .
>
> Two students suffered mild hypothermia, and one of the teachers received a knee injury during the ordeal. . . . Area Commander, Superintendent Pat Paroz, and North West Region Commander Detective Assistant Commissioner Denis Clifford said on Sunday they wanted to know what planning was in place for the walk, which proved risky for participants and rescuers.
>
> However, Mr Goddard maintained on Monday: "The students were never in danger". (*Sydney Morning Herald* 18 June 2007)

The article makes no reference to the aims and objectives of the activity, focusing more on the dangers encountered by rescuers and participants, but it does highlight a difference of opinion in the severity of the situation between the parties involved. The first paragraph also raises an interesting perspective into who has responsibility for the decision to postpone the walk. The question this situation does raise is: if an alternate walk had been used (e.g. no creek crossings) then could the aims and objectives have been met, without necessitating a rescue and encountering additional dangers?

Information and communication

Information on predicted and recent rainfalls, current river heights, historical averages and flood warnings is readily available on the BOM website. This information is frequently updated and often involves live information from automated equipment. Obviously, as with all such information, it is only as useful as its ability to be communicated and used in decision-making.

Trigger points and responses

Establishing trigger points relating to flooding is a very localised process and depends greatly on the planned activity outcomes as well as the participant group. Usually a specific value, such as a river height at a particular point or a certain amount of rainfall in a particular period, is the basis for a trigger point in this area. Local knowledge and historical experience are obviously key factors in further developing these trigger points, such as knowing what the river height in your hiking area may be when it is forecast to peak at a certain time on the main river system.

It also must be considered that the dynamic nature of flooding does not always comply with predicted models or previous experiences. When a river floods, for example, it is affected not only by the rainfall occurring upstream and causing it to rise but also by the rivers that it connects with downstream and allowing it to drain. As such, any trigger point relating to flooding should comprise of two factors, rainfalls and river heights being observed remotely (the bigger picture) and observation of the actual conditions encountered on the ground (dynamic risk assessment).

Figure 10.3 is an example of river heights reported on the BOM website and is a good example of a tool that may be used for the basis of a trigger point of activities conducted on that river.

It is important at this point to acknowledge that 'on the ground' knowledge is a powerful part of trigger points and response to floods. An organisation may have in place a policy that if the gauge reads 1.6 metres then a river crossing can still safely be affected – however, only the leader standing at that river at that time can make the final decision about the safety of that crossing.

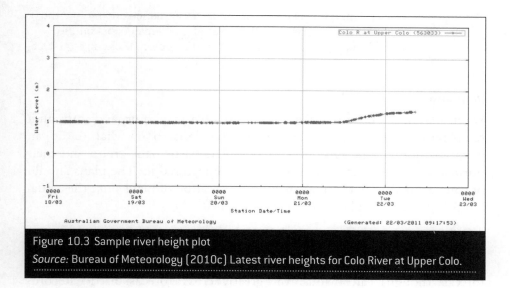

Figure 10.3 Sample river height plot
Source: Bureau of Meteorology (2010c) Latest river heights for Colo River at Upper Colo.

Review

With flooding, reviewing is a critical part of establishing local and historical knowledge as highlighted above. The difficulty of a particular crossing when a river was recorded at a particular height is a critical factor in developing trigger points relating to when that crossing may or may not be attempted.

Review also helps to develop knowledge of local conditions that are not factors recorded on a larger scale. For example, understanding how 25 millimetres of rain in 24 hours affected a particular perennial creek is an immensely valuable piece of information for planning and developing trigger points for that particular walk in the future, and it is the sort of information that is typically not available from any other source.

3 Extreme temperatures

It is easy to think of temperature as something that affects comfort more so than increasing risk, but extremes of temperature should be considered severe weather and warrant risk management just as much as the other events highlighted in this chapter.

The following from a US study into heat stress in youth football helps to highlight this point:

> From 1995 to 2001, 21 young football players . . . died from heat stroke in the US. Since that time, the media has highlighted a number of similar incidents, as well as other heat-related problems with young players on the football field, such as exertional collapse. Despite the recognized benefits of sufficient fluid

intake and precautionary measures to optimize performance and reduce the risk of heat illness, heat- and dehydration-related problems persist on the football field – particularly in preseason practice. (Bergeron, McKeag et al 2005, p. 1421)

Planning

When planning outdoor activities, the possible maximum and minimum temperatures should be considered in the decision of what to do, in what location and at what time of year. The participant group and their normal location of residence should also be factored in. The plans should of course remain flexible to allow for the alteration of plans once the actual temperature for the planned activity is reached.

Information and communication

Temperature is obviously an easy thing to measure and is often accurately forecast, though it can obviously vary greatly across a forecast district. Recording temperature at key locations in a particular area of operations and comparing this to forecasts can be a useful tool in developing local knowledge.

Trigger points and responses

The school I attended had a policy for hot weather that helps to highlight temperature trigger points and responses: when it reached 32 degrees Celsius, boys were permitted to loosen their top buttons, at 35 you could remove your tie entirely – a simple example of using trigger points to manage the risks associated with high temperatures.

The nature of temperature makes it very easy to establish numerical trigger points, although obviously further development is needed. The activity, the participants, their previous experience, the desired outcomes and the control measures put in place are all factors to consider in conjunction with the actual temperature when considering trigger points and responses in this area.

Review

How we manage uncertainties related to temperature in the outdoors is vastly affected by the individual participant group, leader and organisation. For example, a ski instructor may not consider a particular day to be cold, but the group being instructed, having just arrived from the tropics, will have a very different perspective.

The ongoing review of risk management associated with extreme temperature should draw guidance from how participants of the outdoor activity or programme respond to the temperature. Likewise the clothing and equipment that participants actually bring to an activity to protect them from extremes of temperature (as opposed to the equipment that they should bring) should guide organisation in the development of procedures and control measures.

4 Bushfire

Bushfire is accepted as a part of Australian life. Given that outdoor programs and activities are generally conducted in the bush, often in remote areas, the management of uncertainties associated with bushfire is something we must readily accept, and carefully consider where to go at times of high fire danger, ensuring there are plans in place for evacuation and refuge should a fire start.

Planning

When planning any activity in the outdoors, the potential impact of bushfire needs to be evaluated. Walking routes, camping areas and activity sites are conducted in locations that have the potential to be impacted by fire or be isolated because of fire. In these circumstances plans should be put in place to ensure that there is always an evacuation plan and an identified area of refuge for protection should fire actually impact on that location.

It is, however, a much better concept to have alternate locations planned for use on days of higher fire danger.

Information and communication

Information of bushfire danger, as well as the details of fires that may be burning, is made available via the websites of the relevant authorities in the various states. Organisations conducting outdoor activities should familiarise themselves with where to access bushfire information for the area in which they intend to operate well in advance of a time when they may need to find the information quickly. It should also be kept in mind that often bushfires start and move quickly and the information relating to their location and activity may take some time to assemble and make available.

In terms of communicating bushfire information to those in the field, it should be considered that, as in the case of severe thunderstorm warnings, a two-way method of communication may be needed to pass information to groups in the field concerning bushfire activity or threats.

Trigger points and responses

The threat of bushfire on any particular day is expressed as a Fire Danger Rating (FDR), developed in line with a rating system called the Fire Danger Index (FDI). The FDR is described by the New South Wales Rural Fire Service as follows:

The Fire Danger Rating (FDR) is an assessment of the potential fire behaviour, the difficulty of suppressing a fire, and the potential impact on the community should a bushfire occur on a given day. The FDR is determined by the Fire Danger Index (FDI). The FDI is a combination of air temperature, relative humidity, wind speed and drought. An FDI of 1 (Low–Moderate) means that a fire will not burn, or will burn so slowly that it will be easily controlled, whereas an FDI in excess of 100 (Catastrophic) means that a fire will burn so fast and so hot that it is uncontrollable (NSW Rural Fire Service 2009).

The Fire Danger Rating system provides an excellent framework for establishing trigger points and planning responses relating to bushfire. An example of an organisation's trigger point and response plan, developed in line with the FDR is outlined in Figure 10.4.

Adapted from the NSW Rural Fire Service Prepare. Act. Survive. campaign 2009.

Review

Reviewing risk management strategies relating to bushfire is an integral process. Bushfire risks in any area are affected by the fire history and fuel loading of that particular piece of land as well as the long-term climactic conditions. As such, plans put in place at a particular time will need to be reviewed each time that activity is undertaken in that place to ensure the risk management strategies used previously are still appropriate.

Points for action for practitioners

The following is a list of ideas for practitioners to put in place:
- Review the likely weather, severe or otherwise, that will be encountered on each of the outdoor activities you conduct. Determine if that is the right place to be conducting that activity with that group and plan accordingly.
- Consider the possible weather that may be encountered and ensure your risk management plans extend beyond just the likely. Hope for the best, plan for the worst is a good philosophy to follow.
- Establish systems to gather the most up-to-date and accurate weather information possible and determine ways to communicate this in a timely and practical manner to those 'in the field'.
- Train, empower and equip leaders to make weather observations and exercise dynamic risk management in response to the actual weather encountered in the field.
- Constantly review procedures and risk management strategies in response to realisations of actual weather and organisational response to forecasts and warnings.

FIRE DANGER RATING	FIRE DANGER INDEX	KEY ACTIONS	PROGRAMME CHANGES	MANAGEMENT STRATEGIES
CATASTROPHIC	100+ / 100	Organise Evacuation of Camp	• Cease all current programming • Arrange evacuation (if safe to do so) • Consider future and upcoming programmes	• Confirm updates with emergency services, including access, current fire status and location • Contact emergency services and local Rural Fire Service to update our situation and gain advice • Plan and conduct an evacuation of all persons from the property • Organise movement to safety refuge if evacuation is unsafe or impractical • Account for all persons and monitor their wellbeing • Communicate with all relevant stakeholders of our current situation
EXTREME	75 / 74	All Groups moved to Base Camp	• Move all Groups to Base Camp • Conduct local activities on the main property • Camp all groups at main property campsites	• Confirm updates with emergency services, including access, current fire status and location • Contact emergency services and local Rural Fire Service to update our situation and gain advice • Keep all staff, teachers and students informed • All group leaders to leave radios on and monitor for updates and information • Plan potential evacuation and maintain contact with the School • Account for all persons and monitor their wellbeing • Communicate with all relevant stakeholders of our current situation
SEVERE	50	No Groups out on Ridge or in Remote Locations	• Cancel all ridge bushwalks • Change programme to avoid Meroo campsites	• All groups in locations with vehicular access • All group leaders to leave radios on and monitor for updates and information • Plan potential relocations to Base Camp if necessary • Communicate with all relevant stakeholders of our current situation
VERY HIGH	48 / 25	No Camping on Ridge and Morning Bushwalks Only	• Change campsites to avoid Wheelbarrow and other ridge campsites • Early starts on bushwalks to avoid walking in the afternoon	• Inform group leaders during call in to implement early morning walks and rest in the afternoon heat • Plan potential programme changes to avoid ridge walks and remote campsites if necessary
HIGH	24 / 12			
LOW / MODERATE	11 / 0	Programme As Planned	• Programme run as planned • Monitor fire danger meter	• Programme run as planned • Monitor fire danger meter

Figure 10.4 Sample bushfire trigger point and response plan

Source: Somerset Outdoor Learning Centre, used with permission.

- Ensure that the perception of risks associated with severe weather and the outdoors does not impact on the organisation's and individual's ability to venture into the outdoors for recreation, education and development.

Further questions

1 How does the weather add value to a program conducted outdoors? Consider the experience of feeling the rain, experiencing strong winds on a beach or sitting in a warm tent when there is a storm outside.
2 Should outdoor activities be cancelled when there are severe weather warnings? Why or why not?
3 What alternative activities may be conducted to achieve similar outcomes if severe weather limits outdoor activities?
4 What additional training or development activities can you conduct with staff to support their decision-making skills in the face of severe weather events?

References and further resources

References

Bergeron, MF, McKeag, DB, Casa, DJ, Clarkson, PM, Dick, RW, Eichner, ER, Horswill, CA, Luke, AC, Mueller, F, Munce, TA, Roberts, WO & Rowland, TW 2005. 'Youth football: heat stress and injury risk'. *Medicine and Science in Sports and Exercise*, vol. 37, no. 8, pp. 1421–30.

Bureau of Meteorology 2010a. 'About graphical severe thunderstorm warnings in New South Wales. Retrieved 29 November 2010 from <http://www.bom.gov.au/catalogue/warnings/GSTW/graphicalproductsnsw.shtml>.

Bureau of Meteorology 2010b. 'Bureau of Meteorology: severe weather warning education'. Retrieved 29th November 2010 from <http://www.bom.gov.au/catalogue/warnings/WarningsInformation_SW_Ed.shtml>.

Bureau of Meteorology 2010c. 'Latest river heights for Colo River at Upper Colo'. Retrieved 29 November 2010 from <http://www.bom.gov.au/fwo/IDN60233/IDN60233.563033.plt.shtml>.

Devenport, CJ 2010. 'Written findings of Coroner in the matter of the deaths of seven people in Mangatepopo Gorge'. Available from <http://www.opc.org.nz/uploads/content/Coroners%20Report.pdf>.

Director of the Bureau of Meteorology 2000. 'Report by Director of Meteorology on the Bureau of Meteorology's forecasting and warning performance for the Sydney hailstorm of 14 April 1999'. Available from <www.bom.gov.au/amm/docs/2000/publications.pdf>.

Geoscience Australia 2010. 'What is severe weather?' Retrieved 29 November 2010 from <http://www.ga.gov.au/hazards/severe-weather/severe-weather-basics/what.html>.

NSW Rural Fire Service 2009. *Fire Danger Rating*. Available from <http://www.rfs. nsw.gov.au/file_system/attachments/Attachment_FireDangerRating.pdf.>

Further resources

Accidents in North American Mountaineering <http://www. americanalpineclub.org/pt/accidentsinnorthamericanmountaineering>

Australian Journal of Emergency Management <http://www.ema.gov.au/>

Australian National Weather and Warnings <http://www.bom.gov.au/ australia/>

Canadian Avalanche Association <http://www.avalanche.ca/>

Emergency Management in Australia <http://www.ema.gov.au/>

Environment Canada: Get Your Weather <http://ec.gc.ca/meteo-weather/ default.asp?lang=En&n=A0679957-1>

International Journal of Emergency Management <http://www.inderscience.com/ browse/index.php?journalCODE=ijem>

Journal of Emergency Management <http://www.pnpco.com/pn06001.html>

New South Wales Rural Fire Service <http://www.rfs.nsw.gov.au>

New Zealand Mountain Safety Council <http://www.mountainsafety.org.nz/>

New Zealand Severe Weather Warning Service <http://www.metservice.com/ national/warnings/index>

Outdoor Recreation Centre, Victoria Inc <http://www.orc.org.au>

Severe Thunderstorms: Facts, Warnings and Protection <http://www.bom.gov. au/info/thunder/>

Learning from injury surveillance and incident analysis

Tracey J. Dickson

And the trouble is, if you don't risk anything, you risk even more.

Erica Jong, *How to Save your Own Life*, 1977

FOCUS QUESTIONS

1   What is an acceptable level of physical risk in your context? Who considered and determined that the risk is acceptable: management, participants, society?
2   How can you determine the level of physical risks in your activity or program?
3   On what basis do you design and implement strategies to improve physical safety?
4   How can culture, organisational learning, learning organisations and knowledge management support injury prevention outcomes?
5   How can you assess whether injury prevention strategies are having an impact?

CASE STUDY

In 2008 six high school students and a teacher died in a flash flood in Mangatepopo Gorge in New Zealand. The trip started at a dam and was a climb up the gorge to a halfway ledge and back – a distance of just 200 metres each way, an activity that normally only takes two hours. But the instructor with just three months experience had not been trained to access the high water escape route 100 metres along the gorge. The school was on an outdoor education program run by an outdoor centre with extensive experience in the region. The Coroner concluded: 'Regrettably, lack of environmental awareness, lack of instructional use of historical information, instructor inexperience, lack of proper assessment before the gorge was entered to ensure there was no significant chance of water levels rising above a safe level during the trip, lack of or inadequate communication when in the gorge between the instructor and the Field Manager or . . . base staff, failure to implement a crisis plan and dispatch response teams in a timely manner, under-estimation of risks, and complacency contributed to the tragic deaths of [the seven people] in the Mangatepopo gorge on 15 April 2008'. Further the Coroner noted that 'Even if . . . risk management strategies are in place, complacency can defeat them. Continual awareness is required'. Amongst the observations made and the 29 recommendations from the Coroner included staff turnover, staff training and experience, taking a conservative approach in challenging environments, staff to student ratios, communication strategies, organisational learning and industry safety audits.

Introduction

In order to fully understand and effectively manage the real physical risks, it is imperative to have accurate and reliable data that may be tracked over time. It has been suggested that what is needed is:
- information on the frequency of injuries
- the circumstances at the time of the injury
- contributing factors to the injury
- factors that mitigate or worsen the injury severity. (Driscoll, Harrison & Langley 2004)

However, this is just the first step, as it is also important to take that information, investigate, learn from it and where necessary, change policies, practices and cultures. It is these latter parts of injury surveillance and incident analysis that may be most painful for individuals and organisations. No one wants to hear that they might have been able to prevent serious injury or death of one or more people. What is central to this chapter is not creating a scenario whereby blame is placed on one or more people, but looking at the situation from a systemic perspective to enable readers to analyse where injuries occur and to begin to ask questions about what the contributing factors were to an event so that individuals and the organisation can learn from them. It is not about 'safety', but about learning in order to inform future injury prevention strategies consistent with organisationally acceptable levels of risk.

Learning may be viewed as either an outcome or a process. As an outcome, it might be considered that learning may be achieved at some point in time. In contrast, as a process, learning is ongoing and lifelong. Kolb defined learning as 'the process whereby knowledge is created through the transformation of experience. Knowledge results from the combination of grasping and transforming experience' (Kolb 1984, p. 41). The idea of learning as process is reinforced by Shaull when he suggested that education can become the '"practice of freedom", the means by which men and women deal critically and creatively with reality and discover how to participate in the transformation of their world' (1972, p. 14). This notion of learning informs this chapter – ongoing learning in order to bring about change. Prior to exploring this further, it is necessary to consider the current situation in injury and incident investigation and whether safety is the desired outcome.

Are we 'safe'?

In the context of outdoor activities or programs, it has to be questioned whether being safe is a desired outcome, given that the Oxford dictionary defines safe as being not 'damaged, hurt or lost [or] not likely to cause or lead to damage, injury or loss' (Crowther 1995, p. 1035). Achieving this understanding of safety may require staying indoors, in order to ensure that no damage, or injury may occur. In Chapter 1, the story attributed to Willi Unsoeld and the concerns of George Trevelyan highlight the importance of adventure and uncertainty for individuals and society. The concept of safety, or rather the management of physical risks, needs to be balanced with the desirable outcomes of learning, adventure and development achieved in and through the outdoors.

While this does not advocate pursuing sports or activities which might reasonably be expected to lead to injury, the expectation that they could be 'safe' may be in direct contrast to the desire for participants to experience the reality of challenge and adventure. Additionally, to say an activity is 'safe' may undermine any efforts taken to inform participants that there is may be an element of risk through Risk Waivers or Risk Warnings. Understanding the uncertainties related to an activity and potential outcomes is an important element of risk management, as is the need to clearly communicate those uncertainties and outcomes to participants so that they may be part of the risk management process (refer to Chapter 8). Part of the process involves the understanding of what risks there are to the physical wellbeing of participants and staff, hence the need to gather data, investigate and learn.

Why investigate injuries and incidents?

It is not enough to merely count injuries and incidents, the ultimate aim must be to support the prevention of the frequency and severity of injury in the future. The desire to prevent harm to others is important for several reasons:

- People who are injured, in addition to the discomfort and distress from the injury, may be discouraged from ever participating in that sport or recreation activity again which has long-term lifestyle and health implications. (Andrew, Gabbe, Wolfe, Williamson, Richardson, Edwards & Cameron 2008)
- In many circumstances the place in which an injury occurs (indoors or outdoors) may be classified as a workplace, thus there may be obligations under occupational, health and safety legislation to protect the health and welfare of employees and those visiting a workplace.
- From an organisational perspective, the treatment of injuries is a distraction from the goals of the program or event, they consume resources in time and personnel and in the case of serious injury, may become a public relations nightmare.
- There is often a social cost associated with the transport and initial and ongoing treatment of injured people that draws on the resources of the public health system. (Finch & Cassell 2006)

To date there have been a range of approaches or paradigms applied to injury prevention in many industries, as explained in the following section.

Different paradigms

Injury prevention has evolved through a range of paradigms that have been influenced by different professions. As a result, the strategies or solutions discussed within these paradigms reflect the dominant skills and knowledge within those professions (Hanson, Vardon & Lloyd 2002). Some of the major paradigms have been:

- legal: focuses upon who is at fault
- medical: focuses on the physical event and often results in blaming the 'victim'

- health education: grew out of the medical paradigm emphasising the consequences of a person's behaviour, thus education becomes the focus of preventative efforts
- bioengineering: focuses on minimising the injury through engineering solutions, such as car air bags or protective equipment, which avoid the need for individuals to change their behaviour
- systems engineering: emphasises that injury events are normally a result of a sequence of events that may include system weaknesses (latent conditions) and individual behaviours (active failures) (Reason, 1997)
- sociological: recently re-emphasised by the World Health Organization (2009), and considers the impact of factors such as education, income, and politic stability upon injury risk and health outcomes
- social ecological: considers the individual within the physical and sociological environment and interactions between each.

An early example of the application of epidemiological principles to injury prevention is Haddon's Matrix, which linked three injury factors: humans, 'vehicle' and environment, across three time frames, before, during and after the event. The three factors are reflected in later outdoor literature where the emphasis is upon people, equipment and the environment (e.g. Haddock 2004). The factors have since been expanded to include the socioeconomic environment, which introduces a more socio-ecological framework. An example of the application of Haddon's Matrix to road traffic accidents that result in childhood injuries is shown in Table 11.1. This analysis could give rise to a multifaceted and multi-organisational approach to safety to address injury prevention as well as post-event treatment and care.

Ecological and social ecological approaches to injury prevention

Ecology broadly refers to the interrelationships between organisms and their environments, while social ecology broadens environment to include the social, institutional and cultural contexts and highlights the interaction of the individual with the physical environment and social environments across all five levels. As noted by Hanson et al, 'attempts to modify injury risk at one level in isolation (e.g. individual behaviour) will be resisted by the rest of the system, which will attempt to maintain its own internal stability (homeostasis)' (Hanson et al 2002, p. 28). Thus, injury prevention interventions need to consider how to engage all levels across all dimensions. This process reflects the focus of James Reason (1997, 2000, 2008) and the Swiss Cheese Model that considers both latent conditions in the system and active failures by

Table 11.1 Haddon's Matrix applied to the risk factors for road traffic crash injuries among children

	Child factors	Vehicle and safety equipment	Physical environment	Socioeconomic environment
Pre-event	Age, gender, lack of supervision, risk-taking, impulsive behaviour	Lack of roadworthiness of vehicles, poor lighting, poor state of brakes, speeding, overloading	Poor road design, lack of public transport, no enforcement of speed limits, no safety barriers, lack of alcohol laws, poor infrastructure for pedestrian safety	Poverty, single-parent family, large family size, poor maternal education, lack of awareness of risks among caregivers, childcare providers and educators
Event	Size and physical development of child, lack of equipment to protect occupants, or equipment improperly used, underlying conditions in child	Child restraints, seat-belts or helmets not fitted or incorrectly used, poor design of vehicle for protection in crashes, no rollover protection	Roadside objects: trees and poles	Lack of safety culture in the car and on the road
Post-event	Child's lack of resilience, child's general condition, lack of access to appropriate health care, post-injury complications	Difficult access to victim, lack of trained health-care and rescue workers	Lack of adequate pre-hospital care, acute care and rehabilitation	Lack of culture of supporting injured people, no first aid given at scene

Source: Peden, Oyegbite, Ozanne-Smith, Hyder, Branche, Rahman, Rivara & Bartolomeos (2008), Table 2.2, p. 37.

people. To prevent injuries or incidents, or minimise their impact, it is essential to understand what are the contributing factors across the dimensions of the people, environment and equipment.

Similar to Haddon's Matrix, a social ecological approach has three dimensions (Green & Kreuter 1999):

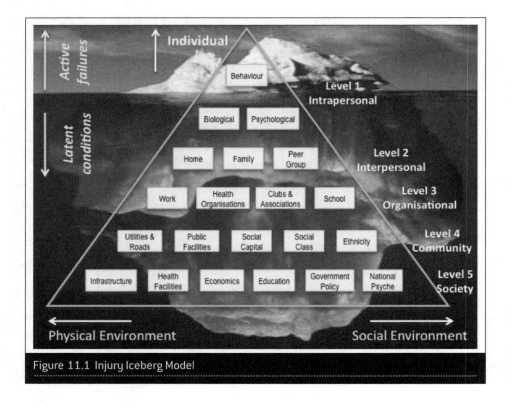

Figure 11.1 Injury Iceberg Model

- the individuals and their behaviour
- the physical environment
- the sociological environment.

These dimensions can then be analysed across five levels: intrapersonal, inter-personal, organisational, community and societal factors and public policy (e.g. the Injury Iceberg Model, Figure 11.1).

Injury surveillance

An example of the misuse of data is evidenced in a British newspaper report that hinted that Australia may be an unsafe place for tourists to visit (Case study, Chapter 5). The journalist selectively used available data that indicated that 2433 international visitors, including 25 children, had died in the previous seven years. What was not reported was that on average, 76 per cent of deaths of international visitors are a result of natural causes and that of the 20 per cent that are the result of accidental causes over half are attributed to traffic incidents (Dickson & Hurrell 2008). The most common activity at the time of death was sleeping! This media manipulation highlights the need for accurate data to be collected, collated and communicated to ensure that correct messages are sent to the parties who are concerned about people's physical wellbeing, such as participants, land managers and insurers.

What is needed is an effective injury surveillance system at the organisational level, but preferably one that is collated at the national level to help inform others in similar circumstances. Injury surveillance requires a systematic approach to collecting, analysing and disseminating injury data with the aim of preventing injuries and controlling the outcomes of injurious events.

To clarify, an accident is an unexpected and uncontrollable event that results in injury or damages while, technically speaking, injuries are caused by

> an acute exposure to physical agents such as mechanical energy, heat, electricity, chemical, and ionizing radiation interacting with the body in amounts or at rates that exceed the threshold of human tolerance (Baker, O'Neill, Ginsburg & Li 1992, p. 4)

Injuries may be the result of intentional or unintentional activities. An incident is often considered to be an event which is not an accident, but may also include non-injurious events, such as a near miss or a close call where no injury, harm or damage occurred but had the potential to do so.

Some characteristics of an effective incident and injury surveillance system are: simple, gathers relevant data, cost and time effective, sustainable given the resources of the organisation and used for injury prevention and control (see also Holder, Krug, Lund, Gururaj & Kobusingye 2001).

Injury rates and levels of exposure

Injury rates are calculated by relating the number of injuries or cases (numerator) to the level of exposure to the risk of injury such as the hours or days of participation (denominator). Incident/injury rates (incidents per number of participants) or accident frequencies do not indicate the real level of risk, which is why exposure measurements are important. Examples of measures that have been used in the snow sport industry include:

- injuries per 1000 skier days (a skier day is an estimate of exposure) = (total number of injuries/total number of 'skier' days) x 1000
- mean days between injuries (MDBI) = number of skier days/number of injuries.

For example, if 150 injuries were reported over a period where there were 40 000 skier days, this would be an injury rate of 3.75 injuries per 1000 skier days, or 266.66 MDBI.

Using skier days as the measure of exposure highlights the problems associated with having an accurate and consistent measure for the denominator. For example:

- a 'day's' skiing or snowboarding for one person may be two to three hours, while for another may be eight or more hours, yet they would treated equally as a skier day
- the distance travelled during a 'skier day' will vary greatly for a beginner vs an experienced participant or if the lifts queues are long or short or if they are skiing in a resort with lifts or backcountry hiking up the mountains
- the lift and trail lengths vary greatly between resorts and countries, so 10 runs in one resort may take the same time as 20 in another. To have an accurate estimate of 'runs' completed would require electronic ticket surveillance, or GPS technology.

However 'it is always problematical to compare injury statistics across sports because of the additional factors of the number of people involved, the time played, and variable injury definition' (Phillips 2000, p. 133). For lay people, there is the additional challenge of accurately 'diagnosing' the injury and having some degree of consistency of interpretation across the data (see Chapter 5). Ultimately, though, what is important is that the data for both what is a reportable injury and the exposure measures are clearly defined and able to be collected regularly and in a cost effective and consistent manner over time in order to inform future injury prevention strategies.

Injury severity

Injury severity can also be a complex issue with many detailed medical classification systems being available such as the Injury Severity Score (ISS) and the Abbreviated Injury Scale (AIS) (Table 11.2). These have been designed for use by highly qualified personnel working in highly controlled environments, but they provide some direction for an injury severity system.

The New Zealand Mountain Safety Council's National Incident Database Project uses a 10-point scale, with severity ratings above three being recorded on the central database. What this means is that the most minor of incidents are excluded from the database. To determine the incident severity, descriptors are provided for injuries, illnesses, social/psychological damage, equipment and environmental damage (Table 11.3).

Another measure of severity is 'time lost'. This would include time lost from participation in a program, game, training, school or work. For example, an injury may be deemed reportable if it results in absence from work or school for a day or more.

Table 11.2 Summary of Abbreviated Injury Scale (AIS)

AIS Score	Injury
1	Minor
2	Moderate
3	Serious
4	Severe
5	Critical
6	Unsurvivable

Table 11.3 Extract from the New Zealand Incident Severity Scale

Severity ranking	Impact upon participation	Injury
1	Minor/short term impact on individual/s that doesn't have a large effect on participation in activity/program	Splinters, insect bites, stings
2		Sunburn, scrapes, bruises, minor cuts
3		Blisters, minor sprain, minor dislocation, cold/heat stress
4	Medium impact on individual/s that may prevent participation in the activity/program for a day or two	Lacerations, frostnip, minor burns, mild concussion, mild hypo/hyperthermia
5		Sprains and hyperextensions, minor fracture

Source: Incident Severity Scale <http://www.incidentreport.org.nz>.

Accident and incident prevention

Any incident prevention strategies need to build on information gathered from the analysis of previous incidents. Occupational health and safety literature provides a hierarchy of hazard controls which emphasises that controlling the hazard at its source rather than the moment of the incident is most important (Figure 11.2). This means that controls like personal protective equipment (PPE) are the last step in the prevention process and should not be relied upon as the only strategy. Having an effective 'safety culture', appropriate policies and procedures, suitable time and funding for staff training in supervision, hazard identification and risk management may be more important to prevent the incident. These may be supported by PPE use and post-event incident management: first aid and crisis response.

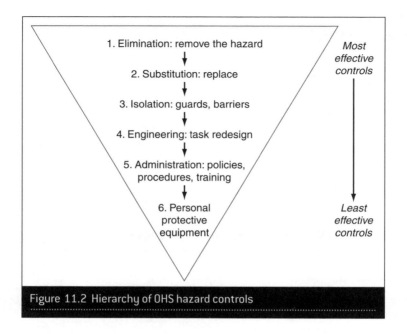

Figure 11.2 Hierarchy of OHS hazard controls

Contributing or risk factors

Previous research has highlighted how risk factors such as an event, condition or a characteristic may result in a particular outcome or condition. They increase the risk or probability that an outcome may occur, in this case an injury (Stevenson, Ameratunga & McClure 2004). Sports research highlights the wide range of risk factors that may be associated with an injury (Gissane, White, Kerr & Jennings 2001). These may be intrinsic factors, i.e. internal to the person (e.g. height, weight, skill) or extrinsic factors, i.e. external to the person (e.g. environment, equipment) (Table 11.4).

Latent conditions and active failures

James Reason, a key author on large-scale organisational accidents, suggests that there are often 'holes' in the layers of defence that at some moment in time 'line up' like Swiss Cheese (Reason 2000). Some of these 'holes' are latent in the system and are a result of managers/supervisors not being able to foresee all possibilities when establishing systems and policies. Others are a result of active failures by individuals, unsafe acts, such as mistakes and breaches in procedures. Reason suggests that latent conditions may result in two unforeseen situations: 'error provoking conditions within the local workplace (e.g. time pressure, understaffing, inadequate equipment, fatigue, and inexperience) and... longlasting holes or weaknesses in the defences (untrustworthy alarms and indicators, unworkable procedures, design and construction deficiencies)' (Reason 2000, p. 320).

Table 11.4 Injury risk factors in contact sports

Intrinsic risk factors	Extrinsic risk factors
Physical characteristics	Exposure
Age	Type of sports/activity
Sex	Playing/participation time
Somatotype [body type]	Position in team
Body size	Level of competition
Previous injury	Warm-up
Physical fitness	Personal equipment
Joint mobility	Training
Muscle tightness	Coaching
Ligamentous laxity	Refereeing
Malalignment of lower extreminities	Control of game
Dynamic strength	Opponents
Static strength	Foul play
Skill level	Opponent's physique
Psychological characteristics	Environment
Psychosocial characteristics	Type and condition of playing surface
Skill level	Weather conditions
Willingness to take risks	Time of day
Interaction with other players	Time of seasons
Experience of sport	Equipment
	Protective equipment
	Footwear
	Orthotics

Source: Gissane, C, White, J, Kerr, K & Jennings, D (2001) 'An operational model to investigate contact sports injuries', *Medicine and Science in Sports and Exercise*, vol. 33, no. 12 (1999–2000).

In outdoor pursuits, Jed Williamson has been analysing alpine accidents in North America for many years to explore those factors that may contribute to mountaineering accidents in order to enable others to learn from these incidents (e.g. Williamson 2007). Based upon this analysis and building upon earlier work by Dan Meyer (1979), Williamson has developed a matrix of causes of accidents which include unsafe conditions, unsafe acts and errors in judgment (Table 11.5). There are connections in this matrix to the active failures mentioned by Reason.

Table 11.5 Potential causes of accidents in outdoor pursuits

Potentially Unsafe Conditions Due to:	Potentially Unsafe Acts Due to:	Potential Errors in Judgment Due to:
Falling objects (rocks etc.)	Inadequate protection	Desire to please others
Inadequate area security (physical, political, cultural)	Inadequate instruction	Trying to adhere to a schedule
Weather	Inadequate supervision	Misperception
Equipment/clothing	Unsafe speed (fast/slow) (includes panic, fear)	New or unexpected situation
Swift/cold water	Inadequate or improper food, drink, medications	Fatigue
Animals, plants	Poor position	Distraction
Physical/psychological profile of participants and/or staff	Unauthorised or improper procedure	Miscommunication
	Disregarding instincts	

Source: Meyer & Williamson (2008). Used with permission

Gathering data

It is only on the basis of valid data that appropriate injury prevention strategies may be developed and evaluated (Driscoll et al 2004). Gathering data must be supported by analysis and translation into practice whether that is by elimination, training, procedural changes, screening mechanisms, protective equipment, scheduling or activity selection.

While time-consuming, it may be beneficial to annually capture all injury data for a period (e.g. one season or term) in order to gain an accurate understanding of the breadth of injuries and the spread of severity of injuries, or to compare these across seasons. Table 11.6 summarises the type of data that may be collected which should reflect the type of activity, location, length of the activity or program as well as the severity of the incident. Additional data may include: lost time from activity or program, follow-up medical treatment, mode/s of transport to medical facilities and medical diagnosis.

Another aspect to consider when looking at contributing factors to incidents is the environment in which the event occurred, particularly when the environment may be substantially different from what the injured participant may normally experience. Understanding the impact of the environment

Table 11.6 Data collection

Intrinsic factors	Extrinsic factors
Age	Date
Gender	Time of day
Fitness level	Activity at time of incident, distinguish
Skill level	between:
In previous 24 hours: sleep,	participating in the activity
fluid, food	observing the activity
Time of last meal or snack	travelling to/from the activity
Injury:	Activity duration
Body location	Personal protective equipment, e.g. helmet,
Injury/illness type, e.g.	harness, PFD
bruising, laceration, sprain,	Environmental conditions, e.g. surface: mud,
fracture	snow, ice, grass; water conditions/grade;
Any previous similar injury	weather conditions: temperature, wind,
	rain, humidity
	Group characteristics:
	Group size
	Instructor/teacher in charge of activity
	Staff/student ratios
	Gender mix
	Program:
	Day of program
	Length, e.g. number of calendar days

on the individual helps in both seeking to prevent any environment-related incidents through activity or program design, clothing and equipment selection, transportation management and food and hydration strategies as well as comprehensively analysing any incident that may occur.

Environmental extremes

Activities or programs conducted outdoors are at the mercy of the elements, whether hot, cold, wet, dry, humid, wind or altitude. In some circumstances, extremes of the environment may be an essential aspect of the activity, e.g. altitude and cold are central to many snow sport or mountaineering activities, while moving and sometimes wild water is the feature of some canoeing and rafting activities.

The human body is designed to adapt to external changes, the term homeostasis refers to 'the body's tendency to maintain a steady state despite external changes' (Cannon, cited in Armstrong 2000, p. 2). However, it takes one to two weeks to adapt to extremes such as with acclimatisation and the effect may be lost in two to four weeks (Armstrong 2000). Our ability to adapt to extreme conditions is a result of the following: the meaning we attach to the experience, genetic makeup, age, intelligence, skills and our previous experience in similar environments. This last point is important in today's society where many people live in air-conditioned homes, travel in air-conditioned vehicles and work or go to school in air-conditioned buildings. The majority of their normal life experience is in climate-controlled situations where their bodies are not being challenged to adapt or respond to changes in environmental conditions. When considering the impact of environmental extremes it is important to take into account the relative difference between what is 'normal' for that individual and the compounding effects of other stressors within the activity or program such as fatigue, dehydration and the social context.

Heat and humidity

Heat and humidity, which is associated with increased physical activity, will result in an increase in the body's temperature. If the temperature is not regulated then it is possible that the person may experience a heat-related illness such as hyperthermia. To help regulate the body's temperature, the body will respond by sweating to promote evaporation and an increased heart rate and dilution of the superficial blood vessels (Armstrong 2000; Schimelpfenig & Lindsey 2000). However, these may not be sufficient to manage the increased heat. In a review of the epidemiological literature on fluid and electrolyte imbalances that occur during physical activity Carter (2008) identified a range of risk factors that may contribute to exertional heat illness (Table 11.7). While exertional heat illness is not directly related to any one specific factor, the combination of factors such as lack of acclimatisation, poor physical fitness and increased body weight or an infection, combined with a previous heat-related injury will put participants at a greater risk of heat illness.

Cold

Prolonged exposure to cold air, the effects of wind chill and immersion in water may result in excessive heat loss, which could lead to hypothermia (Table 11.8). The impact of temperatures lower than the body's normal temperature will be exacerbated by wind speed (Sawka & Young 2005). Hypothermia will impact upon a person's ability to continue the same level of physical activity, make sound decisions and to communicate effectively. The body's two main responses to cold are to increase heat production through shivering, and to decrease heat loss by regulating blood flow (Armstrong 2000;

Table 11.7 Risk factors for exertional heat illnesses

Transient conditions		Environmental
Situational	Medical	Prolonged heat waves
Lack of heat acclimatisation	Febrile illness, i.e. fever	High daily temperature and humidity
Low physical fitness	Gastroenteritis (diarrhoea, emesis)	
Excessive body weight, or high Body Mass Index (BMI)	Self-medication (prescription, recreational drugs, ergogenic stimulants e.g. cocaine, heroin)	
Dehydration	Stickle cell trait	
> 1 hour aerobic intense exercise	Inflammation	
Alcohol	Malignant hyperthermia	
Peer pressure/motivation	History of heat-related injury	

Source: Table 1 Risk factors for exertional heat illnesses. Carter, R III (2008) 'Exertional heat illness and hyponatremia: an epidemiological perspective', *Current Sports Medicine Reports*, vol. 7, no. 4, S20–27, p. S22.

Table 11.8 Risk factors in hypothermia

Transient conditions		Environmental
Situational	Medical	Low ambient temperatures
Larger individuals due to having greater surface area	Impairment of thermoregulation or circulation	High humidity
Physical activity increases blood flow	Self-medication (e.g. antihistamines, beta blockers, diuretics, laxatives, amphetamines, cocaine, marijuana)	Altitude
Dehydration		Prolonged exposure
Fatigue		
Alcohol		
Inadequate nutrition		
Non-insulating and/or non-breathable clothing		

Sources: Sallis & Chassay (1999); Sawka & Young (2005).

Schimelpfenig & Lindsey 2000). As with heat-inducted illness, the prevalence of cold-induced illnesses may be reduced through preventative measures, e.g. wearing appropriate clothing, maintaining adequate hydration and nutrition and ensuring people are adequately rested (Sallis & Chassay 1999).

Incident and injury investigation and analysis

Incident and injury analysis seeks to identify what steps may be taken to eliminate or reduce the possibility that a negative outcome could occur in the future. As stated earlier, this information needs to be help individuals and organisations to learn. Root Cause Analysis and Causal Factors Analysis are just two examples of systems used in the industry to analyse incidents. The analysis may involve gathering data on causal factors to help identify and analyse trends in areas such as in Table 11.6 to inform changes in policies, practices, communications and training.

In conducting an investigation, insight may also be sought from peers who may reflect on policies, procedures and practice.

The following steps provide only a brief introduction and should not replace appropriate policy and procedure development, staff training and external consultation as necessary.

Prior to any incident

Well before any incident occurs, there are several steps that must be completed prior to conducting an investigation.

1 Establish the requirements, expectations and current investigation processes of any statutory body, legislation, and the insurance company (e.g. Workcover or Department of Labour), the roles and responsibilities of police and coroner in the case of loss of life and what support an insurer or accident compensation body might provide in the case of an incident.

2 Clarify what incidents will be investigated. Criteria that may trigger an investigation include: serious trauma or loss of life, near misses that if the incident had occurred it may have led to trauma or loss of life, incidents involving impacts with man-made or natural obstacles or other people, transport incidents, incidents involving other built structures such as slips, trips and falls, equipment failure, incidents involving illegal activity.

3 Ensure that there are relevant policies, procedures and forms available for reporting incidents, gathering statements and analysing incidents. An online search will lead to many examples of incident report forms.

4 Establish the criteria for being part of the team that is conducting the investigation. For example, roles and responsibilities of team members, the mix of staff and/or external personnel, desirable skills and qualifications for individuals and the team as a whole (such as judgment, discretion, interpersonal and interviewing skills, photography skills, report writing), training needs, confidentiality requirements, knowledge of operational areas. For smaller organisations, it may be more effective to develop strategic relationships with like organisations and establish a network of investigators who are able to support one another in the case of an incident and participate together in training exercises.

5 Conduct regular staff training in incident analysis. This may involve external trainers, but may also include regular analysis of case studies, either previous events within the organisation or others such as those listed in the resources at the end of the chapter. The regular analysis of cases may help create a culture of sharing ideas and learning from one another. To avoid one person or persons from always being seen as the 'expert' cases could be prepared and presented by different people to enhance their learning but also to create a community of learners.

Investigation scope

Prior to commencing an investigation, it is necessary to clarify the scope of the investigation. Building on Haddock's suggestions (2008, p. 13), the scope may include:

- organisational documentation
- program objectives and outcomes (e.g. evaluations, client feedback)
- participant and leader preparation for an activity of this nature (e.g. qualifications, experience)
- the organisation's understanding of the risks involved and their management systems to mitigate risk (e.g. risk assessments, risk management plans)
- the participants/parents understanding of the risks involved and informed consent procedures (e.g. pre-course documentation)
- formal approval processes in place for activities of this nature (e.g. land access, licenses, excursion polices)
- competence of staff to deliver the program and deal with emergencies meets relevant industry standards (e.g. wilderness first aid qualifications, rescue training)
- consistency of practices used in the activity with current accepted practices and relevant standards in the outdoor sector (e.g. benchmarking with other organisations)
- the role of outside agencies in planning, execution, response and review (e.g. emergency services)

- commendations – all the things the organisation/s did well in managing and resolving the incident
- recommendations for the organisation, relevant government agencies and the wider outdoor sector as a result of the findings
- timeframe for any reporting
- confidentiality requirements.

Once any injured parties are properly cared for, it is important to start gathering information as soon as possible to get the most accurate information to support the investigation. For example, statements from injured parties, witness statements, responders' statements, photographic records of the physical site (including damage), events leading up to the incident for the injured person or the group (up to 24 hours prior), management of the injured parties and diagnosis of the injury by medical personnel. This will need to be in line with the previously documented organisational procedures.

Other documentation that may need to be gathered includes pre-course information provided (e.g. permission forms), assumptions of risk, insurance documentation, weather reports for the time of the incident, equipment maintenance schedules, risk assessments for the activity, location and/or event, training and qualifications of staff, volunteers, supervisors, instructors, coaches who were involved in the sequence of events leading up to the injury or incident, reports, recommendations and actions from previous similar events.

Reports of investigations conducted by external parties may be available to help inform any internal investigation and organisational learning including police, insurers, land managers, ambulance, other emergency services, reports by the client and coroners.

All the information then needs to be collated, and the sequence of events established, remembering Reason's work on latent conditions and active failures and that most incidents have multiple causes. A roundtable conference of the investigation team may enable different scenarios to be developed and to clarify how they perceive the sequence of events, this would then need to be confirmed with those involved. Depending on the culture of the organisation this may require one-on-one conversations or it may be conducted in an open forum.

As indicated earlier, from the findings of the investigation, both commendations about what was done well and recommendations for improvement will form part of the final report. For major incidents such as loss of life or major trauma the report will then need an official response, either from senior management or a board to indicate what actions will be taken on the recommendations, determining the timeframe, allocation of resources and an indication of who is responsible to ensure that all insights can be appropriately acted upon, and a timeframe allowed for reviewing the changes. Where possible, a presentation to those involved may also be appropriate to provide feedback on both the commendations and recommendations.

Organisational learning, learning organisations and knowledge management

A key aspect of incident prevention is learning from what has happened before. Argyris defined organisational learning as the process of 'detection and correction of errors'. In his view individuals were the agents through which organisations 'learn' to the extent that 'individuals' learning activities, in turn, are facilitated or inhibited by an ecological system of factors that may be called an organisational learning system' (Argyris 1977, p. 117). Ang and Joseph suggest that organisational learning emphasises a process, 'a sequence of activities in which an organisation undertakes to learn. In contrast, 'learning organisation' emphasises unique structural characteristics of an organization that has the ability to learn' (1996, p. 3).

Another aspect to consider is the concept of 'knowledge management' which involves not just analysing an incident but putting those insights into policy and practice through effective communication strategies, training, organisational cultures and policy and practice changes, as necessary. However, it is not possible, nor necessarily desirable, to document every action or strategy required in every context, in part because the process may result in such a large document that is of no practical use. That is not to suggest that documentation should be avoided. Documentation helps people know *what* to do, theoretically. Knowing *how* to do it in real situations depends upon practical experience.

An example of how *planning* and *action* may play out differently is provided by Suchman (1987), in planning to canoe a rapid. Even though the plans may be well constructed, in the end what prevails is the application of the individual's tacit and embodied skills (based upon experience), at that time and in that place or environment.

> 'I'll get as far over to the left as possible, try to make it between those two large rocks, then backferry hard to the right to make it around that next bunch.' A great deal of deliberation, discussion, simulation, and reconstruction may go into such a plan. But, however detailed, the plan stops short of the actual business of getting your canoe through the falls. When it really comes down to the details of responding to currents and handling a canoe, you effectively abandon the plan and fall back on whatever embodied skills are available to you. The purpose of the plan in this case is not to get your canoe through the rapids, but rather to orient you in such a way that you can obtain the best possible position from which to use those embodied skills on which, in the final analysis, your success, depends (p. 52).

In the coroner's report on the incident that opened this chapter two other instructors related that part of their decision-making process that fateful day had involved gut instincts. Training, qualifications, supervision, policies and procedures are all-important, but so are individual experience, intuition and gut feelings. For these to prevail, there must be an organisational climate to allow and support such non-cerebral decision making influences.

Conclusion

Physical wellbeing is only one aspect of the overall risk management in an organisation or program. While important, it should not be the only focus of the organisation, but should be considered in the context of program objectives, organisational and staff experience and abilities and participant's knowledge, skills and attitudes. Ongoing incident and injury surveillance is important to identify trends, implement new prevention strategies and evaluate the effectiveness of previous strategies. To achieve this, consistency in data collection and analysis will aid any potential knowledge that may be acted upon, as will having a system and culture in place that supports the education of individuals who are working together and who are able to learn from past incidents to make changes in policies, procedures and practices which support incident and injury prevention strategies. This reflects the views of the Royal Society for the Prevention of Accidents who place 'an emphasis on equipping people with the skills to ensure informed choices of behaviour. It is important that society becomes risk aware, not risk averse, and this begins with safety and risk education' (Royal Society for Prevention of Accidents 2010). This enables individuals, staff and participants to be part of the solution and not just to be considered part of the problem.

Points for action for practitioners

1 Gather data from a challenging adventure that was successful, such as a program, an expedition or an event:
   • What were the contributing factors for success?
   • How was the knowledge of these factors shared and imbedded into the organisational culture, policies and process?
   • If you were to have that adventure again, would the result be the same? Why or why not? What would you need to change to increase the likelihood of success?
2 Gather all available data from a previous incident that you would now deem reportable:

- Was any investigation conducted? If so, what conclusions or recommendations emerged? To what extent were they implemented?
- Use it as a staff training exercise to investigate how new or other staff may interpret the contributing factors. How similar or different are their conclusions? If people see the situation differently, what has influenced those different perspectives?

3 If there are no incidents, create a realistic scenario for your situation that may result in large losses either financial or threats to human life:

- What are the potential positive outcomes from pursuing this scenario?
- What strategies may be put in place to prevent the negative outcomes and enhance the likelihood of achieving the positive outcomes?
- What resources would be needed, e.g. time, money and human?
- In what time frame would these need to be implemented?
- What will the indicators that you achieved your aims?

Further questions and activities

1 Think of an incident you or someone familiar to you has been involved in, such as a car crash, sporting injury or a near miss:

- Document the sequence of events leading up to the incident, considering who was involved (e.g. age, gender, experience), their roles, the culture of the group, familiarity with the environment, levels of food, drink and fatigue, previous experience of participants, prior planning, and correct use of appropriate equipment.
- At what points along that sequence of events do you think different decisions or choices could have been made that may have altered the outcome?
- What would need to be different next time to support individuals making those difference choices or decisions?

2 Read one of the books listed in Further resources:

- Analyse what were the factors that contributed to the success or failure of the adventure.
- What recommendation would you put in place to prevent the failures or enhance the likelihood that successes would be repeated?

Glossary of terms

The following definitions are drawn from McClure, Stevenson and McEvoy (2004), Pless and Hagel (2005) and the Australian sports injury data dictionary (Australian Sports Injury Data Working Party, 1998):

Accidents: unpredictable and therefore not preventable events.

Exposure figures: used as the denominator in many injury rates and may be estimates of participation 'days' or hours. Consistency of calculation is important to ensure that data from different activities is comparable.

Injuries: the result of the transfer of energy (e.g. mechanical, chemical, thermal etc.) or the lack of essential energy, such as oxygen, that is beyond human tolerance.

> *Intentional injuries*: those that are the result of purposeful action such as homicide, violence, abuse and suicide.
>
> *Unintentional injuries*: those that are not purposely inflicted by the patient or someone else.

Injury control: what happens after the injury occurs that may impact upon the eventual outcome from the injury, including first aid, medical treatment and rehabilitation.

Injury prevention: measures taken to prevent the injury in the first place and efforts to limit the outcome from the injury.

> *Primary prevention* relates to preventing the (uncontrollable) 'accident' event.
>
> *Secondary prevention* relates to laws, designs and protective equipment usage that reduce the impact of the event.
>
> *Tertiary prevention* relates to reducing the long-term impacts of the injury.

Injury rate: calculated by dividing the number of injuries by the relevant exposure figure, such as injuries per thousand employee hours, or may be calculated as the mean days between injuries.

Injury surveillance: an ongoing and systematic process of gathering, analysing, interpreting and communicating data about injuries in order to facilitate injury prevention and control.

Mechanism of injury: the way in which a person is injured, such as a fall, hit by something, a chemical or thermal effect.

Morbidity: injury caused by disease or illness.

Mortality: death caused by injury or illness.

Risk homeostasis: the theory that increased safety measures are met with increased risk-taking (see also Wilde, Robertson, & Pless 2002).

Safety: the state of being free from damage, injury or loss and is the result of successful injury prevention.

References and further resources

References

Andrew, NE, Gabbe, BJ, Wolfe, R, Williamson, OD, Richardson, MD, Edwards, ER & Cameron, PA 2008. 'Twelve-month outcomes of serious orthopaedic sport and active recreation–related injuries admitted to Level 1 Trauma Centers in Melbourne, Australia'. *Clinical Journal of Sport Medicine*, vol. 18, no. 5, pp. 387–93.

Ang, S & Joseph, D 1996. 'Organizational learning and learning organizations: trigger events, processes, and structures'. Submitted for the Academy of Management Meeting, August 1996, Organizational Development and Change Division. Retrieved from <http://www3.ntu.edu.sg/home/adjoseph/Webpages/Publications/aom10.pdf>.

Argyris, C 1977. 'Organizational learning and management information systems'. *Accounting, Organizations and Society*, vol. 2, no. 2, pp. 113–23.

Armstrong, LE 2000. *Performing in extreme environments*. Human Kinetics, Champaign, IL.

Australian Sports Injury Data Working Party 1998. 'Australian sports injury data dictionary: guidelines for injury data collection and classification for the prevention and control of injury in sport and recreation'. Working document Available from <http://www.sma.org.au/information/ssinjury.asp>.

Baker, S, O'Neill, B, Ginsburg, MJ & Li, G 1992. *The Injury Fact Book*, 2nd edn. Oxford University Press, Oxford.

Carter, R, III 2008. 'Exertional heat illness and hyponatremia: an epidemiological prospective'. *Current Sports Medicine Reports*, vol. 7, no. 4, S20–7.

Crowther, J (ed) 1995. *Oxford Advanced Learner's Dictionary*. Oxford University Press, Oxford.

Dickson, TJ & Hurrell, M 2008. 'International visitors to Australia: safety snapshot 2003–05' in C Cooper, TD Lacey & L Jago (eds) *Technical Report*. Available from <http://www.crctourism.com.au/>.

Driscoll, T, Harrison, J & Langley, J 2004. 'Injury surveillance' in R McClure, M Stevenson & S McEvoy (eds), *The Scientific Basis of Injury Prevention and Control* (pp. 87–109). IP Communications, Melbourne, Victoria, pp. 87–109.

Finch, CF & Cassell, E 2006. 'The public health impact of injury during sport and active recreation'. *Journal of Science and Medicine in Sport*, vol. 9, no. 6, pp. 490–7.

Gissane, C, White, J, Kerr, K & Jennings, D 2001. 'An operational model to investigate contact sports injuries'. *Medicine and Science in Sports and Exercise*, vol. 33, no. 12, pp. 1999–2003.

Green, LW & Kreuter, MW 1999. *Health Promotion Planning: An Educational and Ecological Approach*, 3rd edn. Mayfield Publishing, Moutain View, CA.

Haddock, C 2004. *Outdoor Safety: Risk Management for Outdoor Leaders*. New Zealand Mountain Safety Council, Wellington, NZ.

Haddock, C 2008. 'Incident reviews: aspects of good practice'. *Ki Waho – Into the Outdoors*, vol. 2, Spring/Water, pp. 10–3.

Hahn, K 1947. 'Training for and through the sea'. Address given to the Honourable Mariners' Company in Glasgow, 14 February 1947. Retrieved from <http://www.kurthahn.org/writings/train.pdf>.

Hanson, D, Vardon, P & Lloyd, J 2002. 'Safe communities: an ecological approach to safety promotion' in R. Muller (ed), *Reducing Injuries in Mackay, North Queensland*. Warwick Educational Publishing, pp. 17–34.

Holder, Y, Krug, MPE, Lund, J, Gururaj, G & Kobusingye, O (eds) 2001. *Injury Surveillance Guidelines*. World Health Organization, Geneva.

Kolb, DA 1984. *Experiential Learning: Experience as the Source of Learning and Development*. Prentice Hall, Englewood Cliffs, NJ.

McClure, R, Stevenson, M & McEvoy, S (eds) 2004. *The Scientific Basis of Injury Prevention and Control*. IP Communications, Melbourne, Victoria.

Meyer, D 1979. 'The management of risk'. *The Journal of Experiential Education*, vol. 2, no. 2, pp. 9–14.

Peden, M, Oyegbite, K, Ozanne-Smith, J, Hyder, AA, Branche, C, Rahman, AF, Rivara, F & Bartolomeos, K (eds) 2008. *World Report on Child Injury Prevention*. World Health Organization, Geneva.

Phillips, LH 2000. 'Sports injury incidence'. *British Journal of Sports Medicine*, vol. 34, no. 2, pp. 133–6.

Pless, IB & Hagel, BE 2005. 'Injury prevention: a glossary of terms'. *Journal of Epidemiology and Community Health*, vol. 59, no. 3, pp. 182–5.

Reason, J 1997. *Managing the Risks of Organizational Accidents*. Ashgate Publishing, Aldershot, UK.

Reason, J 2000. 'Human error: models and management'. *BMJ*, vol. 320, pp. 768–70.

Reason, J 2008. *The Human Contribution*. Ashgate Publishing, Aldershot, UK.

Royal Society for Prevention of Accidents 2010. The Royal Society for the Prevention of Accidents. Retrieved 28 April 2010 from <http://www.rospa.com>.

Sallis, R & Chassay, CM 1999. 'Recognizing and treating common cold-induced injury in outdoor sports'. *Medicine and Science in Sports and Exercise*, vol. 31, no. 10, 1367.

Sawka, MN & Young, AJ 2005. 'Physiological systems and their responses to conditions of heat and cold' in CM Tipton, MN Sawka & CA Tate (eds), *ACSM's Advanced Exercise Physiology*. Lippincott Williams and Wilkins, Baltimore, MD, pp. 535–67.

Schimelpfenig, T & Lindsey, L 2000. *Wilderness First Aid*, 3rd edn. National Outdoor Leadership School and Stackpole Books, Mechanicsburg, PA.

Shaull, R 1972. 'Foreword' in P Freire (ed), *Pedagogy of the Oppressed*. Penguin Books, London, pp. 9–14.

Stevenson, M, Ameratunga, S & McClure, R 2004. 'The rationale for prevention' in R McClure, M Stevenson & S McEvoy (eds), *The Scientific Basis of Injury Prevention and Control*. IP Communications, Melbourne, Victoria, pp. 34–43.

Suchman, A 1987). *Plans and Situated Actions: The Problem of Human-machine Communication*. MIT Press, Camdridge, MA.

Wilde, GJS, Robertson, LS & Pless, IB 2002. 'For and against: does risk homoeostasis theory have implications for road safety?' *British Medical Journal*, vol. 324, no. 7346, pp. 1149–52.

Williamson, J 2007. 'Accidents in North American mountaineering'. *American Alpine Club*, vol. 60, Golden Co.

World Health Organization 2009. 'Social determinants of health'. Retrieved from <http://www.who.int/social_determinants/en/>.

Further resources

Injury surveillance, databases and incident registers
  Abbreviated Injury Scale, Association for the Advancement of Automotive Medicine, US <http://www.carcrash.org/>
  The Australian Accident Register, <http://www.accidentregister.info/index.html>

Australian Sports Injury Data Dictionary, Sports Medicine Australia
    <http://www.sma.org.au/information/ssdatadict.asp>
International Incident Database Project, US <http://www.
    incidentdatabase.org/>
National Incident Database Project, New Zealand Mountain Safety Council
    <http://www.incidentreport.org.nz/>
Outdoor Medical Incident Database, Forecast Systems Australia, <http://
    www.forecastsystems.com.au>
Wilderness Risk Management Committee (WRMC) and the Association for
    Experiential Education (AEE) Incident Data Reporting Project <www.
    aee.org/accreditation/wildernessCommittee>

Books: potential case studies

Ajango, D. (Ed.). (2000). *Lessons Learned: A guide to Accident Prevention and Crisis Response*.
    University of Alaska, Anchorage.
Blum, A 1980. *Annapurna: A Woman's Place*. Sierra Club Books, San Francisco, CA.
Brown, I 1999. *Extreme South: Struggles and Triumph of the First Australian Team to the
    Pole*. Australian Geographic, Terrey Hills, NSW.
Gammelgard, L 1999. *Climbing High: A Woman's Account of Surviving the Everest Tragedy*.
    Pan Books, London, UK.
Hall, L 2008. *Alive in the Death Zone: Mount Everest Survival*. Random House, Sydney.
Simpson, J 1989. *Touching the Void: The True Story of One Man's Miraculous Survival*.
    Perennial: New York.
Krakauer, J 1996. *Into the Wild*. Pan Books, London.
Krakauer, J 1997. *Into Thin Air: A Personal Account of the Everest Disaster*. Macmillan,
    London.
Peters, M & Pikkemaat, B 2005. 'Crisis management in Alpine winter sports resorts –
    the 1999 avalanche disaster in Tyrol'. *Journal of Travel & Tourism Marketing*,
    vol. 19, no. 2/3, pp. 9–20.

Online resources

Accidents In North American Mountaineering Statistics <http://www.
    americanalpineclub.org/pt/accidentsinnorthamericanmountaineeringstatistics>
Bennett, S 1999. 'Disasters as heuristics?: a case study.' *The Australian Journal of
    Emergency Management*, vol. 14, no. 3, pp. 32–6. Retrieved from <http://www.
    ema.gov.au>.
Bennett, S 2000. 'Learning from "near-misses": a case study'. *Australian Journal of
    Emergency Management*, vol. 15, no. 3, pp. 7–9. Retrieved from <http://www.ema.
    gov.au>.
Good Sports Case Studies <http://www.goodsports.com.au/goodsports/pages/
    case-studies.html>.
Health and Safety Executive: Case study index <http://www.hse.gov.uk/slips/
    experience.htm>.
Marine Accident Investigation Section Marine Department: Hong Kong Special
    Administrative Region 2005. 'Report of investigation into capsizing of the sailing
    dinghy Stratos No. 9 in Stanley Bay to the west of Bluff Head on 18 August 2005'.
    Available from <http://www.mardep.gov.hk>.

Reports on maritime accidents and incidents investigated by Maritime New Zealand <http://www.maritimenz.govt.nz/Publications-and-forms/Accidents-and-investigations/Accident-and-investigation-reports.asp>.

Savive Pty Ltd Case Studies <http://www.savive.com.au/casestudy/>.

NOVA Online, 'High exposure, humans at altitude'. <http://www.pbs.org/wgbh/nova/everest/exposure/>.

NSW Department of Sport and Recreation, Sport rage case studies <http://www.dsr.nsw.gov.au/sportrage/casestudies.asp>.

Wall, M 2006. 'The case study method and management learning: making the most of a strong story telling tradition in emergency services management education. *The Australian Journal of Emergency Management*, vol. 21, no. 2, pp. 11–6. Retrieved from <http://www.ema.gov.au/www/emaweb/emaweb.nsf/Page/Publications>.

Videos/DVDs

Butler, M (writer) 1994. *White Mile* [video]. A. Santa Croce (producer). HBO: New York, NY.

Dennison, R (writer) 1999. *Risk: Yelling in the Face of Life* [video]. J Heyward (producer). Wild Releasing, Sydney, NSW.

Godi Productions, *Outdoor Alert!* [DVD Series] <http://store.goldiproductions.com/store_outdoor_dvd.html>.

Judson, S & Breashears, D 1998. Imax – Everest [DVD]. Buena Vista Home Entertainment.

Appendix

Examples of risk analyses

Risk Scores based upon ISO 31000:

    Low = C1, D1, D2, E1, E2: Manage by routine procedures
    Moderate = C2, D3, E3: Management responsibility must be specified
    High = A1, A2, B2, B3, C3, D4, E4, E5: Senior management attention needed
    Extreme = A3, A4, A5, B4, B5, C4, C5, D5: Immediate preventative action required

Chapter	Activity, action or process	Potential risks	Potential outcome	Likelihood	Consequence	Risk Score	Possible Risk Management Strategies (RMS)	Risk score after RMS	Responsibility
1	Organisational planning	1 Risk management not integrated into all aspects of organisation	Inability to respond to uncertainty	C	4	C4	Risk management is an integral part of all organisational processes Risk management is part of everyone's role	D2	Board, executive and senior staff
2	Planning, implementing sustainability	2.1 Failure to recognise, act on and reap the benefits of sustainability	Failure to reap the benefits of sustainable operations and outcomes Possible criticism and adverse publicity from stakeholders Possible adverse impacts from government and other compliance agencies	C	4	C4	Awareness raising and education Engagement with stakeholders Engagement with relevant compliance and policy making agencies and organisations	D4	Stakeholders Management All workers (employed and volunteers)

3	Risk waivers	Undermining risk waivers by saying programs or activities are safe	Law suits in the case of injury, illness or deaths	C	3	C3	Instruct staff about the implications of using the word 'safe' Provide material for participants that clearly outline the types of experiences they may have Delete 'safe' from all information and marketing materials	Program managers Staff
4	Strategic planning	4.1 Lack of innovation or creativity 4.2 No new ideas for generating snow on the appropriate hills	Lose competitive advantage and thus market share The event doesn't run	C	4	C4	Environmental scanning What is already available to help mitigate the problem? Where might we need to innovate? Regular review of client feedback Speak with sport organising bodies about the best way to handle problems with snow Attending external training and development Look into the 'latest and greatest' that the refrigeration industry has to offer	D4 Senior management Marketing All senior staff

Chapter	Activity, action or process	Potential risks	Potential outcome	Likelihood	Consequence	Risk Score	Possible Risk Management Strategies (RMS)	Risk score after RMS	Responsibility
5	Full day hiking activity	5.1 Participants experience blisters	First aid treatment Delayed activity Evacuation	B	2	B2	Participants briefed to wear clean socks and worn-in shoes Preventative taping Establish culture that it is OK to stop and treat Equipment check prior to departure	C2	Program manager & students Teachers Teachers & instructors Instructors
6	Flying fox equipment mainte-nance & storage	6.1 Exceed equipment manufacturer's use by dates	Equipment failure, participant injured Equipment warranty invalid	C	4	C4	Equipment retirement policies Budget allocation to replace equipment Staff training regarding expectations	D4	Maintenance Finance HR (training)
7	Program evaluation of achieve-ment of program objectives	7.1 Program may not be effectively delivering claimed outcomes	Students not experiencing claimed outcomes Stakeholder criticism of program processes Poor marketing	B	4	B4	Commit to a systematic program evaluation process by: stating the purpose of the evaluation developing a written plan for a program evaluation process conducting an evaluation cycle. Address issues arising from the evaluation e.g. through program design changes	E3	Quality manager

| 8 | Informed consent | 8.1 | Parents not being clear about the objective hazards being faced | Students not being prepared for their program
Media criticism of program processes | C | 4 | C4 | Ensure effective risk communication pre, during and post program.
Do this by: offering face-to-face meetings with parents at times that are likely to suit them
Ensure the program's website is accurate with program information, activities and forecasted/likely conditions
Treat the informed consent information sheet seriously by having the principal sign a covering letter and ensuring it gets home separately (not with other permission forms at the beginning of the year) | D4 | Program manager (pre and post)
Field staff (during program) |

(cont.)

Chapter	Activity, action or process	Potential risks	Potential outcome	Likelihood	Consequence	Risk Score	Possible Risk Management Strategies (RMS)	Risk score after RMS	Responsibility
9	Allowing participants to use mobile phones on outdoor programs	1.1 Negative risk: may distract and interfere with participants' engagement with the program activities. 1.1 Participants may leak news about the program rather than news going through official channels. 1.2 Positive risk: Strategic use of mobile phones may help towards program goals, e.g. taking photos, audio and video to document and reflect on the experience.	Allowing use of mobile phones is likely to alter the participants' experience – depending on how this is done it is likely increase both negative and positive risks.	A	4	A4	Investigate and assess potential positive and negative risks of allowing mobile phone usage during programs. Develop policy, principles and guidelines for use of mobile phones during programs. Develop action plan for dissemination and training of staff and participants for mobile phone policy.	D3	Risk manager Quality manager Program instructors Participants

10	Bushwalking Expedition	10.1 Consistent heavy rain	Isolation Exposure	B	3	B3	Establish alternative walking routes Create trigger points Enact alternate plans	D3 Management Leaders Students
10	School Camp in National Park during January	10.2 Severe thunderstorm	Tree fall Lightning Strike Isolation due to flash flooding	C	5	C5	Gather and communicate forecasts and warnings Establish Severe Weather sites Prepare participants	C2 Management Leaders Students
11	Injury surveillance	11.1 Collecting insufficient data	Putting risk management efforts and resources in the wrong place	C	3	C3	Implement an injury surveillance system Train staff about data collection and analysis Review major incidents and implement changed as necessary	D3 Management Staff
11	Incident analysis	11.2 Not learning from previous incidents	Repeating previous mistakes Serious injury or death	C	4	C4	Implement risk management across the organisation as part of all job descriptions Develop a 'safety culture' Provide resources (time and money) to implement risk management strategies	D3 Board/council Management Staff

Index

accident and incident prevention
  contributing or risk factors, 214–16
  data collection, 216–17
  hazard controls, 213–14
  see also injury prevention
accidents and incidents
  definition of accident, 93
  investigation and analysis, 220–3
  in New Zealand, 104
  potential causes in outdoor pursuits, 216
  reasons for investigating, 207
  research into, 95, 109–11
  see also deaths; injuries; injury prevention;
    injury surveillance
accreditation, 76–7
action research, program evaluation, 141
adventure
  commodification of, 4, 10–11
  conditions for, 5
  core qualities of, 5
  as essential part of personal growth and
    experience, 4–5
  and legal concept of 'reasonableness',
    45–6
  nature of, 4–5
  and uncertain outcomes, 6–7
  see also outdoor activities and programs
Adventure Activity Standards, 125
adventure tourism, 10–11
Agar v Hyde, 63
Andersen v R, 64
anti-discrimination legislation, 68
Army cadet program, 43–4
AS/NZS ISO 31000: 2009 Risk
    Management – Principles and
    Guidelines, 3

as benchmark for legal interpretation,
    46–7
communication and consultation, 14,
    151
definition of risk, 3, 46
definition of risk management, 4
establishing the context, 14
key steps in risk management process,
    13–16
monitor and review, 16
principles of risk management, 71–2
risk analysis, 15
risk evaluation, 15
risk identification, 14–15
risk management framework, 47
risk treatment, 16
Association for Experiential Education (US),
    108
Australian Bureau of Meteorology (BOM),
    criteria for issuing severe weather
    warnings, 185–6
Australian Bureau of Statistics (ABS), 95,
    101
Australian Consumer Complaints
    Commission (ACCC), 63
Australian Defence Force (ADF), 44
Australian Institute of Health and Welfare
    (AIHW), 102

Banksia Awards, 39
biodiversity, 30
Blake v Galloway, 65
British Canoe Association, 126
Brundtland Report (UNWCED), 26, 27
bush adventure therapy (BAT), 116–17
bushfires

impact of, 187
risk management strategies, 199–200

Canadian Ski Instructors Alliance, 126
carbon footprint, 30
Carson, Rachel, 30
Cathedral Ranges tragedy, 118–19
Causal Factors Analysis, 220
child protection, and the nanny state, 10
civil liabilities legislation, 59–62
civil liability, workplace health and safety, 55
Civil Liability Act 2002 (NSW), 63
climate change, 31
coercive power, 85
cold, risk of injury or illness, 219
common law, 56
communication and consultation
    ISO 31000 definition and examples, 14
    see also risk communication
communication devices see technological and communication devices
consultation with workers, 53
context, establishing, 17
    ISO 31000 definition and examples, 14
Contiki Holidays, 63
contributory negligence, 59
corporate social responsibility, 32
Cosgrove, Peter, 82
creativity, 80–1
criminal liability, workplace health and safety, 55
Crocker v Sundance Northwest Resorts Ltd, 64
culture, 78–80

dangerous recreational activities, 60–1
deaths
    community injury-related deaths, 101
    injury-related deaths among young people, 101
    in sport and recreation activities, 95–6
    of tourists in Australia, 91–2, 210
    of young people engaged in sporting/leisure activities, 102
    see also names of specific incidents, e.g. Lyme Bay canoeing tragedy
Duckworth, Eleanor, 7
due diligence, 52
duty of care
    breach of, 55–8
    and occupier's liability, 58–9
    and risk management, 56–8

Earth Summit (Rio 1992), 26
economic sustainability, 33, 39
economic sustainability indicators, 35
Ecotourism Australia, 38–9
'Education for Life: the Year 9 Experience', 132–3
Emergency Position Indicating Radio Beacons (EPIRBs), benefits of, 165–7
employees see staff; training, development and education
environmental extremes
    cold, 219
    heat and humidity, 218–19
    risk factors, 217–18
    see also severe weather
environmental sustainability, 30–1, 39–40
environmental sustainability indicators, 35
equipment
    minimal footwear, 177–8
    positive and negative risks associated with, 167, 174–7
    and program design, 125–6
    and risk management, 9
    see also technological and communication devices; technology
evaluation see program evaluation
exertional heat illness, risk factors, 219
experiential knowledge, 78
experiential learning cycle, stages, 134
expert power, 85
extreme temperatures, risk management strategies, 197–9

Falvo v Australian Oztag Sports Association, 63
Fédération Internationale de Football Association (FIFA), 73, 74
finance sector, lessons from, 2
financial sustainability, 33, 39
Fire Danger Index (FDI), 199
Fire Danger Rating (FDR), 199
first aid training, 8
floods
    information and communication, 196
    planning for impact of, 195–6
    reviewing knowledge gained, 197
    risk management strategies, 194–7
    trigger points and responses, 196
'Food Miles', 30
footwear, minimal, 177–8
foreseeability, 56

generations
  characteristics of, 11
  and understanding target market or
    clients, 11–13
Geoscience Australia, 185
Gleeson CJ, 43, 44
goals and objectives, 74
Green and Gold Inc. (Canada), 27
Gulf of Mexico oil spill, 150–1

Haddon's Matrix, 208–9
Hahn, Kurt, 5, 11
hazard controls, 213–14
Health and Safety Employment (HSE)
    Act 1992 (NZ), 104–5
heat, and risk of injury or illness, 218–19
'helicopter parents', 10
Home Office (UK), Vetting and Barring
    Scheme, 18
human factors engineering, 9
humidity, and risk of injury or illness,
    218–19
hypothermia, risk factors, 219

incident prevention see accident and incident
    prevention
Incident Severity Scale (NZ), 213
incidents see accidents and incidents
indoors, evolution of, 170
'industrial manslaughter', 55
industry-led sustainability, 71
informed consent, 118
injuries
  in adventure programs in US, 105–7,
    108–9
  in challenge rope courses in US, 107–8
  and changing societal context, 94–5
  children and adolescents in wilderness
    programs, 109
  contributing or risk factors, 101, 110–11,
    214–16
  definition, 93
  frequency across selected sport and
    recreational activities, 99–100
  hospital separations due to injury and
    poisoning, 99–100
  hospitalised sports injuries, 96–9
  indicators of severity of injury, 101
  key indicators for sports-related
    hospitalisations, 99
  reasons for investigating, 207
  resulting in hospitalisations, 96

resulting in hospitalisations in Australia,
    96–100
serious injury in sport and recreation
    activities, 95–6
see also deaths
Injury Iceberg Model, 210
injury prevention
  in children's sport, 93–4
  developing strategies, 100
  Haddon's Matrix, 208–9
  Injury Iceberg Model, 210
  major paradigms, 207–8
  reasons for, 207
  social ecological approach, 208
  see also accident and incident prevention
injury surveillance, 210–12
  injury rates and levels of exposure, 211–12
  injury severity, 212
  need for effective system, 211
innovation and creativity, 80–1
Intergovernmental Panel on Climate Change
    (IPCC), 31
International Classification of Diseases –
    Australian Modification (ICD-10-AM),
    96
intuitive knowledge, 78

Jesus, 82

Key Performance Indicators (KPIs), 34
  for risk management, 47
  SMART indicators, 34
  for sustainability, 34–6
knowledge management, 78, 223–4
knowledge transfer, 78

Lao-Tzu, 82
Larner v Parks Victoria, 63–4
law of negligence see negligence
leadership
  and power, 82–6
  responses to different types of power, 85
  sources of power, 84
leadership styles, 83–4
learning
  from past incidents and injuries, 205–6
  as a process, 206
learning organisations, 223
legitimate power, 84
Life Effectiveness Questionnaire (LEQ),
    139
lightning, risk management strategies, 191

location tracking devices, 165–7, 178–9
Lyme Bay canoeing tragedy, 55, 127

McAvoy, Leo, 173
Mangatepopo Gorge tragedy, 77, 187, 204–5
message maps, 159
Mikronos v Adams, 63
mission statements, 73–4
Model Work Health and Safety Act 2010 (Aust), 48, 54
monitoring and review, 21
    ISO 31000 definition and examples, 16
Mortlock, Colin, 4–5
Mountain Safety Council (NZ), National Incident Database Project, 212
Murao v Richmond School District No 38, 64
Myers v Peel Country Board of Education, 64

the nanny state, and child protection, 10
National Coroner's Information System (NCIS)v(Aust), 95, 96, 102
National Hospital Morbidity Database (Aust), 96
National Outdoor Leadership School (NOLS), 126
National Safety Network (US), 105
nature, disconnection and alienation from, 5
'nature deficit disorder', 5
negligence
    breach of duty of care, 55–8
    contributory negligence, 59
    liability in, 57–8
New Zealand National Incident Database Report (2005), 99–100
NSW Caravan and Camping Industry Association, 'Gumnuts' accreditation program, 34

Obama, Michelle, 18
objectives
    factors that may impact on, 18
    and strategic direction, 74
obvious risks, and civil liability legislation, 60
occupational health and safety *see* workplace health and safety
Occupational Health and Safety Act 1991 (Cth), 44
occupier's liability, 58–9, 68
Ochoa v Canadian Mountain Holidays Inc, 64

Orchard v Lee, 65
organisational culture, 79
organisational learning, 223
organisational sustainability, 34
    indicators of sustainability, 34–6
    and risk management, 28–9
Our Common Future Report (UNWCED), 26
outdoor activities and programs
    and civil liability legislation, 61–2
    different uses of, 5–6
    duties and obligations associated with different roles, 51–4
    importance of legal context, 44–5
    key operational areas of responsibility, 49–50
    liability of providers: recent cases, 62–5
    relationship with technology, 168–9
    special characteristics of participants, 50–1
    statutory liability for health and safety, 48–9
    see also accidents and incidents; program design; program evaluation; sport and recreation; technology
Outdoor Council of Australia (OCA), 126
outdoor industry, and severe weather events, 186–7
Outdoor Recreation Industry Council of New South Wales, 3
the outdoors, adventure and risk management, 5
Outward Bound, 5, 6, 73

Paralympic Organisation, 73
personal power, 85–6
PEST analysis, 72
philosophy, 9
physical risk
    balancing with physical challenge, 92
    learning from past incidents and injuries, 205–6
    need for accurate and reliable data, 205
    real and perceived, 93
podcasting, 179
pollution, 30
Poppleton v Trustees of the Portsmouth Youth Activities Committee, 65
Porter's Five Forces, 72
positional power, 84–5
power
    and leadership, 82–6
    sources of, 84

program design
  activity design, 123–4
  activity standards and industry norms,
    124–6
  aims and objectives of organisation,
    119–22
  dramaturgy wave, 122–3
  equipment choices, 125–6
  holistic program design, 122–3
  one-size-fits-all approach, 120–1
  school-based programs, 127
  staff skills and qualifications, 126–7
program evaluation
  action based on results, 144
  action research, 141
  approaches to, 137–41
  common practices, 145
  continuum of motivation for research in
    evaluation, 136
  data analysis, 144
  data collection, 143
  dissemination of findings, 144
  historical dimensions, 135
  Life Effectiveness Questionnaire (LEQ),
    139
  literature review, 142
  measurement tools, 138
  methodology selection, 143
  mixed methods research design,
    140–1
  nature of evaluation, 135–6
  needs assessments and checklists,
    144–5
  problem identification, 142
  qualitative methods, 140
  qualitative vs quantitative methods,
    137
  and quality control, 134
  quantitative methods
  reasons for, 136
  research question/hypothesise
    formulation, 142–3
  steps in, 141–4
  and three stage experiential learning cycle,
    134
  tips, 145
  types, 136
Project Adventure Inc (PA), 107

qualitative methods
  program evaluation, 140
  vs quantitative methods, 137

quantitative methods
  program evaluation, 138
  vs qualitative methods, 137
Queenstown Lakes District Council v Palmer, 64

reactive risk management, 8
Reason, James, 214
reasonable care, 52–3, 56
'reasonableness', legal concept of, 45–6
'reasonably practicable', in health and safety
    legislation, 54
reassurance–arousal paradox, 153
recreational activities, 60–1
  see also sport and recreation
referent power, 85
'rescue-free wilderness', 173
reviews, 76–7
reward power, 84
Riding for the Disabled Association (RDA
    NSW), 74
risk
  contextualising, 118–19
  defined, 3, 93
  nature of, 118, 154, 156–7
  and social and cultural context, 94–5,
    117–18, 153
  and technology, 174–7
risk analysis, 19
  examples, 231–7
  ISO 31000 definition and examples, 15
risk analysis matrix, 19, 20
risk assessment, 53
risk communication
  acknowledging uncertainty, 161
  collaborative approach, 154–5
  communication and consultation with
    stakeholders, 151
  communication methods, 159–60
  competence and language use, 160
  deficit model, 155
  definition, 153
  four 'generations' of, 153–4
  inclusiveness, 160
  informed consent, 118
  lessons learned, 152
  listening well, 160
  message maps, 159
  need for, 153–5
  practical strategies, 158–61
  program benefits, 160
  reassurance–arousal paradox, 153
  research findings, 157–8

review theoretical perspectives, 153–7
risk comparisons, 159
with stakeholders, 21, 151
trust and relationships, 155–6
risk comparisons, 159
risk elimination, 52
risk evaluation, 20
acceptable and unacceptable levels of risk, 20
ISO 31000 definition and examples, 15
risk factors
Causal Factors Analysis, 220
for exertional heat illness, 219
for injuries, 101, 110–11, 214–16
intrinsic or extrinsic, 214–15
latent conditions and active failures, 214
Root Cause Analysis, 220
risk identification, ISO 31000 definition and examples, 14–15
risk management
AS/NZS ISO 31000 framework, 47
balancing physical risk with physical challenge, 92
definition, 4
external context, 71
key performance indicators, 47
and liability for negligence, 57–8
and limiting civil liability, 62
nature of, 4
organisational context, 70–2
and organisational sustainability, 28–9
people, equipment and environment, 9
principles of, 71–2
reactive risk management, 8
responding to incidents, 62
and safety, 7
social and political context, 9–10
strategies for severe weather events, 191
and sustainability, 28–9
three-legged risk management stool, 8
weather-related risks, 187–91
whole-of-organisation approach, 3–4, 7–8
risk management process
key steps, 13–16
nature of, 3
proactive nature of, 7–8
risk management programs, 53
risk management standards, 3
risk minimisation, 52

risk perception, 156–7
'risk society', 153
risk-taking
nature of, 117–18
reasons for, 3
risk treatment, 20–1
ISO 31000 definition and examples, 16
Root Cause Analysis, 220
Royal Society for Prevention of Accidents (RoSPA), 12, 224

safe
definition, 93
expectation of being 'safe', 94–5, 206–7
safety
and risk management, 7, 9–10
and technology, 174–7
safety gap culture, 79–80
safety legislation, 67–8
Sandman, Peter, 155
Saxentenbach River canyoning tragedy, 63
school-based programs
designated 'teacher in charge', 119–22
lessons learned, 152
staff training, 127
Scurfield v Cariboo Helicopter Skiing Ltd, 56
serious harm, definition, 104–5
servant leaders, 82–3
severe weather
BOM criteria for issuing warnings, 185–6
managing associated risks, 187–91
nature of, 185
severe weather events
bushfires, 199–200
extreme temperatures, 197–9
floods, 194–7
and the outdoor industry, 186–7
risk management strategies, 191
wind, thunderstorms and lightning, 192–3
severe wind, thunderstorms and lightning, risk management strategies, 192–3
Shackleton, Ernest, 1
Silent Spring (Carson), 30
SMART indicators, 34
SMART objectives, 74
social ecological approach to injury prevention, 208
social sustainability, 31–3, 40
social sustainability indicators, 35
Society for Risk Analysis, 153

sport and recreation
  deaths of young participants, 102
  frequency of injuries across selected
      activities, 99–100
  hospitalised sports injuries, 96–9
  key indicators for sports-related
      hospitalisations, 99
  participation rates, 93–4
  research on incidents, 95
  serious injury and death, 95–6
sporting events, factors that may impact on
    objectives of, 18
sporting injuries *see* deaths; injuries
SPOT Satellite Messenger and Personal
    Tracker, 178
staff
  consulting with over health and safety
      issues, 53
  skills and qualifications, 126–7
strategic management
  accreditation and reviews, 76–7
  definition, 72
  goals and objectives, 74
  knowledge management and knowledge
      transfer, 78
  mission statements, 73–4
  planning, 74
  policies, procedures and practice, 75
  strategic analysis, 72
  strategic direction, 73–4
  strategic implemetation, 74–5
  strategy evaluation, 76
  vision statements, 73
sustainability
  concept of, 25–7
  economic and financial sustainability, 33,
      39
  environmental sustainability, 30–1, 39–40
  indicators of, 34–6
  industry-led sustainability, 71
  organisation sustainability, 28–9, 34
  in organisational sense, 29–30
  policy development, 38
  reviewing your own operation, 36–8
  and risk management, 28–9
  simple model, 27
  social sustainability, 31–3, 40
  spatial dimension, 28
  staff training and development, 38
  strategies to assist, 36–9
  temporal dimensions, 27–8
  three-pillar model, 29–30

sustainable development, 26
sustainable tourism, 26
SWOT analysis, 72
Sydney to Hobart yacht race (1998), 176

tacit knowledge, 78
target market, understanding nature of,
    11–13
Taylor J, 56
technological and communication devices
  audio and video availability, 178–9
  benefits and pitfalls of, 168–9
  as intrusions in wild places, 176–7
  location tracking, 165–7, 178–9
  podcasting in outdoor education, 179
technology
  definition, 169
  evolution of, 170
  level of technologies used in outdoor
      programming, 173–5
  low to high technology spectrum, 168
  obsolecence, 177–8
  overdependence on, 172
  reasons for not using in the outdoors,
      171–3
  reasons for using in the outdoors, 171
  relationship with outdoor experience
      programs, 168–9
  risk and safety, 174–7
  types used in outdoor programming,
      173–4
technophiliacs/techno-addicts, 173
thunderstorms, 192–3
  risk management strategies, 192–3
tourists, causes of death, 91–2, 210
training, development and education,
    86–7
  and health and safety, 53
  and learning, 86–7
  staff skills and qualifications, 126–7
  and sustainability, 38
'Triple Bottom Line', 26
triple bottom line accounting, 36

UN Commission on Sustainable
    Development (UNCSD), 26
UN World Commission on Environment
    and Development (UNWCED), 26
uncertain outcomes, and adventure, 6–7
Union of International Mountain Leader
    Associations, 126
Unsoeld, Willi, 7

Vairy v Wyong Shire Council, 43, 44
value statements, 9
Victorian Institute of Forensic Medicine, 102
Victorian State Trauma Registry (VSTR), 95
vision statements, 73
volunteers, use of
    establishing context for risk management,
        17
    identifying risks, 17–19
    risk analysis, 19
    risk treatment, 20–1

waste management, 30
Watson v British Boxing Board of Control, 65
weather
    associated risks, 184–5
    communicating information to those 'in
        the field', 190
    information sources on, 189–90
    as integral part of outdoor experience,
        184
    and planning of outdoor activities, 188–9
    reviewing responses and building
        knowledge, 191

trigger points and responses, 190–1
see also environmental extremes; severe
    weather
Wilderness Risk Management Committee
    (US), 108
Williamson, Jed, 215
Winter Olympic and Paralympic Games
    (Vancouver 2010), 70, 71, 73
    planning for sustainability,
        37
Wong v Lok's Martial Arts Centre Inc,
    64
Woodroffe-Hedley v Cuthbertson, 65
Woods v Multisport Holdings, 64
workplace health and safety
    civil liability, 55
    criminal liability, 55
    hierarchy of OHS hazard controls,
        213–14
    legislation, 67–8
    notes for outdoor program providers,
        65–6
    statutory liability, 47–9
World Tourism Organisation, 26